The Hymns of Zoroaster, Usually Called the Gathas

1 431959.

The
Hymns of Zoroaster
usually called the GATHAS

1776
4048

For the first time discovered to be

DUPLICATE BIOGRAPHIES
PERSONAL AND PRIESTLY

THE HYMNS THEMSELVES
For the first time made entirely accessible by

Transliterated Text, Translation.
Dictionary and Grammar.
Introductory Tables, Analysis.
Higher and Biblical Criticism.
Revealment of Zoroaster's Sociological Significance
Origin of the Zoroastrian Pantheon.
Also a Small Concordance, yet Unprinted
(Ready to print when means are supplied)

by

KENNETH SYLVAN LAUNFAL GUTHRIE
Revealer and Translator of Plotinus, Numenius, Pythagoras and Proclus

THE PLATONIST PRESS
Teocalli, No. Yonkers, N. Y., U. S. A.

Kenneth Sylvan Launfal Guthrie

A. M. (Harvard and Sewanee) ; Ph. D. (Columbia and Tulane) ; M. D. (Pennsylvania).
Professor in Extension, University of the South, Sewanee.
Address: Teocalli, 1177 Warburton Avenue, North Yonkers, N. Y.

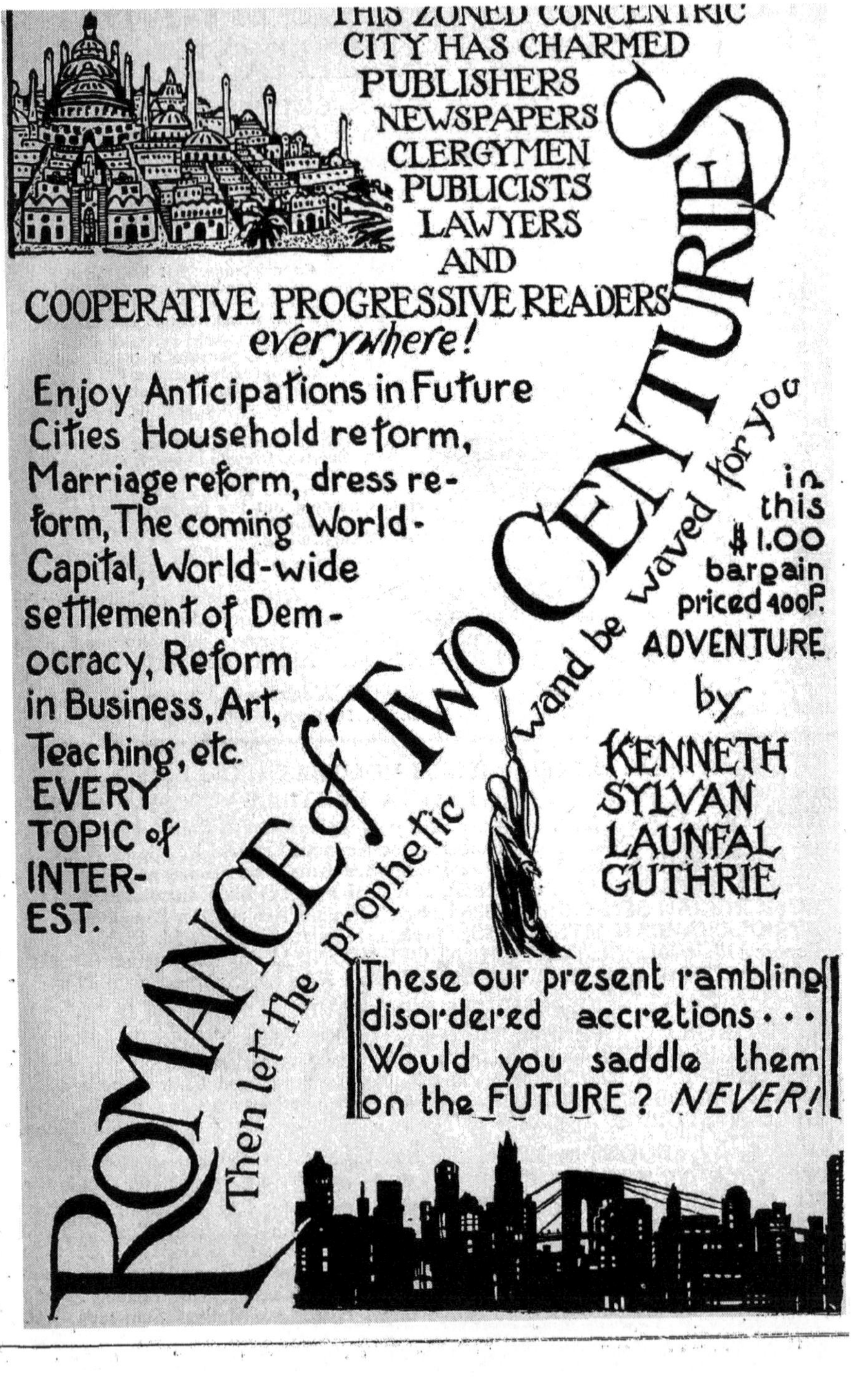
THIS ZONED CONCENTRIC
CITY HAS CHARMED
PUBLISHERS
NEWSPAPERS
CLERGYMEN
PUBLICISTS
LAWYERS
AND
COOPERATIVE PROGRESSIVE READERS
everywhere!
Enjoy Anticipations in Future Cities Household reform, Marriage reform, dress reform, The coming World-Capital, World-wide settlement of Democracy, Reform in Business, Art, Teaching, etc.
EVERY TOPIC of INTER-EST.
ROMANCE of TWO CENTURIES
Then let the prophetic wand be waved for you
in this $1.00 bargain priced 400P. ADVENTURE
by
KENNETH SYLVAN LAUNFAL GUTHRIE
These our present rambling disordered accretions . . . Would you saddle them on the FUTURE? NEVER!

PLOTINUS, the FOCUS of GREECE and the DAWN of THEOLOGY

is now accessible in the Magnificent Complete GUTHRIE ONE VOLUME TRANSLATION at the Net Bargain Price of $6.25, postpaid

(which will last only till the present remainder is exhausted)

WHAT ARE THE SPECIAL MERITS OF THE GUTHRIE PLOTINUS?

1. It is the only complete one, and will always be the cheapest. It is the famous edition of which Stephen McKenna said, 'I congratulate you; you have gotten ahead of me.'

2. It is the best for the student, as it has a 60 page Concordance, and has the first explanation of Plotinic philosophy's origin, development, and destiny. Only Dr Guthrie could do this, because it was he who dug out Plotinus's master Numenius. Also, his version is representative of contemporary language and ideas, and is not merely turning puzzles into modern dialect.

3. It is the best for him who wishes to understand Plotinus, because it is the only edition that unscrambles, chronologically, Plotinus's 4 progressive stages of development from Porphyry's frightful hotch-potcht of 9 medleys. Other translators who perpetuate this disorder after Dr Guthrie's discovery seem to be keeping the subject hazy purposely, not for the reader's benefit.

4. It is the most faithful version, because Dr. Guthrie's sole object was to focus the labors of the best students,—Marsilius Ficinus, Mueller, Drews, Bouillet, Chaignet, Taylor, and others; but one only thing he does claim,—that he has not knowingly left any obscurity. Otherwise he glories in this subservience to all the best that had been done before him, and for himself he claims nothing but the unappreciated production of what nobody else would do, and the critical discovery of Plotinus's progress. To be original is to be mistaken and misleading.

READER, DO YOU NEED AN INTRODUCTION TO THIS PLOTINUS?

Then send for the free booklet 'Names to Conjure With', which explains why he s of interest to all religious people; also why **PROCLUS**, now accessible in Master-Key form at $3.00, is of permanent, universal importance; and why you need **PYTHAGORAS's Source-book and Library, $3.00.** Also **NUMENIUS at $2.00.**

PLATONIST PRESS, Teocalli, 1177 Warburton Avenue
North Yonkers, N. Y., U. S. A.

LIBRARY EDITION OF UNIFORM VOLUMES, at One Dollar each

By KENNETH SYLVAN GUTHRIE

1. **TEMPLE GATES AJAR, or Introductory Religious Instructions,** with completing Corroborative Outlines of all other great Kenneth Guthrie Religious Works.
2. **PAGAN BIBLE, or Angel Belief as Inheritance from Greco-Romans.**
3. **WHAT BECAME OF KITCHENER,** Novel of Faith, & **Six Educational Playlets.**
4. **ROSICRUCIAN MYSTERIES,** Playlets on Original Rosicrucian Documents.
5. **SHAKESPEAREAN MYSTERIES,** Playlets. Hamlet, Tempest, M. S. N. Dream.
6. Popular Illustrated **HISTORY OF NEOPLATONISM,** comprehensive (details).
7. **APPROACHES to the MYSTERIES OF ALL NATIONS,** complete outline.

By THOMAS KIP TURVEY

1. **TEMPLE GATES OPENED,** Experiences, Conservation, Temple-Travel.
2. **TEMPLE PLAYLETS and RITUALS** for Personal Achievement.
3. **DISCOVERIES & INSIGHTS** in Theology, Literature, and Character Study.
4. **CHARACTER-STUDY MANUAL,** Zodiac's Origin, Meaning and Results.
5. **OCCULT STORIES,** Apollonius of Tyana, Hurrah for God, Reuniting Pilgrimage.

BOOKS by KENNETH SYLVAN GUTHRIE

A ROMANCE OF TWO CENTURIES, an Utopia of A.D. 2025	**$2.00**
VOTIVE GARLANDS, Collected Poems, with Frontispiece, in Gift-form....	**2.00**
MITHRAIC MYSTERIES, Restored and Modernized, with Exercises; Illustr...	**3.00**
ANGELIC MYSTERIES, Nine Angel-Degrees of Initiation; Illustrated	**3.00**
SPIRITUAL MESSAGE of LITERATURE, 1st Text-book of Comp. Literature	**2.00**
PROGRESSIVE COMPLETE EDUCATION, Marriage as Supreme School..	**1.50**
TEACHERS' PROBLEMS, How to Solve them, Historical Method Summary	**1.50**

SPICY SITUATIONS, and Dr Kenneth Guthrie's REMEDIES

The Board of Education's Examiner had just turned down the blushing Miss Teacher Candidate. Weeping, she wailed. *Is there no hope at all for me?* Oh yes, purred he. Try again next year! *What could I study in the meanwhile?* Dr Guthrie's TEACHERS' PROBLEMS & HOW TO SOLVE THEM, $1.25; Value and Limits of the History of Education.' and 'The Mother-Tongue Method of Teaching Modern Languages.' each 30 cents. *Will that pass me?* Really, Miss, you are too pretty to teach school. Get his Progressive Complete Education, or Marriage as the Supreme School of Life, $1.25. *And if I pass examination on it?* Then I will marry you. *Thanks, kind sir!*

How a Pessimist Became an Optimist. The theological student had just been preparing a thesis by cribbing the wittiest passages from **Discoveries & Insights**, Essays Theological, Literary, and of Character-Study, $1. Nettled at the undeserved praise, he blushed at the second-handedness of his religion. So at midnight he went to the Bishop's study, and said that he would leave the Church because he was honest. 'Ignorant, you mean!' corrected the adviser. 'Do a little first-hand reading yourself!' *'That's where the trouble lies,* bellowed the martyr. *I can't hunt the manuscripts!* 'Unnecessary nowadays!' soothed the Bishop, 'I know of a wizard who can summon to your room for conference all the greatest but neglected philosophers of antiquity. Shall I have him send them to you? *Oh yes, please!* gasped the theolog. *All my life I have dreamed of those sublime leaders of the race, but who were inaccessible.* 'Very well, the wizard shall send you Zoroaster, teacher of purity and angels, $3; Pythagoras, the Sage, & Philosopher, $3; Numenius Comparative Religionist, $2; Plotinus, Greek Combiner, $12 cl, $9 pp; Proclus, Universal Hierophant, $3; Zoroaster Translation only, $1.25; Apollonius of Tyana, Life, $1; Plotinus, Outline $2; Philo Judaeus, Outline, $2.' *Stop! If they came all at once, it would be tragic. Is there no guide to all this?* 'Write for a free copy of Names to Conjure With, which will open the whole subject.'

This is what occurred at the Masonic Club after last night's Lodge-Meeting

The Master was entertaining the just initiated Candidate who asked him, *Where could I read up on the meaning and historic origins of initiations such as ours?* Well, said the Master, the best book is **The Pagan Bible** an Anthology of the Soul and its Helpers, Gathered from Ethnic Sources $1. *That sounds good,* said the novice. *But I would like to see the original rituals.* You can, explained the Master, by reading **The Modernized Mithraic Mysteries**, Dramatic Sketches of Historic Initiation, $3. *But are the Christians entirely excluded?* No, no! laughed the Master; whatever exclusion there is, is of their own making. *Good; but are any Christian Mysteries accessible?* Certainly, and good ones! Get the **Angelic Mysteries** of the Nine Heavens, a Drama of Interior Initiation, $3. *But how do you advise all this, when you yourself are a Rosicrucian?* retorted the persistent Candidate. 'I was only trying to please you!' winked the Master. 'I myself prefer the **Rosicrucian Mysteries**, $1, a dramatization of the original documents.' *But I am a modern man!* sobbed the querulous Candidate. 'Nothing is easier,' comforted the suave Master. 'You need only get the **Modern Mysteries**, $1, alluring and thrilling Mystical Playlets of Experiential Religion: also the glorious **Shakesperean Mysteries**, $1. *Thanks!*

Savanarola's Ghost met Giordano Bruno's, still reeling from the fire's agony 'Cheer up, friend,' consoled he: 'you are now safe from persecution!' *Perhaps; but I am homeless.* 'Oh no, friend; look!' As he waved his hand, there appeared a glistering Temple. *What's that building?* gasped Bruno. 'Your home!' comforted Savanarola. *But the door is locked, and I want to get a look in!* 'It's your own fault,' rebuked the Florentine: 'didn't you while on earth read **Temple-Gates Ajar**, $1?' *But a look-in is not enough; I would want my whole body in.* 'Very well: I shall send for a copy of **Temple-Gates Opened**, $1.' *But in the meanwhile?* whined Bruno. 'I'll lend you **Prayers, Visions & Aspirations**, $2.' *Please, I don't want merely to aspire, I want to DO something!* 'Then I will lend you **Regeneration** the Gate, Applied, and Special Methods, $2 each, $5 all three.' *Oh thank you! Then I won't lose any time.*

A Fundamentalist-Modernist Fracas. In a recent rail-road wreck near Albany the Modernist Rev. I. Catchem, of St Shark's-in-the-Mill-pond for hours lay waiting for rescue, cheek by jowl with the renowned Fundamentalist Rev. U. Cheatem. Fellow-misery broke down the barriers of orthodoxy, and I Catchem said, My injuries are due to over-fascination while reading occult stories entitled **Hurrah for God**, $1. 'My fatuous friend,' in shocked tones retorted self-righteous U. Cheatem, 'you better sober up by exchanging books, for the faith-strengthening **What Happened to Kitchener**, $1, whose hypnotic charm immobilized me during the accident.' Conversation revealed they were both about to be ousted, and a flash of genius bade them exchange: but this flop implied two reeducations, betraying secret tricks of the craft. So U. Cheatem babbled. 'To be a Fundamentalist all you need to do is to keep people distracted by anything absorbing, such as **Romance of Two Centuries**, $2. **Reuniting Pilgrimage**, $1, Stories for Young People, $1.25, eerie **Votive Garlands**, $3: and then you can fulminate from Why You Really Want to be a Churchman, $1.25.'—'Thanks,' chortled I. Catchem. 'Now I will tell you how to succeed as a Modernist. Shed tears while haranguing over your honesty, and inability to be convinced by any reasonable arguments. In the meanwhile cribbing from The Ladder of God, & Other Sermons, $1. The Message of the Master, $1.25. & How the Master Saved the World, $1.25. Then you can make a reputation as a pundit by judiciously using **The Spiritual Message of Literature**, $2.50, it's convenient. *But shouldn't I seem somewhat saintly?* 'Transcribe Of Communion With God, 50 cts, and Of the Presence of God, $1.25.' Pray? That was the only point where Fundamentalist and Modernist agreed: Let us prey on the

PLATONIST PRESS, Teocalli, 1177 Warburton Ave, No. Yonkers, N.Y.

Kenneth Sylvan Launfal Guthrie

A. M. (*Harvard and Sewanee*) ; Ph. D. (*Columbia and Tulane*) ; M. D. (*Pennsylvania*).
Professor in Extension, University of the South, Sewanee.
Address: Teocalli, 1177 Warburton Avenue, North Yonkers, N. Y.

The
Life of Zoroaster

in the words of his own Hymns, the Gathas

according to both Documents,
the Priestly, and the Personal, on parallel pages,
(A new Discovery in Higher Criticism,)

Translated by

Kenneth Sylvan Guthrie

A.M., Harvard; Ph.D., Tulane; M.D., Medico-Chirurgical, Phila.
M.A., G.D., Professor in Extension, University of the South, Sewanee

This is one of the great scriptures of the world, but has until this present translation been practically inaccessible. There is a translation by an Englishman, but it is not only more puzzling than the original, but it makes Zoroaster speak like an Anglican theologian, instead of the pre-historic bard who was conducting a crusade against nomadicism, and for a cow-herding civilization. Besides, the acknowledged authorities on the subject do not hesitate to acknowledge openly that it is to their financial interest to keep the text from the public. Anyone who desires to question this easily understood translation can purchase the author's larger book which contains the full transliterated text, dictionary, grammar, criticism, outlines, and tables of all available kindred information.

Net price, cloth bound, post free, $1.10.

The Comparative Literature Press

182 Monroe Street, Brooklyn, N.Y.

At the end of the book will be found more extended
notices of the following works by the same author:

Of Communion with God

Life, Times and Philosophy of Plotinos

The Message of Philo Judaeus

Numenius of Apamea, Works, Life and Teachings

The Gathas, or Hymns of Zoroaster, in English

The Greek 'Pilgrim's Progress,' or, the Picture, by Kebes

A Garland of Fancies;   A Garland of Aspirations

Friendship

Hymns to the Universal Divinity

Avesta. Gathas.

The Hymns of Zoroaster

Usually called the Gathas,

For the first time made entirely accessible by

**Transliterated Text, Translation,
Dictionary and Grammar,
Introductory Tables, Analysis,
Higher and Biblical Criticism,
Complete Concordance, and Subject-Index**

Kenneth Sylvan Guthrie,

A.M., Harvard; Ph.D., Tulane; M.D., Medico-Chirurgical, Philadelphia.
M.A., Grad. Div., Professor in Extension, Univ. of the South, Sewanee.
Member Am. Historical Ass'n, Society for Biblical Literature and Exegesis.

LONDON: George Bell and Sons,
Portugal House, York Street, Kingsway, W.C.
BROOKLYN: COMPARATIVE LITERATURE PRESS,
182 Monroe Street.

Dedicated to

Elizabeth Hayes Fracker
Friend, Sister, Mother, Critic, Helper,

the Serenity of whose Tranquil Home sheltered me
during the rare hours I could
snatch myself away from the whirlpool of duties;
And Who, under God, thus enabled me to accomplish
Whatever Missions for which I may have
been Destined by

My Revered Dead
and the
Inscrutable Divine.

Stern **Zarathushtra**, Prophet of Iran,
Which is the title dearest unto thee?

Dispenser of a blest eternity?
Or, **Mediator** between God and Man?
Teacher of law of heavenly righteousness?
Helper, and **Savior**, or **Life-healing Friend**?
Judge who condemn'st to tortures without end?
Redeemer of the Race to Usefulness?

Yet all these titles leave me cold.

                        The best
Of all, is that thy **heart** did ever keep
Time and compassion for advocacy
Of gentle Cow and unresisting Sheep
Whose cry to Heaven reached Divinity
Which, from all men, chose **thee** as **Tenderest**!

PREFACE

ZOROASTER is a name to conjure with. Yet, strange to say, what may be considered his authentic hymns, beautiful and inspiring as they are, are but little known. The retirement of these from the public, partly due to the commendable hesitation on the part of scholars to hazard a translation, is however, after all, as unreasonable as would be the withdrawing from circulation of other scriptures merely because of unsettled conditions of critical problems. Hence this popular edition, with all necessary helps, in the hope of adding to the available inspiration of the world.

During the winter 1907-1908 the writer was fortunate enough to have the opportunity to study the elements of Avestan, especially in connection with some of the Gâthas, under Professor A. V. W. Jackson of Columbia University, New York. The purpose of this Gâthic study was chiefly a desire to grasp, with as much clearness as possible, their significance for Comparative Religion. Such masterly analyses of Mazdean doctrine as Bishop Casartelli's draw from Mazdean sources of all periods, yielding a composite picture as inconclusive as the parallel traditional method of treating the Hebrew scriptures. The writer first attempted to establish a distinction between the older and later Avestic elements, as has been done in the Pentateuch, with the intention of confining his analysis to the older portions. Pursuant to this plan, Professor Jackson very kindly went over the Avestan text with him, indicating a provisional separation of the older from the newer portions. However, after careful examination, even these older portions seemed to yield results both uncertain and unsatisfactory. It was, therefore, ultimately decided to limit the present analysis strictly to the Gâthas, about whose age there would naturally be less question.

Let it at once be understood that this very practical interest precluded even a faint hope of any final scholarly results. Only those who have devoted most time to Gâthic accidence and lexicology are the most conscious not only of how little in this field is known definitely, but how little, perhaps, can, or ever will be known. We are uncertain as to the precise meaning of some of the chief terms — such as, for example, those that are usually translated *spirit, righteousness,* or *covenant,* and the result is that the more literary and attractive the translation, the less actual value it has. The frequently irreconcilable conflicts of the translations of Spiegel, Mills, Darmesteter, de Harlez, and Bartholomae are sufficient justification for the refusal of our ablest scholars to make any version whatever — and yet they are the only persons who could properly be trusted with so delicate a task.

But, obviously, we who are living at the present day cannot wait for centuries for the doubtful event of the finding of solutions to riddles that are possibly or probably unsolvable. The importance of the Gâthas as one of the springs of the world's religious thought will force some practical access to them; this work was inevitable, and would ultimately have been done by somebody else, if not by the writer. Let none therefore quarrel with this undertaking.

So popular a presentation, necessarily so imperfect, was, naturally enough, repugnant to Professor Jackson; and it was only the writer's pressing need of a clear understanding of what the Gâthas do teach that forced him to continue this costly work. Let it be repeated that this book is not for scholars, who will want the alternate text-readings which Geldner gives; it is for the average intelligent man and woman who should not be defrauded of their spiritual birthright merely because of the unsettled condition of abstruse and probably hopeless critical problems.

In keeping with this, every unnecessary difficulty has been cleared away. The German text-books show the difficult Avestan characters may be dispensed with, especially as in our transcription every form of each letter is accounted for, which is more than Reichelt does. Everything that could be reduced to order and ready reference has been alphabetized. Even the infinitely superior and eventual order of the alphabet as used in oriental works, has been sacrificed, not without keen regret. Words have been indexed according to the text, and not according to their derivations, which are sufficiently indicated by references. All the numerous forms of the pronouns have been given alphabetically, as also all occurring forms of the verb *to be*—it is hoped that none have been omitted. While no one can be more conscious than the writer is of the many imperfections of this work, he believes that it points the way to the *kind* of Gâthic work which will eventually be written by some scholar fortunate enough to have his pleasure *coincide* with his business, instead of *conflicting* with it, as with the present writer.

It is self-evident that in a work involving so stupendous a mass of details and so delicate problems of judgment, the present writer could not possibly have avoided all oversights or blunders. It must suffice for him to announce his gratitude to any who will enable him to correct any and all.

To this unstinted acknowledgment of shortcomings, the writer would nevertheless add that, within the very narrow limits left him for legitimate endeavor, he has done his best to be accurate and thorough; the work done was certainly painstaking and laborious.

The book should, of course, have been dedicated to the pioneers in the work—Spiegel, Geldner, Darmesteter, de Harlez, Casartelli, Bartholomae, Mills; but more particularly to Professor Jackson, whose unwearied kindness and consideration deserves particular mention. But he is too conscious of his own failings to venture to embarrass such men by connecting them with these efforts, however laborious, earnest, and conscientious. Yet it is these qualities which embolden him to advance the critical results to which he has been led. They are mostly due, not to any special cleverness of his, but to his thorough and relentlessly followed determination clearly to understand his own translation; and no doubt if he does, others will too. When the Gâthas are clearly understood, the present critical results will no doubt be confirmed by their own weight. However, once more is the reader cautioned of the hopeless uncertainty of many material points ; yet must we do our best to cope with the situation.

The writer is fully conscious that in thus making the Gâthas accessible he is only carrying out the unspoken intention of the above master-scholars, who do not have the time for so much drudgery as this book has entailed. To them, therefore, be attributed any credit that may accrue; for, after all, without their guidance, the present work would have been impossible.

And indeed the writer would not have had the courage to continue and complete these unremitting labors if he had not sunk personal considerations in the broader realization of the ever-enduring importance of the Gâthas as one of the great scriptures of the world which ought, must and will be interpreted to humanity. Nor will the writer count his labors entirely lost if he have been able to add even one grain to the walls, now building, of the *City of God.*

INDEX.

Part I. Introductory Tables, Outlines and Summaries.

Part II. Text, Translation, Life of Zarathushtra.

Part III, Higher Criticism of the Gathas.

Part IV, Dictionary and Grammar.

Part V, Subject-Index and Concordance to the Gathas.

This part has not yet been set in type because the author's health, time and money gave out. It will be printed if there is sufficient popular demand for it. To purchasers of the book it will be fifty cents; to others, one dollar. Notices of subscription should be sent in immediately, but money will not be accepted until the volume is ready for delivery.

It is the most important part of this work. It summarizes Zarathushtra's significance on every topic he touches in clear, compendious form, with full references. It was indeed only to furnish a reliable basis for this that the present study was undertaken. Although the author cannot yet see it, there is no doubt some divine blessing lurking in this untoward delay of the chief purpose of this heart-breaking effort and lonely venture of faith.

Abbreviations

Z, Zarathushtra. AM, Ahura Mazda. A, Asha. Am, Ameretat. Arm, Armaiti. As, Ashay. AkM, Aka Manah. AnM, Angro Mainyu. GU, Geus Urvan, the Soul of the Cattle. H Haurvatat. SM, Spenta Mainyu. VM, Vohu Manah. X Xshathra.———B, Bartholomae. J, Jackson. M, Mills. Sp, Spiegel.

The figures after Avestan Words are the columns of Bartholomae's Dictionary where they may be found.

Figures after an M stand for pages of Mills' Zarathushtrian Gathas in Metre and Form, unless referring to his translaof, or oomment on, some particular Gatha, such as, 28.10.

The figures after each line of the translation assist the reader in referring to the corresponding line of the Text; but even so the exigencies of the English idiom have led to further unmarkable transpositions.

Traditional Arrangement

I. Gatha Ahunavaiti, Yasnas 28-34   ———
II. Gatha Ushtavaiti, Yasnas 43, 44, 46.   The Wish.
III. Gatha Spenta Mainyu, Yasna 47-50.   The Holy Spirit.
IV. Gatha Vohu Xshathrem, Yasna 51, The Good Kingdom
V. Gatha Vahishta Istish, Yasna 53.   The Best Wish.

Provisional Chronological Succession of Scriptures

I. Gathas, Yasna 28-53; and formulas in 27.13,14; 54.
II. Haptanghaiti, Yasna 35-42; 12; 58; 4.26.
III. Metrical: Yasnas 9,10,11,57,62,65
      Yashts 5,8,9,10,13,14,15,17,19
      Scattered verses in Vispered, Nyaishes, and Afringans.
IV. Remaining prose portions of the Avesta.

𝕮𝖍𝖗𝖔𝖓𝖔𝖑𝖔𝖌𝖞 (after Casartelli)

I. MEDES, 700-559 B.C.

1. Contact between Medes and Semitic peoples.
2. Zarathushtra in Western Iran, 660-583 ? B.C.
3. Propagation of his religion in Bactria. Longer Gathic document?
4. Establishment thereof. Shorter, priestly Gathic document?

II. ACHAMENIANS, 559-331 B.C.

Cuneiform inscriptions of Darius I, Xerxes I, Artaxerxes I, Artaxerxes III. Development of Avesta, Haptanghaiti (Yasna 35-42)?

III. SELEUCIDS, 331-250 B.C.

Greek kings. Decadence of Mazdeism under Alexander.

IV. ARSACIDS, 250 B.C.—225 A.D.

Parthian kings, Religious doubt. Avesta translated into Pehlevi.

V. SASSANIDS, 226-651 A.D.

Mazdean kings, State Religion.

226-241, Ardeshir I, heresy of Mani.

238, Text of Avesta gathered under the high-priest Tansar.

369-379, Shahpur II, Text corrected under Aderbad Marehspand.

438, Yezdegerd II. Edict of his minister, Mir Narseh, 440. Writings of the Armenian Eznig.

490, Kobad. Heresy of Mazdak, 488. Formation of Avestan alphabet.

531, Khosrav Anosharevan. Golden age of Pehlevi literature. Redaction of principal treatises. Greek and Syriac civilization in Persia.

632, Yezdegerd III, Paul the Persian of Dair-i-shar.

651, Arab Conquest finally suppresses Mazdean establishment.

𝕮𝖍𝖗𝖔𝖓𝖔𝖑𝖔𝖌𝖞 𝖔𝖋 𝖙𝖍𝖊 𝕰𝖑𝖊𝖒𝖊𝖓𝖙𝖘 𝖔𝖋 𝕸𝖆𝖟𝖉𝖊𝖆𝖓 𝕽𝖊𝖑𝖎𝖌𝖎𝖔𝖓

I. Old Gathic Y43-53, Zarathushtra's experiences, Fire, Prayer.

II. Late Gathic, Y28-34, Priest, Sacrifice, Penances, Resurrection, Daenas, or individualities.

III. Old, Haptanghaiti, Y35-42, Personification of the Ameshaspentas. Worship of Fravashis, fire, earth and grass. 'Yazamaide' or praise to waters, Geus Urvan, and to all holy and clean beings.

IV. Doubtful, Haoma, the Death-repeller; Misvan, or limbo.

V. Recent, Bundahish, 6 creation-days; 5 divisions of day; and five Gathas. Baresman.

VI. Sassanian. Crystallization of definite doctrines.

Home and Age of Zarathushtra

Jackson, in his book on Zarathushtra gives the life-time of Zarathushtra as B.C, 660-583; the tradition states he was 42 years of age on the conversion of Vishtâspa, the chief of the Magians, while he received the vision when 30 years of age.

The place of his birth seems to be Atropatene, or Adarbaijân, the region to the West of Media, the neighborhood about Lake Urumiah. This is to the West of the southern third of the Caspian Sea. His mother was said to hail from the Median Ragâ or Raî.

Turan is Turkestan, on the opposite, eastern side of the lower third of the Caspian Sea.

The location of the Vision of Vohu Manah is traditionally to the South of the Caspian Sea, in the Alborz Mountains (that is, Hara Be-rezaiti), whose two peaks are Hûgar, and Aûsind.

The location of the Vision of Asha, is 'at the Tôjân water,' and is probably the Tajan, or Thejend, river. This is in Turan. It flows westwards, and does not reach the Caspian Sea, but loses itself in the desert of Turan. This location would allow good opportunity for Zarathushtra's acquaintance with the 'friendly' tribes of Fryana the Tura.

The third Vision, or conference, was with Ahura Mazdâh, and took place in Zarathushtra's home, already mentioned, to the West of the southern third of the Caspian Sea, called Adarbaijân, or Aîrân-Vêj, on the river Dâitê, or Dâityâ, the Jordan of Zoroastrianism.

The traditional seven questions addressed to seven divinities in seven different places must have been derived from the above three experiences.

Bibliographic Suggestions

Text: Westergaard, Copenhagen; Geldner's, Strassburg, is the best.

Bartholomae, Christian, Karl Teubner, Strassburg, publisher.

Translation: Gathas des Awesta.   Grammar: Handbuch.

Dictionary: Alt-Iranisches Woerter-buch.

Geiger und Kuhn (and Jackson), Grundriss der Iranischen Philologie. Strassburg, Karl Teubner, 1896-1904.   Exhaustive.

Jackson, A.V.W, Columbia University, New York City, Macmillan, Persia, Past and Present, a book of Travel and Research. 1906.

Zoroaster, the Prophet of Ancient Iran.   Both excellent.

Justi, Handbuch der Alt-baktrischen Sprache.   Old, but excellent.

Mills, Lawrence H. Oxford University, England.   Has published: Dictionary of Gathas, yet in press.

Text: A Study of the Five Zarathushtrian Gathas, with Text and Translations. Epoch-making edition of all the critical material.

Translations: in Sacred Books of the East 31, and 'Zarathushtrian Gathas in Metre and Rhythm,' Open Court Co, Chicago.

Numerous books on Zoroastrianism as compared with other religions

Reichelt, H. Awestisches Elementar-buch. Winter, Heidelderg.

Translations: Spiegel, de Harlez, Darmesteter.

Boeklen, Ernst, Die Verwandschaft der Juedisch-Christlichen mit der Persischen Eschatologie. Goettingen, Vandenhoeck u. Ruprecht,02

Casartelli, L-C, La Philosophie Religieuse du Mazdeisme sous les Sassanides. Louvain, Vanlinthout Freres, 1884.

Darmesteter, James, Ormuzd et Ahriman, leurs Origines, et leur Histoire. Paris, F Vieweg, 67 Rue Richelieu, 1877.

Haug, Essays on Sacred Language, Writings and Religion of Parsees

Jackson, AVW, Doctrine of the Future Life. Biblical World, Aug96

Moffat, James, Zism and Primitive Christianity, Hibbert Journal, 1,2

Stave, Erik, Einfluss des Parsismus...Haarlem, 1897, Erven F Bohm.

Soederblom, Nathan, at Leroux, Paris

Les Fravashis, Etudes sur. .la Survivance des Morts, 1899.

La Vie Future d'apres le Mazdeisme, 1901.

Zartushti, Bombay, India, Parsee periodical.

Outline of the GATHAS

YASNA 28

SELF-CONSECRATION
OF PRIEST AND CONGREGATION

I. Self-consecration of the Priest Zarathushtra.

1 Z prays for the Holy Spirit, so as to satisfy both VM and the Soul of the Bovine Creation.

2 As reward for his willingness to serve Z demands both worlds.

3 Z will sing praises as never before, if the Gods support him when he calls.

4 Z, watching over mens' souls, will teach them to seek Asha,

5 Converting them by the promise of the beatific vision of VM, AM, and his retinue.

II. Prayer of the Congregation for Help and Mercy.

6 The Congregation prays: for Z, that he may receive support; and for themselves, that they may be protected from enemies;

7 For Vishtaspa, that he attain his wishes; for Z, that he obtain a hearing;

8 For the hero Frashaoshtra, and all other members, the good of VM for ever.

9 In order to avoid angering the Gods, the Congregation placates them with praise, as being best able to promote Utility.

10 May the Clever attain their objects, inasmuch as wise prayers are fruitful.

III. Zarathushtra's Prayer for Efficiency.

11 Z will preserve the believervs' good actions and thoughts, and he prays for knowledge that he may proclaim the destiny of life.

YASNA 29

THE EXTERIOR CALL OF ZARATHUSHTRA

DRAMA IN HEAVEN. New 'Dramatis Personae' are: the deified Soul of the Archetypal Bull, as the advocate of the earthly Cattle; and their Creator technically termed their 'Shaper'.

I. The Cattle demands protection.

1 The Cattle demand the introduction of agriculture as protection from human maltreatment.

2 The Shaper-of-the-Cattle consults Asha as to whether there is no legal process to enforce protection for the Cattle.

3 Human moral limitations are so great that Asha knows of no help. Then the Creator of the Cattle decides to undertake this defence,

4 Asha refers suppliants to AM whose omniscience decides of all.

5 The Creator of the Cattle addresses his plea to AM, who answers that

6 Legal process exists only for men, not also for Cattle, who are men's property, being intended to furnish him with flesh and milk for food;

7 But only according to merciful provisions; who will teach these?

II. The Call of Zarathushtra as Teacher and Protector.

8 VM selects Zarathushtra, and would confer on him prophetic ability and dignity.

9 The Soul of the Cattle weeps at receiving, as protector, not a warrior, but a priest; and prays that, at least, this priest may be endued with power sufficient to protect the Cattle.

10 Zarathushtra proclaims absolute reliance on the divine power and efficiency;

11 But men should do their part by accepting and practising his teachings. The Soul of the Cattle wails that the Cattle are willing to serve AM if He will but protect them.

YASNA 30

THE PROCLAMATION OF DUALISM
TEACHING THE NECESSITY OF TAKING SIDES

I. Exhortation to the Faithful to Open their Ears to the Mystery.

1 Z proposes to teach *a*, what is necessary for praise to AM, and for prayer to VM, and *b*, the bliss of the believer in beholding Asha.
2 *c*, for discrimination between the two Parties, and for
  d, the eventuating of the fate of the ages in their favor.

II. Revelation of the Doctrinal Root of the Division of the Parties

3 The Twin Spirits are the good and bad in 'thought, word, deed'.
4 They determined *a*, life and death; *b*, ultimate reward and punishment.
5 The Opponents chose the Bad Spirit, while Asha chose the Best.
6 The Daevas, being deceived, went over to Aeshma, author of sickness.
7 X, VM, and A then visited the sick man; Armaiti gave him vigor, that he might attain health or paradise, even if only through the test of retribution by fire.
8 At the time of punishment mercy shall be shown to them who deliver their Drujist-opponents into the two hands of Asha.

III. Zarathushtra hopes for Universal Conversion by Choice between Eternal Bliss and Woe.

9 Z prays for God's help in making life progressive, and in confirming the wavering.
10 The good shall receive the promised reward in heaven, while the bad shall suffer destruction.
11 The Cause will progress only when the believers fully realize the significance of eternal bliss or woe.

YASNA 31
PRAYERS FOR ENLIGHTENMENT
AND EXHORTATIONS TO PARTISANSHIP

**I. Practical Introduction: Enlightenment Claimed
As no more than Justice to Zarathushtra.**

1 Zarathushtra proposes to preach.
2 His mission is demanded by the natural difficulties of search for truth.
3 But before he can preach, he must have a divine revelation of his message,
4 In order to prosper the Coming Kingdom.
5 He himself must meditate over his message before going out.

II. First Call for Enlightenment, and Answer from Within.

1. Call.

6 Z offers a reward for an explanation of 1, Health and Immortality,
7 2, Creatorship; 3, Origin of Asha; 4, Maintaining of Vohu Manah; 5, the Prospering of these through the Holy Ghost.

2. Answer.

8,9a From within Z himself comes the answer to all these:
9b,10 Agricultural Civilization solves these problems, while
11 Mazdah is the Creator of all.

III. Second Call for Enlightenment.

1. Introduction.

12 The Opinions of Men are divided, while
13 Mazdah is all-detecting, and omniscient.

2. Second Call.

14 Z asks about 1, Compensations;
15 2, Punishment for his Opponents;
16 Whether his Followers may attain God-likeness;
17 Which is the more important Object of Choice—a good, but unscrupulous living, or Improvement of State or Self?

IV. The Partisan Close: Choose Sides, Take Zarathushtra's Word

18 Oppose the Drujists with weapons, for they would destroy your settlements.
19 But hearken to Z, who is able to Enforce his words at Latter Day
20 The Drujists shall in hell be tormented, while
21 Those will be rewarded who are Friendly to God in word and deed
22 All this will be Accepted by the Well-disposed.

YASNA 32

AT A PARLEY, VITUPERATION OF
THE RIVAL PROPHET, GREHMA

I. Public Self-consecration, and its Acceptance.

1 Priests, warriors, and farmers, as servants of AM, separate from Daevas.
2 AM publicly accepts their devotion: 'it shall be Ours'.

II. Zarathushtra Vituperates his Rival Grehma to the Daevas.

3-8 The Daevas are warned to renounce the actions and teachings of the rival prophet Grehma, who, however high he stands at present, has incurred eternal punishment for meat-eating, and
9-12,14, for many other misdeeds, and who shall yet
13 be brought, when in company with the rich in hell, to desire the message of Zarathushtra, who then will hinder Grehma from beholding Asha.
14 Hence the Karpanite and Kavayite is condemned to destruction, while those who suffered by them are taken to heaven by Haurvatat and Ameretat.

III. Zarathushtra will Exult in Executing this Final Judgment

15 Zarathushtra hopes soon to be able to limit the Drujists' violence against his own beloved.
33.1 Zarathushtra will exult to act as judge to the Drujists, his followers, and to the 'mixed'.
33.2 Whoever either injures a Drujist by thought, word, or hand, or converts a brother, he fulfils the good pleasure of AM.
33.3 Whoever does good to any one of the congregation, or zealously tends cattle, shall be admitted to the pasture of Asha.

YASNA 33

HIGH-PRIESTLY PRAYER FOR
ACCEPTANCE, CONVERSION, and PARADISE

I. Prayer for Acceptation.

4 Through the might of his prayer,
5 And through his praise of Obedience, when he reaches Paradise,
6 And by divine teaching initiated into the mysteries of Agriculture,
7 Zarathushtra hopes to attain a more extensive hearing.

II. Prayer for General Conversion.

8,9 He prays that universal conversion may already improve then contemporaneous conditions
10 in matters of comfort and bodily well-being.

III. Prayer for Paradise.

11 But, for the other world beyond also, may the Gods grant mercy
12 to him and his, with grant of eternal reward.
13 He hopes yet to convert many a person.
14 He promises to do all in his power to show himself worthy of the favor of the Gods

YASNA 34

CONGREGATIONAL PRAYER

FOR   PROTECTION and INSTRUCTION

I. Congregational Prayer for Protection and Instruction.

1 In view of the equivalent interchange of work, word and prayer for divine rewards, the believers will earn as many as possible; hence,

2 May the Gods grant that no merit be lost.

3 As dutiful observers of all that is right we hope for eternal reward

4 And to pass through the fire-ordeal comforted, not injured.

5 Have You the power to preserve the poor who trust in You, and have renounced all relations with the Daevas?

6 If so, show Your power by improvement of conditions not only beyond, but even here!

7 Defend us from those who spread false teachings,

8a And are dangerous because richer than Zarathushtra,

8b,9 But even on that account they shall lose the rewards of Paradise

10,11 Which are for those who hold the true teaching, and who oppose the enemy.

12a Inform us of what Thou requirest, that we may give it;

12b,13 Teach us the paths of VM on which the Helpers will go to Paradise.

II. Zarathushtra Closes with a Prayer for Congregation and Humanity.

14 Let the Congregation assure themselves of reward by good care of the Cattle,

15 And by fulfilling the divine commands to attain perfection—efficiency and utility.

YASNA 43

THE INTERIOR CALL OF ZARATHUSHTRA

I. Prayer for Fulfilment of Human Aspirations.

1,2 Prayer for the fulfilment of the wishes of all who are present.
3,4 Zarathushtra prays for the fulfilment of his own wishes, especially for knowledge of AM's power and greatness.

II. Reminiscences of Six Visions.

5,6 FIRST. AM at the very beginning plans rewards and punishments
7,8 SECOND. Zarathushtra takes sides with the Ashaists, and determines never to cease seeking instruction.
9,10 THIRD. Visible revelation of Asha is granted.
11,12 FOURTH. The Gods promise to support him in the prophetic office which he has undertaken.
13,14 FIFTH. Prayer to VM for ultimate Paradise, and immediate victory over his opponents.
15,16 SIXTH. Armaiti promises the latter if Zarathushtra will break off all intercourse with the unbelievers. He makes confession of faith, and looks forward to the establishment of the Kingdom.

YASNA 44

ORACULAR CONSULTATION AS TO ADVISABILITY
OF CONVERSION THROUGH WAR

I. Questions about Theology.

1 What is the proper method of prayer to the Gods, so as to induce them to help him to attain VM?
2 Will the rewards begin in the second life? Z is Watcher and Savior.
3 Who is the first creator and energizer of Nature?
4 Who is the Preserver, and creator of VM?
5 Who created light, waking and morning?
6 Is his own message genuine? For whom was the Cattle created?
7 Whose wisdom made sons reverence parents? AM is creator.
8 Z would know the words of life to attain ultimate rewards.
9 Will Z be able to perfect his individuality?
10 Will his religion of practice and reverence find acceptance?
11 Will his religion spread to the pagans? He has a right to expect this, for the Gods chose him; he is an enemy to all other prophets

II. Questions about Propaganda by War.

12 Must not the other prophet who opposes Z be an enemy to God?
13 Will it be possible to drive the dissidents from home into the camp of the avowed opponents?
14 Z would hand over these Druj to Asha for torment and punishment
15 In this religious war, which side shall gain the victory?
16 Prayer that a vision reduce the people to obedience to himself.
17 Will he succeed in establishing salvation for himself and his?
18 Will he, while yet in this life, receive his reward?
19 Z takes it for granted that whoever fails to pay him due reverence will have to suffer for it at the end of life; why not now also?

III. Loyalty to Zarathushtra is Profitable.

20 The management of the Druj always resulted in 'hard times'; why side with them?

YASNA 45

SERMON ON DUALISM, TEACHING
AGRICULTURE AS ROAD TO PARADISE

I. Repeated 'Open Your Ears to the Mystery'.

1 Z preaches to multitudes from far and near lest the Druj prophet
mislead them.

II. The Doctrinal Dualistic Foundation of Partisanship.

2 The Good Spirit sets up a total disagreement with the Bad Spirit.

III. The Good Spirit Teaches the Best Word of Agriculture.

3 Whoso disagrees with Z's revelation shall suffer at the end of life.
4 The best in this life is the efficient VM (doctrine) and beneficent
Armaiti (agriculture).
5 The Best Word to hear is obedience to It; that will earn Health
and Immortality.

IV. AM will Vindicate Z as Judge by Reward and Punishment.

6,7 This has been revealed through AM who disposes of final rewards
and punishments through his Kingdom.
8 AM should be won by prayer.
9 We should seek contentment through VM, and efficiency thro' AM,
10 Who, through Asha and VM, promised H and Am in his realm.

V. Zarathushtra Remains Mediator.

11 The attainment of all this depends on enlisting the support of the
Prophet and Redeemer-Helper, by being devoted to him alone.

YASNA 46

WAR PRELIMINARIES OF
HEART-SEARCHINGS and ENCOURAGEMENTS

I. Failure in Conversion and Demand on Mazdah for Vindication
1 Conversion lags; all the Estates oppose the Prophet.
2 Z's poverty diminishes his influence so that he depends on God
3,4 Who is expected to stem the tide, and break the power of the prince who is the chief obstacle.

II. Rules How to Treat Converts.
5,6 Converts are to be protected from injury by former associates.

III. Actual Struggle to Protect Converts (against Bendva ?)
7,8 Hope that all will turn out well, and that opponents will meet with punishment.

IV. Z is the First Prophet: Obedience to him Gains Paradise.
9 He himself was the first to proclaim the truths of salvation.
10 Whoever obeys him attains Paradise.
11 His opponents will, on the Judgment-bridge, be sifted into hell.
12 But he hopes that the descendants of Fryana the Tura will be converted, and gain Paradise.
13 Whoever obeys Z is worthy to be heard of, and will attain both worlds.

V: Praise for the Supporters of his Cause.
14 Kavay Vishtaspa will be rewarded by union with AM in Heaven.
16 Frashaoshtra Hvogva is to attain both his wishes and the Gods.

VI. Partisanship with Zarathushtra Essential to Gain Paradise.
15 Haechataspas are to learn discrimination, and attain Asha
17 Jamaspa Hvogva's prayers and docility to be remembered beyond.
18 Zarathushtra promises friendship to friends, enmity to enemies.
19 Whoever satisfies Zarathushtra shall attain future life and a pair of cows which AM will know how to procure.

YASNA 47

SONG OF THE SPIRIT AS INSPIRER OF WAR.

1 Whoever evidences the right spirit in thought, word and deed shall receive from AM the highest reward.

2 Hence that right spirit should be evidenced, because AM is the father of all who hold to Asha.

3 AM is also father of that Spirit who created cattle for men, and pasture for the cattle.

4 All Ashaists should separate from the Opponents who have fallen away from that Spirit,

5 And who will have no share in the rewards of the Ashaists.

6 It is to be hoped that the expectation of reward may yet convert many.

YASNA 48

INCOHERENT APPEAL FOR
CHAMPIONS and DEFENDERS

I. Hope for Rewards in This Life.

1 Ultimate victory of Asha is certain.
2 The lot of the Faithful should improve in this life already.

II. Punishment for Opposers and Waverers.

3 It is wisdom to hold to the secret teachings of AM.
4 Persons who waver between these divine teachings and their own inclinations, wishes and convictions shall be—separated?

III. Right of Believers to Present Comfort.

5 Through good princes Armaiti is to provide pasture for cattle, and for men, the earning of Paradise.
6 The earth was designed as residence for men, as pasture for cattle
7 All who seek eternal reward must protect cattle from cruelty.

IV. Uncertainty Here and Hereafter.

8 Is the realm of AM certain for his prophet Zarathushtra? Will the Judgment favor his own followers?
9 How will his life shape itself in this world? Will he be able to protect himself from his enemies?

V. Nobles must resign Luxury, enforce Security, gain Salvation.

10 When will the Nobles absent themselves from the ceremonies of the opposing priests and rulers?
11 This alone will enforce security.
12 Helpers of the land are those who practice enforcement of AM's laws. They are conquerors of Aeshma, destined rulers and saviors.

YASNA 49

ZARATHUSHTRA, DEFEATED BY BENDVA,
APPEALS FOR DEFENDERS

I. Zarathushtra Utters Imprecations on his Successful Opponent.

1,2 Perdition to Bendva, the Chief Obstacle, and to his hired prophet Grehma,

3 Whose teachings promote perdition; wherefore both deserve excommunication.

4 To them violence to cattle seems meritorious; they might yet gain the upper hand.

5 Bliss awaits those who hold to the true belief.

II. Frashaoshtra is Urged to Become Defender.

6 Z seeks to know clearly God's plans so that he may proclaim his religion acceptably to God.

7 Whom, among noble or commoner, does God choose as champion?

8 Z prays that Frashaoshtra may attain union with Asha, and that he himself may attain the Kingdom. Both of them would be God's ambassadors for eternity.

9 Jamaspa also is called; may he remember what the Prophet can, at the latter end, do for those who follow him faithfully.

10 Z will take pains to see to it that all good deeds are remembered and rewarded,

11 While the unbelievers may expect the worst.

YASNA 50

ORDINATION OF DISCIPLES TO FORM SETTLEMENTS

I. How to Form New Settlements.

49.12 Z asks what help is coming to him from the Gods he worships.
50.1 From whom else can he expect help?
2 How shall new settlements be started? By 'just' living, and by 'clever' aggression.
3 Ultimate possession will result from gradually dispossessing the Druj from neighboring lands.

II. These Settlers are to Act as Missionaries.

4 Z praises the Gods for the Settlers' joy at their establishment.
5 The Gods' responsive joy leads Z to encourage the Settlers to manual labor.
6 May the Settlers propagate Z's commands in a prophetic manner!
7 These missionaries are compared to steeds whom Z will yoke for the Gods.
8 As priest, Z presents to the Gods the devoted prayers of humanity.

III. But Zarathushtra Remains the Only Mediator.

9 So Z again stands before the Gods as mediator; but to the congregation he promises that when he is among the Gods he will then still more energetically see to it that his followers get their reward
10 Z's past and future actions, and Nature's beauties praise the Gods
11 Z would for ever remain the eulogist of the Gods.

YASNA 51

ENEMIES, HEROES, AND SAINTS OF THE KINGDOM

I. The Children of the Kingdom.

1 Z's object is to gain the heavenly kingdom for himself and his.
2 Assure us that we will be received, O AM, if we serve faithfully.
3 Prayers of those who serve Thee by deeds should be heard.
4 Where is retribution, forgiveness, the Gods, and the kingdom?
5a To the pious farmer grant a cow in his paradise
5b,6 Inasmuch as Z is appointed Judge and Distributor at the end.
7 Z invokes on himself strength and judgment.

II. Opposition to the Prophet is Enmity to Humanity.

8,9 Clear knowledge of reward and punishment is the chief issue.
10a Hence an opponent to its teacher Z is an enemy to humanity,
10b,11 Against whom Z summons Asha and every friend of his.
12 One of these opponents was inhospitable to Z;
13 Which act will deprive him of reward, and dooms him to terrors.
14 The Karpans will not practice agriculture or spare cattle; by one
   word shall they be condemned to the House of the Druj.
15 Z claims for himself that which he has promised to the believers
   and which AM was the first to attain in heaven.

III. Supporters of the Prophet are Heroes and Saints.

16 Praise for Vishtaspa, the political chief of the congregation.
17 For Frashaoshtra, the noble of the Hvogva family
18 Who promised him his daughter; and for Jamaspa, his son-in-law;
19 Also for Maidyomangha the missionary.
20 These four leaders produce prosperity, which results in godliness
21 Which results in attainment of the Kingdom.
22 Z will reverence those who, like the above four heroes, have acquired AM's recognition.

YASNA 53

ZARATHUSHTRA GIVES HIS DAUGHTER
TO SECURE A CHAMPION

I. Marriage Ceremony.

1,2 The Prophet is assured of a most excellent lot beyond, as are also his followers and supporters, the heroes Vishtaspa, Frashaoshtra, and Maidyomangha.

3 Z gives away Pouruchista, exhorting her that she grow wise by obedience to her husband as mediator towards Gods and the Cause.

4 By serving him, the believers and relatives Pouruchista will attain divine blessing.

5 By common life the married pair are to cherish each other, and to encourage each other to good works.

6 The pleasures of the evil are short, and lead to tortures in hell.

7 If you are constant to the Cause, you shall be happy; but woe be to you, if you abandon it!

II. The Bridegroom is Goaded to Conversion by the Sword.

8 Renewed encouragement to Vishtaspa to promote peace for the faithful by slaughter of the enemy; and quickly, too!

9 It is certain the evil shall go to hell; but where is the prince who, to anticipate that doom of theirs, will rid the earth of them immediately? AM has the power to give to the Poor that Better Part.

Summary of Zarathushtra's Message.

We cannot leave these sublime hymns without indicating summarily the chief motives which prompted them, which they embody, and which they still preach to futurity.

Root-Principle : Protection of Animals from Cruelty.

It was the call of the Cattle, Yasna 29, which led to Zarathushtra's external call as prophet to teach men to protect the cattle; those are called 'enemies' who treat the cattle with violence, 31.15; 32.12; 49.4; 51.14; the members of the congregation are to assure themselves of eternal reward by care of the cattle, 33.3; 34.14.

First Result : Vegetarianism.

It is enemies who kill the cattle, 32.12, and eat them, 31.15, and who teach others to eat the pieces of flesh, 32.8, possibly at sacrifices.

Second Result : Settling of Land, and Agriculture.

Cattle need pasture, stables, and fodder; consequently protection of cattle implies settling on definite pieces of land, and practice of the laws of agriculture, 29.1; 31.9,10. This fact attests that, far from being recent productions, these hymns are possibly some of the most venerable of human documents; echoes of the religious dialect of man's first steps in civilization.

Third Result : Forming of Parties by Patriotic Partisanship.

Inevitably settlers of one valley form a community; and love of home develops into a patriotism which considers their own valley paradise or heaven. The contiguity of other valleys, however, brings home to them the outside universe which appears as hell or limbo according as its inhabitants are enemies or indifferent friends.

Fourth Result : Dualism.

Clothed in religious verbiage, these practical needs (see Y 30.9-11 connected with 30.3-8) appear as two divinities, the Good, and the Evil, representing Agriculture versus Nomadism (the dualism of 45.2 connected with the agriculture of 45.3-5).

Fifth Result : Need of Leader and Teacher calls Zarathushtra.

But the 'good' peaceable agriculturalist needs a leader against the warlike nomad who to him is evil. Zarathushtra's recognition of this need expresses itself in Y 29.8.

Sixth Result : Zarathushtra's Struggles Emphasize his Personality

Although Zarathushtra was called forth by the need of a teacher of kindness to cattle, and of a prophet of Dualism, his labors by peaceful means were fruitless, Y 44 and 45; see 53.8,9. Unfortunately, this standing still became retrogression before the aggressiveness of the enemy. To attain no more than peace, 53.8, he must incite to war and slaughter. As tho enemies' damnation is inevitable the sooner they are butchered, the better, 53.9. It was fated, however, that he himself should perish by the sword he had thus drawn.

To support these doctrines of damnation and blood there is needed an authority greater than that of teacher or prophet—that of priest, 28.1-5; 33; 50.7,8; of redeemer, 45.11; of mediator, 50.6,9; and of advocate. Let us hope that it is only because of this that heresy is constituted by mere opposition or discourtesy to Zarathushtra, 51.10, 12; who even becomes the Judge at the end of things.

Seventh Result : The Prophet's God becomes Supreme.

While the Gathas remain polytheistic to the end, yet do they teach the supremacy of Mazdah; but they do so in a manner such as to suggest it was either novel or questioned. The heat of the prophet's championship of Mazdah betrays his originality in superimposing Mazdah over the Iranic pantheon.

Eighth Result : This God's Will Thereby Becomes Righteousness.

When we have raised a divinity to the position of supremacy, his will thereby becomes transformed into the standard of righteousness or Asha. Hence, in an ever widening stream, flow duty, conscience, merit, and freedom of the will.

Ninth Result : Rightness Appears in Thought, Word and Deed.

A triple psychology makes three avenues for Virtue: spirit manifests in thought, soul in word, and body in deed. This triplicity reappears in their eschatology—the blessed, the damned, and the indifferent; Paradise, Hell, and Misvan or limbo.

Tenth Result : Future Rewards and Punishments.

With unerring instinct Zarathushtra played boldly on the one chief human longing, that for a blissful eternal life. The prophet's main object is to obtain the Kingdom of Heaven for himself and his, 51.1. The glory of both worlds is a twofold division found again in the two-foldness of reward and punishment. If this be clearly realized, 31.22, there will be no need of further exhortations to partisanship for or against the prophet. The eternal reward is vision of, and communion with the Gathic Pantheon, especially Ahura Mazdah.

Eleventh Result : Practical Prosperity.

Except divine names, one of the most common words is deeds. One argument against the Druj is that under their management there were hard times. It is the function of Armaiti to prosper house and land. The calving, fortune-bringing Cow is fruitful. It is hoped that future promises will begin to manifest already here on earth.

What the Gathas do not Contain.

Asceticism, scorn of riches, race suicide, love, independent thought.

From our Modern Point of View.

This great teaching of the protection of the brute creation is a gospel which even to-day is not needless or dead, nor ever will be, and which, to the remotest generations, will carry the long revered name of Zarathushtra as the first to make a religion of kindliness to helpless, self-sacrificing animals.

We may reflect that this gospel was needed peculiarly at a time when the sickening details of unorganized butchery were daily re-peated in range of sight and hearing. The modern prudery of the abattoir has not solved the moral aspect of butchery—vegetarian-ism alone will do that. The principle involved is however not only compassion for animals, but self-respect and personal purity, principles also taught by Zarathushtra.

EPOCHAL DISCOVERY

in the Zoroastrian Scriptures

by KENNETH SYLVAN LAUNFAL GUTHRIE

That the two Yasna Sections in which the Gathas appear are

PARALLEL BIOGRAPHIES OF ZOROASTER

The Shorter Mark-like Personal   and the Longer Luke-like Priestly

Harmony of *the* GATHAS

PART II

Text, Translation, *and*
The Life *of* Zarathushtra

TRANSCRIPTION OF AVESTAN ALPHABET

a	ᴜ			n	﹖ *n*	
ā	ᴜ			ñ	﹖*n*	
a	ᴂ	*a*		n	﹐*w*	
āe	ᴜ	*ā*		ng	ʊ *ŋ*	
b	⅃ *b*			o	﹋	
c	⅌ *c*			ō	﹋	
d	⅃ *d*			p	ᴕ *p*	
d	ᵴ *d*			r	﹨ *r*	
e	ᴫ			s	ᴂ *š*	
ē	ᴕ			s	ᴠ *s* (*c*)	
e	﹩ *ə*			sh	ᴕ *š*[8]	
ê	﹩ *ə̄*			sh	sht	ᴕ *š*[3]
f	ᶂ *f*			t	ᴫ *t*	
g	⅊ *g*			t	ᴇ *t*	
g	ᴛ *ǰ*			th	ᶀ *þ*	
h	ᴕ *h*			u	'	
h	ᴔ *h*			ū	﹏	
hv	ᴕ *hv* (*q*)			v	ᴗ (*ʋ*) *v* (*u̯*)[2]	
i	·			w	ᴕᴕ *w*	
ī	ᴔ			x	ᶀ *h*	
j	ᴛ *j*			y	ᴕᴕ (*ʋ*) *y* (*i̯*)[2]	
k	ᴤ *k*			z	ᶊ *z*	
m	ᴛ *m*			z	ᴕ *ž*	

INTRODUCTION to *the* TRANSLATION

I. The Translation Undertaken in Self-defence, Not Bravado.

It is well-known who they are who 'rush in where angels fear to tread'; and this translation would never have been attempted had not the writer faced the alternatives of leaving incomplete the labor of years in the domain of comparative religion, or make a translation sufficiently comprehensible and still faithful to serve as working basis for even approximate results. So far is this removed from being intended as a criticism of translations existing, that chiefly out of modesty in the presence of Masters so accomplished and renowned, and partly out of an overwhelming sense of his own limitations, the present writer had based the first draught of his CONCORDANCE OF THE GATHAS on a painstaking collation of all the chief recognized translations. The criticism passed on this effort was that it was indefinite, because it was not based on the text. There was therefore no other resort left but to give, besides the fresh translation, the full text, with sufficient apparatus in the way of vocabulary and grammar, to enable every intelligent man both to check this translation's reliability, and to defend it from the attacks of interested parties who till now have succeeded in keeping the text inaccessible. If therefore the writer has made this translation, it has not been out of bravado, but in sheer self-defence.

II. Why the Vocabulary is Based on Bartholomae's Dictionary.

The kindly, unprejudiced general reader would never suspect the groundlessness of whatever attacks this work may receive, unless he is informed of the incredible animosities that obtain among Avestan scholars. For instance, a certain German scholar did not forgive a brother scholar for a difference of opinion about some trifle, even after his demise. It would seem almost as if the intolerance of Zarathushtra himself had descended on those who study his writings.

The cheapest attack, that the present translation is a romance, has been made impossible by the presence of the text and vocabulary. The next handiest attack will be the pointing out of the oversights of which such a work must no doubt be full. These attacks will cease immediately, as soon as it is realized the writer considers all corrections (that are not disguised differences in matters of opinion) as helps rather than hindrances, his purpose being to perfect his work as far as possible, he himself never having had the false pride which hesitates to acknowledge his errors. Such an acknowledgment is, in effect, as Bacon suggested, an announcement he is a wiser man than he was before. Worthy of careful answer, however, is the logically next attack, to the effect that this translation results from a vocabulary based on Bartholomae's general Iranic dictionary, rather than on a special Gathic dictionary still in course of publication. To this attack there are two answers, one negative, the other positive.

First, Bartholomae has by no means been followed blindly; wherever he has suggested 'special' meanings, they have
been rejected just as thoroughly as if they had been advanced by anybody else. A case in point is DAB, which he in-
terprets 'to practice' for 53.1 exclusively, while the usual
meaning 'to deceive' makes good sense, as Mills has shown.
In other words, the Vocabulary has attempted to combine
the best from the labors of the best scholars.

On the whole, however, general dictionaries are, as a
rule, more reliable than special dictionaries; what we gain
in depth we lose in breadth. The more special a meaning is
the less likely is it to be of general usage. To the unso-
phisticated, dictionaries are fetishes to conjure with, whereas
there are venerable doctrines which have survived merely
because dictionaries bulky enough have been compiled by
their champions. The more special a dictionary is, the more
does it represent its compiler's bias, and the less is its value
for comparison with the whole language and literature —
which is of especial importance for the Gathas, whose many
peculiar words, not found elsewhere, must otherwise, for
their interpretation, depend on prejudiced commentaries or,
worse yet, on pure fancy.

The present Vocabulary does not claim to be more than
a student's practical help to reach and then interpret the
roots from which the Gathic forms are derived. The English interpretations were the simplest that could be used
conscientiously in order to avoid any dogmatic prejudice,
or ecclesiastical association — the purpose of the present
writer being as far as possible to restore the Gathas to that
classification of literature to which they really belong—not
dogmatic theology, but world-wide prophecy.

III. Why the Translation is not in Verse.

Why is this translation not in verse, when rhythm is commended by Zarathushtra himself (50.8, 51.16)? Chiefly because of the exceptional difficulties of the Gathas.

Poetry has its recognized advantages; but in certain fields these very qualities operate as disadvantages:

1 The danger of subordinating sense and message to the mechanical exigencies of versification. How fatal the effects of this tendency are will appear from consideration of the chaotic traditional arrangement of the text itself, produced (for memnonical purposes?) by neglect of every consideration other than similarity in metre. This is, indeed, generally recognized.

2 The chief element of poetry is suggestiveness, that is, punning on words. Where, however, we are laboriously trying to enter fully into the exact meaning of an author, suggestiveness is treacherous and unfaithful. Each language has its peculiar repertory of groups of word-associations which mislead when they are set down as corresponding. This is apparent in the existing verse-translations whose very eloquence is sometimes formed by ideas probably foreign to the text. We are fortunate enough if we succeed in catching the author's meaning; more fortunate still, if we can express it in English words; and most fortunate, if the prose-version even is not unidiomatic.

3 Even in English poetry rhyme and metre have, during the last century, been openly repudiated by recognized writers; why therefore should we feel ourselves under the slight-

est obligation to undertake trammels, so fatal to accuracy, which are recognized to be unnecessary and artificial?

4 Evidently the Gathas belong to the same general category as the Biblical Psalms. The ludicrous failure of the early Calvinistic metric versions should prove a wholesome deterrent from following in their foot-steps.

5 The linguistic genius of English (analytic) and Avestan (synthetic) differ so much that the greater the slavishness in imitation of the technicalities of Avestan poetics, the greater would be the essential unfaithfulness to English understanding. So true is this that Mills' praiseworthy zeal for faithfulness misled him into putting his standard version in another synthetic language, Latin. This, however, was a fundamental error, as it interposed between the two idioms a third, which must inevitably add to the already grave confusion of thought-associations. A good translation should act as a clear lens in a pair of spectacles; the interposition of a third idiom would act as a smoked glass, which changes all the colours. Besides, the fatal doctrinal results which have resulted from a similar interposition of a Latin version between the Bible and the people should preclude another such misfortune. Nor does Mills escape this fatality: the Latin version which was made as a tool is frequently used as an authority.

6 Poetry, even in English, interferes with the logical word-order, creating unnecessary problems felt very acutely in the interpretation of even English poets. While such unnecessary puzzles may have personal and aesthetic value, they are evidently entirely out of place in a conscientious effort to represent a difficult foreign meaning accurately.

IV. Why the Names of the Ahuras have been Retained.

It would have been very much easier for the present writer to follow the lead of other translators in omitting the names of the Avestan divinities in such passages as he might have thought demanded their supposed psychological equivalents. The chief purpose of such a substitution has been attained by the mere inversion of the order of name and translation, the most suitable, apparently, being given precedence. Omission of the Avestan word, on the other hand, would have put at a great disadvantage the reader, who should be allowed to judge for himself in this matter, wherein the experts have no rule which is not accessible to the amateur. Of course, the writer is not unmindful of that class of readers who PREFER to have their thinking done for them. He regrets he cannot accommodate them.

Nor can he accommodate those who urge the legitimate ground that it makes the style ponderous to give the translation of the divine names in each case. Their problems are far too difficult and important to admit of such a consideration as style.

Comparative religion suggests the improbability of so excessive a degree of spirituality as would result from a free translation of the sacred names. These divinities must be considered tribal fetishes to which only later moral meanings were attributed when, in later times, the original meaning was lost. Indications of such vicissitudes are discoverable in such evident duplications as Asha and Ashay. Comparative religion may yet solve our problem—it must not be hid!

V. Some Results Attained in this Translation.

There are some peculiar difficulties in translating the Gathas, in that it is generally admitted that in later Avestan grammar had degenerated to an extent such that it formed a veritable chaos; while it is apparent that the hymns were, at some later period, torn out of their original interrelations and grouped mechanically according to their rhythms. The results of this general recognition have been fatal to a proper sense, on the part of translators, of responsibility to be accurate and consistent; for it is evident that they could gratify any fancy with such elasticity of form and sequence. As a result, the translations have differed scandalously, and have led to the most bitter recriminations and animosities.

The present writer realized the need, in the Avestan field, of that which has been done for centuries in the Biblical — the comparative Commentary method which, before deciding, gives and compares the opinions of the most memorable scholars in that field. Accordingly, in this translation, occasional initials will inform the reader of the more important differences of opinion; and this effort would like to be regarded as a pioneer commentary, which will no doubt be supplied someday in full detail by some person with greater opportunity and ability than the present writer.

. As to the writer's own translation, while also recognizing the above-mentioned limitations to possible accuracy and consistency, he considers they should not be made use of except as a last resort. Indeed, he has found it possible to account for every case-ending naturally; and by dint of retaining the subject wherever possible a number of new consistent interpretations have been achieved, vindicating the utmost possible limitation of chaos.

1 In 51, stanzas 16-19 mention four heroes. Stanza 21 expresses Zarathushtra's purpose to celebrate all Helpers. Why then should stanza 20 abandon the subject of heroes, and alone treat of divinities (B and M)? From its position, we should expect it be a connecting link between what precedes and follows; and indeed such is the case. The 'like-willed' refers back to the four above-mentioned heroes of the Cause, connecting them to the 'innumerable cloud of witnesses' in the next verse.

2 The context of 46.17 shows that Zarathushtra is planning to reveal how one might discriminate the Wise from the Foolish(15). In 46.9-13,18 he considered unfriendliness to himself as enmity to humanity. It would therefore not be unnatural if we interpreted verse 16, the natural connection between 15 and 17, in the same sense, namely, that the Wise are those who would follow the Preparer, that is, Zarathushtra himself. This reasonable result flows primarily from strict adherence to the Grammar.

3 When we remove 50.3 from the unnatural, artificial eschatological atmosphere by considering it in connection with its context, we find no 'open-laying' at the 'consummation', but plain, sensible, consistently-carried-out advice how to settle agricultural, hence 'sun-exposed' lands amidst the Druj, with 'cleverness' to evade unnecessary friction. This interpretation would have an interesting bearing on the meaning of 'Magian', which might easily be connected with the word for 'hole,' MAGA (1110),—i.e., lands in a deep

valley, not well-adapted to agriculture, which needs the sunshine. Our passage therefore records the time when the Magians, so to speak, 'got out of the hole.'

4 The benefit of this sociological explanation is best seen by its agreement with the equally natural interpretation of 50.4, which ceases to be an entirely uncalled-for vision of Ahuras, standing by the path to heaven, and becomes the natural picture of how the Preparer Zarathushtra will, as result of the success of his 'clever' tactics, rejoice on standing by the path to the new settlements towards which the 'Wisher'-settlers are proceeding with shouts of joy.

5 We have, in 44.20, a case where strict adherence to grammar results in good sense, and agreement with parallel passages, such as 47.3, where Armaiti is created as pasture for the cattle. In contrast with this entirely natural statement, consider the inherent absurdity of cattle being watered in order to promote agriculture (M), or cattle being cherished to promote agriculture, without closer explanation (B). This seems like putting the cart before the horse.

6 We should bring out the purpose of the divine promise of ten mares with stallions—namely, to promote Zarathushtra's own health (Haurvatat) and preservation (Ameretat) (notice the instrumental case in 44.18,c). So keenly did Zarathushtra feel his poverty (34.5, 46.2), as to attribute to it whatever he may have experienced of temporary disappointments.

7 Evidently (29.10,c) Ahura Mazdah is not so much the first possessor of peace, as its source and provider.

8 It is hoped that our translation of 30.9,c is not a thought too beautiful to be considered probably accurate.

Its psychology agrees strikingly with Sidgwick's definition of wisdom as the union of altruism and expediency.

9 Later tradition may have referred the 'death-repeller' of 32.14,c to the ritual Haoma-juice; a strict grammatical construction, on the contrary, demands no more than a reference to the Ashaist repelling the Drujist with the sword.

10 The true significance of 44.10 can be reached only when it is considered as the link connecting stanzas 9 and 11. The former asks how to sanctify the human spirits; the latter, how Armaiti shall, in deeds, spread over those to whom the doctrine is taught. The link connecting these two thoughts is evidently the urgency of adjusting faith and works—the eternal problem that agitated Paul and James.

11 In 45.5,c the word 'this' apparently refers to the MANTHRA as a magic formula.

12 Although the locative case of THWAMI in 48.4 does primarily suggest a local Misvan or Limbo, might that not be translated as being separated 'in Thy estimation'?

13 It would seem as if, in 51.2, Asha and Armaiti should be read in the vocative, not the instrumental case.

14 The full meaning of all the grammatical forms of 53.4 seems to have been brought out, for the first time by our rhetorical arrangement.

15 The Ashaist lord, in 53.9, need not be in hell; it is far more likely that he is yet on earth, as stanzas 8 and 9 consistently refer to the nomads who are opposing the herdsmen; thus one more eschatological reference is avoided.

16 Our grammatically faithful version of the very difficult 31.7 seems to offer a solution both natural and logical.

17 In 31.8 'him' should refer to 'Mind' as last subject.

18 Might not 30.7 refer to an experience in Zarathush-tra's life when he became sick? This would furnish a suffi-cient reason for the apparition of the Gods; their gift of en-duringness and vitality suggests a healing. The molten me-tal test may have been a fever, or something connected with it. If this is right, it furnishes a logical link connecting

(30.6) the partisanship of dualism and the Daeva-sick-ness, which might have been due to a wound caused in an Aeshmic raid; and

(30.8) punishment for violence and 9, desire to improve the world.

The connection between 'molten metal' of 30.7 and a real experience of Zarathushtra is all the more natural as it would explain the origin of the eschatological metal. May it not have been the sword of the combatants? One case in point is 32.7, where Mills translates, Bendva's 'glittering sword', while Bartholomae has the 'glowing metal' of the Judgment-day. The figure would not be unusual, as is at-tested by the traditional fiery sword of the Angel guarding the gate of Eden. A wound burns enough, and brings on sufficient fever to suggest the figure of a molten metal test.

19 May not the ADVAN of 44.3 be the 'Milky Way'? It would follow quite naturally after sun and stars, and avoid the taking of the usually accusative form XVENG as a genitive for this particular place (B), whereas it is in appos-tion with other accusative forms. In this case the plural suns' would be the sunny days, while the singular 'star' de-notes the starry sphere. Thus we preserve the grammatical relations intact.

20 May not the two 'swift ones' 'yoked to the clouds and winds' of 44.4 be thunder and lightning?

21 A misplacement seems to have occurred in 46. Stanza 16 interrupts the connection of 15 with 17, while it continues and closes 14, carrying out the invitation to heaven there given. Then stanza 15 begins a new subject, carried out in stanza 17. Thus is restored logical order.

VI. Why Different Kinds of Type have been Employed.

If the choice of kinds of type employed in this book should fail to commend itself to the reader, he may rest assured that while it may be the result of poor judgment, it certainly is not the result of lack of anxious fore-thought. An effort was made to increase the clearness of the several parts composing this book by using such a face of type as seemed best to fit that particular section.

For instance, the Longer and Shorter Documents are distinguished by size of type. The Outlines of the several hymns are arranged so as to occupy one page each, in order to make more obvious their individual significance. The very difficult text was set in type large enough to remove all unnecessary obstacles. The more academical higher criticism was set in Old Style, while the more practical Concordance was set in clearer Roman. It is hoped that the result of so much effort and fore-thought may justify the time and expense lavished upon it.

In spite of all this, none feels the existing defects more keenly than the present writer; he has done his best, however, under the present circumstances.

VII. Various Details about the Translation.

An effort has been made to reproduce the text with scrupulous exactitude from GELDNER; and whatever deviations therefrom may be discovered are unintentional. It was this consideration which caused the failure to divide each line according to the cæsura. But any reader who may desire to read the lines according to the metre can easily do so by following this scheme of the number of the syllables in each part of each line of the stanza of each hymn.

Table of Gathic Versification.

28-34 has stanzas of three lines of 7 plus 9 or 8 syllables.
43-46 has stanzas of five lines of 4 plus 7   syllables.
47-50 (except **48**.5,6), four lines of 4 plus 7   syllables.
51   has stanzas of three lines of 7 plus 7   syllables.
53 has stanzas of 4 lines, 2 of 7 plus 5; 2 of 7 plus 7 plus 5

The desire to make the text as living and as attractive as possible has led to a cautiously sparing punctuation thereof in accordance with the present translation thereof. This was perhaps an error of judgment for which the writer would atone by cautioning the reader who desires (as he should) to make his own independent version, **to disregard the present punctuation entirely.** Every independent version implies its own punctuation.

The writer's unremitting labors on this book have undermined his health to such an extent that it has been found imperative to postpone the issuance of the VOCABULARY, GRAMMAR and CONCORDANCE OR SUBJECT-INDEX until the accumulation of evidence of sufficient popular appreciation to justify the further sacrifices entailed thereby. A subscription blank for this purpose will be found near the title-page.

Ahunavaiti Gatha

YASNA 28

28. 1

Ahyā yāsā nema*n*hā ustānazastō ra*f*edrahyā   1

manyê*u*s mazdā pourvīm spe*ñ*tahyā ashā vīspê*ñ*g sh*y*aothanā ?

va*n*hêus xratūm mana*n*hō yā xshnevīshā gê*u*scā urvānem, 3

28. 2

yê vā*e* mazdā ahurā pairī-jasāi vohū mana*n*hā   4

maibyō dāvōi ahvā*e* astvatascā hya*t*cā mana*n*hō   5

āyaptā ashā*t* hacā yāis rapa*ñ*tō daidi*t* *h*vāthrē,   6

HYMN 28

Self-consecration *of* Priest *and* Congregation

I. Self-consecration of the Priest Zarathushtra.

XXVIII.—4

To the utmost of my ability, will I teach men to seek Asha (justice)! (And this will I do)   12

XXVIII.—1

With outstretched hands; and by reverent prayer for support, O Mazdâh, (mindful)   1

I will entreat, as the first (blessing) of the Spenta Mainyu (bountiful mentality)—that all (my) actions, (may be performed) with (the aid of) Asha (justice),   2

(That I may receive) the understanding of Vohu Manah (good disposition), and that I may thus satisfy the Soul of the Bovine (creation),   3

XXVIII.—2

(And this do I) who entreat You, O Ahura Mazdâh, (lord mindful) through Vohu Manah (good disposition),   4

To grant me both lives, that of the body and of the mind,   5

With the felicity with which Mazdâh, through Asha, supports (those to whom) Mazdâh (mindful) gives the two-lives for their comfort;   6

Ahunavaiti Gatha

YASNA 28

28. 1

Ahyā yāsā nemanhā ustānazastō rafedrahyā   1

manyêus mazdā pourvīm speñtahyā ashā vīspêñg shyaothanā 2

vanhêus xratūm mananhō yā xshnevīshā gêuscā urvānem, 3

28. 2

yê vāe mazdā ahurā pairī-jasāi vohū mananhā   4

maibyō dāvōi ahvāe astvatascā hyatcā mananhō   5

āyaptā ashāt hacā yāis rapañtō daidīt hvāthrē,   6

HYMN 28

Self-consecration *of* Priest *and* Congregation

I. Self-consecration of the Priest Zarathushtra.

XXVIII.—4

To the utmost of my ability, will I teach men to seek Asha (justice)! (And this will I do)   12

XXVIII.—1

With outstretched hands; and by reverent prayer for support, O Mazdâh, (mindful)   1

I will entreat, as the first (blessing) of the Spenta Mainyu (bountiful mentality)—that all (my) actions, (may be performed) with (the aid of) Asha (justice),   2

(That I may receive) the understanding of Vohu Manah (good disposition), and that I may thus satisfy the Soul of the Bovine (creation),   3

XXVIII.—2

(And this do I) who entreat You, O Ahura Mazdâh, (lord mindful) through Vohu Manah (good disposition),   4

To grant me both lives, that of the body and of the mind,   5

With the felicity with which Mazdâh, through Asha, supports (those to whom) Mazdâh (mindful) gives the two-lives for their comfort;   6

28. 3

yê vāe ashā ufyānī manascā vohū apaourvīm   7

mazdamcā ahurem yaēībyō xshathremcā agzaonvamnem   8

varedaitī ārmaitis ā-mōi rafedrāi zavêñg jasatā,   9

28. 4

yê urvānem mêñ gairē vohū dadē hathrā manaɲhā   10

ashīscā shyaothananam vīdus mazdāe ahurahyā   11

yavat isāi tavācā avat xsāi aēshē ashahyā!   12

28. 5

ashā kat thwā daresānī manascā vohū vaēdemnō   13

gātūmcā ahurāi sevīshtāi seraoshem mazdāi   14

anā mathrā mazishtem vāurōimaidī xrafstrā hizvā.   15

XXVIII.—3

(And this do I) who will sing hymns to You O 'Ahura Mazdâh, through Asha (justice) and Vohu Manah (good disposition), as never before;   7

And (I will) also (sing hymns to) those (faithful believers) for whom Armaiti prospers the never decreasing realm-of-Xshathra;   8

Hither, (O you divinities, come) to my support; come to my call!   9

XXVIII.—4

(And this do I) who with Vohu Manah (good disposition) am mindful to watch over the Soul of the Bovine (creation),   10

And who knows (with what) compensations are rewarded the deeds of (the kind inspired by) Ahura Mazdâh.   11

To the utmost of my ability, will I teach men to seek Asha (justice)!   12

II. Prayer of the Congregation for Help and Mercy.

XXVIII.—5

O Asha (justice)! When shall I through thee behold Vohu Manah (good disposition) as an Expert-knower, discovering-or-attaining, (among the Magian tribe)   13

The throne, and (the tribe-men's) Sraosha-(obedience) for (the prospering of the cause of) the most powerful (mindful)-Mazdâh Ahura-(lord)?   14

With this mystic word (of promise B) I will cause those savages to choose (the cause of) the greatest Mazdâh Ahura-(mindful lord).   15

28. 6

vohū gaidī manaṇhā dāidī ashā-dāe daregāyū   16

ereshvāis tū uxdāis mazdā zarathushtrāi aojōñghvat rafenō 17

ahmaibyācā ahurā yā daibishvatō dvaēshāe taurvayāmā. 18

28. 7

dāidī ashā tam ashīm vaṇhêus āyaptā manaṇhō   19

dāidī tū ārmaitē vīshtāspāi īshem maibyācā   20

dāestū mazdā xshayācā yā vê mathrā srevīm ārādāe! 21

28. 8

vahishtem thwā vahishtā yêm ashā vahishtā hazaoshem 22

ahurem yāsā vāunus narōi ferashaoshtrāi maibyācā   23

yaēibyascā it rāeṇhaṇhōi vīspāi yavē vaṇhêus manaṇhō 24

28. 9

anāis vāe nōit ahurā mazdā ashemcā yānāis zaranaēmā 25

manascā hyat vahishtem yōi vê yōithemā dasemē stūtam 26

yūzêm zevīshtyāeṇhō īshō xshathremcā savaṇham.   27

XXVIII.—6

O Mazdâh Ahura-(mindful lord), come with long life of Asha
(justice) gifts, with Vohu Manah (good disposition),   16
With just utterances, and give (these) to Zarathushtra as the
means-of a vigorous support.   17
(Then, give these) to us, that we (thereby) may overcome the
hostilities of the enemy.   18

XXVIII —7

Grant, O Asha (justice), this compensation: namely, the felicities
.of Vohu Manah (good disposition) ;   19
Grant, O Armaiti (love), the wish of Vishtaspa and of myself; 20
O Thou greatest Ruler, grant a (ready) hearing unto him-who-
prepares with the Word.   21

XXVIII.—8

For the best do I entreat the Lord Ahura, like willed with thee,
the best Manah-disposition,   22
And with the best Asha's-justice, supplicating Asha (justice) for
(1) the hero Frashaoshtra, and (2) me,   23
And (3) for whomsoever thou wouldst grant Asha-(justice) for
all the age of Vohu Manah (good disposition.)   24

XXVIII.—9

We would not vex You by those supplications, O Ahura Mazdâh
(mindful lord), (nor would we vex) the best Manah-(good
disposition),   26
Because of these (expected) benefactions; rather would we haste
to offer praise   25
(To) You, who are the best prosperer of human wishes for profit,
(here below and in) the Xshathra-realm (to come).   27

28. 10

a*t* yeñg ashāa*t*cā vōistā va*n*hêuscā dāthêñg mana*n*hō　28

erethwêñg mazdā ahurā aēibyō perenā āpanāis kāmem　29

a*t* vê xshmaibyā asūnā vaēdā *h*varaithyā vaiñtyā s*r*avāe.30

28. 11

yê āis ashem nipāe*n*hē manascā vohū yavaētāitē　31

tvêm mazdā ahurā frō-mā sīshā thwahmā*t* vaoca*n*hē　32

manyêus hacā thwā êeāe*n*hā yāis ā a*n*hus pouruyō bava*t*.　33

XXVIII.—10

O Ahura Mazdâh (lord mindful), crown with attainments the
desire of such clever (persons)   29

As thou knowest, through Asha (justice) to be both (1) worthy
and (2) of Vohu Manah (good disposition)   28

(And this I pray because) I know that supplicatory words reach
You, and are effective.   30

III. Zarathushtra's Prayer for Efficiency.'

XXVIII.—11

I who am to protect (the worship of) Asha-(justice) and Vohu
Manah (good disposition) for ever,   31

(I beg) thee, Mazdâh Ahura (mindful lord) to reveal to me (the
truth), so that I may (be able) to proclaim   32

What is the development of the (present) first (dispensation of)
life out of thy Mainyu (mentality) (as if it was being uttered)
through thy mouth.   33

YASNA 29

29.1

Xshmaibyā gêus urvā gerezdā: 'kahmāi mā thwarōzdūm
kê-mā tashat?　　　　　　　　　34

ā-mā aêshemō hazascā remō āhishāyā derescā teviscā,　35

nōit mōi vāstā xshmat anyō athā mōi sastā vohū vāstryā!' 36

29.2

adā tashā gêus peresat ashem: 'kathā tōi gavōi ratus,　37

hyat hīm dātā xshayañtō hadā vāstrā gaodāyō thwaxshō　38

kêm hōi ushtā ahurem yê dregvōdebīs aêshemem vādāyōit?'39

29.3

ahmāi ashā nōit sarejā advaēshō gavōi paitī-mrāvat:　40

'avaēsham nōit vīduyē yā shavaitē ādrêñg ereshvāenhō　41

hātam hvō aojishtō yahmāi zavêñg jimā keredushā.'　42

HYMN 29

The Exterior Call *of* Zarathushtra

I. The Bovine Creation Demands Protection.

XXIX.—1

The soul of the Bovine (creation) complained to You:
  For whose benefit did You fashion me? Who shaped me? **34**
Fury (rages) against me; violence and cruelty, maltreatment and
  roughness oppress me;   **35**
I have no herdsman except You: therefore (it is) You (I beg) to
  procure me good pasture.   **36**

XXIX.—2

Then the Shaper of the Bovine (creation) asked Asha (justice),
  "What was thy idea about a judge for the Bovine?"   **37**
"Did You make an energetic herdsman along with the pasture,
  when You made the Bovine (creation)?"   **38**
"On whom have You decided as her lord, who may repel the fury
  (of the attack) by the Drujists?"   **39**

XXIX.—3

(Mazdâh (mindful) who was) with Asha (justice), answered to
  the Shaper of the Bovine creation), For the Bovine do I not
  know of a helper who would not be liable to do harm.   **40**
Those (savages) yonder do not comprehend how just (men
  would) treat their dependents."   **41**
But (if there is no human helper), to whomsoever of living beings
  I come as help, he is the strongest of living beings.   **42**

29.4

mazdā*e* sa*h*vār*ê* mairishtō yā-zī vā*v*erezōi pairī-cithī*t*　　43

daēvāiscā ma*sh*yāiscā yācā vareshaitē aipī-cithī*t*　　44

hvō vīcirō ahurō athā-n*ê* a*n*ha*t* yathā hvō vasa*t*.　　45

29. 5

a*t* vā ustānāis ahvā za*s*tāis frīnemnā ahurāi ā　　46

m*ê* urvā g*ê*uscā azyā*e* hya*t* mazd*a*m dvaidī ferasābyō　　47

nōi*t* *e*rez*e*jyōi frajyāitis, nōi*t* fshuyeñtē dregvasū pairī.　　48

29. 6

a*t* *ê* vaoca*t* ahurō mazdā*e* vīdvā*e* vafūs vyānayā　　49

nōi*t* aēvā ahū vistō naēdā ratus ashā*t*cī*t* hacā　　50

a*t* zī thwā fshuyañtaēcā vāstryāicā thwōreshtā tatashā.　　51

29. 7

t*ê*m āzūtōis ahurō ma*t*hr*e*m tasha*t* ashā hazaoshō　　52

mazdā*e* gavōi xshvīd*e*mcā hvō urushaēibyō speñtō sāsnayā　　53

'kastē vohū mana*n*hā y*ê*-ī dāyāt *ê*eāvā maretaēibyō?'　　54

XXIX.—4

(Asha (justice) interrupts.) Mazdâh (mindful) is the (being)
  most retentive of the plans, which have been performed by
  Daevas, (gods) and men in the past;   43
And also of the plans which shall be performed in the future.   44
(And as to the present it is) he Ahura (Lord) who makes the de-
  cisions; (it is) whatever he wills, (that) will happen to us. 45

XXIX.—5

("If that is so," said the Shaper of the Bovine creation, "then
  shall both) my soul and that of the calving cow, urge Mazdâh
  (mindful) with questions,   47
And placate him with outstretched hands, (praying that)   46
No destruction may affect the just-living farmer (who dwells)
  among the Drujists."   48

XXIX.—6

(In answer to which) Ahura Mazdâh (Lord mindful) who knows
  the decrees which (make) for wisdom, himself spoke: 49
("In as much as) neither overlord, nor rightly appointed judge
  exists for thee,   50
Therefore I, who am the Fashioner, shaped thee for the farmer
  and pasturer."   51

XXIX.—7

This decree, which provided fat (pastoral) food for the cattle,
  (and destined) the (cattle) milk-food for the hungry (farmer
  and pasturer),   52
(Was uttered by) Ahura Mazdâh (lord mindful) in agreement
  with Asha (justice), through his bountiful teaching.   53
(But the Bovine pair were at a loss for some one to enforce this
  decree on earth, so they asked,) "What (man) hast thou O
  Vohu Manah (good disposition) who could tend us both among
  men?"   54

II. The Call of Zarathushtra as Teacher and Protector.

XXIX.—8
(Vohu Manah (good disposition) answered): "The only person
  known unto me here who has hearkened to our teaching   55
Is Zarathushtra Spitama; he is desirous of proclaiming the
  (divine) thought,   56
For Mazdâh (mindful) and Asha (justice); so we will endow his
  words with (attractive) sweetness."   57

XXIX.—9
Thereupon the soul of the Bovine (creation) lamented:
  "(Woe is me that it is I) who must for a Preparer (for my
  needs)   58
Put up with the impotent speech of an impotent man!
  (I) who wished for myself a self depending (divine) ruler;   59
In what age shall he who may give me energetic help arise?"   60

XXIX.—10
(Zarathushtra speaks:) ("I beg) You, O Ahura (lord), and Asha
  (justice) that You will give to these-two, (the soul of the
  Bovine creation and the calving cow)   61
Such vigor and ruling power as gives peace of dwelling through
  Vohu Manah's (good disposition's) assistance.   62
As to me, O Mazdâh, (mindful), I have (in this my call to serve
  thee) recognized thee as the original provider of supplies."   63

XXIX.—11
Where (else, except with thee, O Mazdâh) (mindful) is Asha
  (justice) and Vohu Manah (good disposition) and Xshathra
  (political power)?   64
So, O mortals, receive me among you that I may impart to you
  instruction for the great Magian cause.   65
Grant us help, now O Ahura Mazdâh (mindful lord)! (For) we
  intend to be) of service to such divinities as You.   66

29. 8

aēm mōi idā vistō yê-nê aêvō sāsnāe gūshatā   55

zarathushtrō spitāmō; hvō nê mazdā vashtī ashāicā   56

carekerethrā srāvaye*ngh*ē hya*t* hōi hudemêm dyāi
vax*ed*rahyā.   57

29. 9

a*t*cā g*ê*us urvā raostā: 'y*ê* anaēshem xsha*nm*ênē rādem   58

vācem n*er*es asūrahyā y*ê*m ā vasemī īshā xshathrīm!   59

kadā yavā hvō a*nh*a*t* y*ê* hōi dada*t* zastava*t* avō?'   60

29. 10

yūz*ê*m aēibyō ahurā aogō dātā ashā xshathremcā   61

ava*t* vohū mana*nh*ā yā husheitīs rāmamcā dā*t*   62

az*ê*mcī*t* ahyā mazdā thw*am* m*ê*nghī paourvīm vaēdem!   63

29. 11

k*u*dā ashem vohucā manō xshathremcā? a*t* mā mashā   64

yūz*ê*m mazdā frāxshnenē mazōi magāi ā paitī-zānatā   65

ahurā nū-nā*e* avar*ê* *ê*hmā rātōis yūshmāvat*am*.'   66

YASNA 30

30. 1

Aɬ tā vaxshyā isheñtō yā mazdāthā hyaɬcīɬ vīdushē   67

staotācā ahurāi yesnyācā vanhêus mananhō   68

humazdrā ashā yecā yā raocêbīs daresatā urvāzā.   69

30. 2

sraotā gêushāis vahishtā avaēnatā sūcā mananhā   70

āvarenāe vīcithahyā narêm narem hvahyāi tanuyē   71

parā mazê yāenhō ahmāi nê sazdyāi baodañtō paitī!   72

30. 3

aɬ tā mainyū pouruyē yā yêmā hvafenā asrvāɬem   73

manahicā vacahicā shyaothanōi hī vahyō akemcā   74

āescā hudāenhō eres vīshyātā nōiɬ duzdāenhō.   75

HYMN 30

The Proclamation *of* Dualism, Teaching *the* Necessity *of* Taking Sides

I. Exhortation to the Faithful to Open their Ears to the Mystery.

XXX.—1.

But thus, O (souls) desirous (of hearing), I will utter (1) those
things worthy to be remembered by the Expert-knower   67
(2) The praises for Ahura (lord), and (3) hymns (worthy) of
Vohu Manah (good disposition),   68
And things well remembered with the aid of Asha (justice), and
the propitious (omens) beheld through the lights (of the stars,
or of the altar-flames).   69

XXX.—2

Listen with your ears to the best (information); behold with
(your) sight, and with (your) mind;   70
Man by man, each for his own person, distinguishing between both
confessions,   71
Before this great crisis. Consider again!   72

II. Revelation of the Doctrinal Root of the Division of the Parties

XXX.—3

At the beginning both-these Mentalities became conscious of each
other,   73
The one being a Mentality better in thought, and word, and deed,
than the (other Mentality who is) bad.   74
Now let the just (man) discriminate between these two, and
choose the benevolent one, not the bad one.   75

30. 4

atcā hyat tā hêm mainyū jasaētem paourvīm dazdē 76

gaēmcā ajyāitīmcā yathācā anhat apêmem anhus 77

acishtō dregvatam at ashāunē vahishtem manō. 78

30. 5

ayāe manivāe varatā yê dregvāe acishtā verezyō 79

ashem mainyus spênishtō yê xraozdishtêñg asênō vastē 80

yaēcā xshnaoshen ahurem haithyāis shyaothanāis fraoret
mazdam. 81

30. 6

ayāe nōit eres vīshyātā daēvācinā hyat īs ā-debaomā 82

peresmanêñg upā-jasat hyat verenātā acishtem manō; 83

at aēshemem hêñdvāreñtā yā banayen ahūm maretānō. 84

30. 7

ahmāicā xshathrā jasat mananhā vohū ashācā 85

at kehrpêm utayūitīs dadāt ārmaitis anmā 86

aēsham tōi ā anhat yathā ayanhā ādānāis pouruyō. 87

XXX.—4

But when the twin-Mentalities came together, they produced 76

The first life, and lifelessness, and (settled) (on the state of) the last condition of existence, 77

The worst for the Drujists, but for the Ashaists the best mind. 78

XXX—5

The Drujist chose between these twin-Mentalities, the one who perpetrated the worst (deeds), 79

But he (1) who (was inspired) by the most Bountiful Mentality that is clothed upon by the most adamantine stone-quarried heavens as a garment, 80

And he (2) who cheerfuly satisfied Ahura Mazdâh (lord mindful) with sincere deeds, chose Asha (justice.) 81

XXX.—6

The Daevaists did not discriminate accurately between these two, because 82

Just as they were deliberating, (there) came upon them a delusion so that they should choose the Worst Mind, 83

So that, all together, they rushed-over to Aeshma (fury) through which they afflict the life of man with disease. 84

XXX —7

And to this (man now sick) came (Mazdâh Ahura) (mindful lord) with the Xshathra (power) realm, with Vohu Manah (good disposition) and with Asha (justice), 85

And Armaiti (love) endowed the (sick) body (of man) (with) firmness and endurance 86

So that he may become the first of those (surviving) (the tests of passing) through the metal(lic trials) and through Adânas (the retributions). 87

XXX.—8

And thereupon, when the punishments of those malefactors shall occur, 88

30. 8

atcā yadā aēsham kaēnā jamaitī aēnanham   88

at mazdā taibyō xshathrem vohū mananhā vōivīdāitī   89

aēibyō sastē ahurā yōi ashāi daden zastayō drujem.   90

30. 9

atcā tōi vaēm hyāmā yōi īm ferashēm kerenāun ahūm   91

mazdåescå ahurāenhō ā-mōyastrā baranā ashācā   92

hyat hathrā manāe bavat yathrā cistis anhat maēthā.   93

30. 10

adā-zī avā drūjō avō bavaitī skeñdō spayathrahyā   94

at asishtā yaojañtē ā-hushitōis vanhēus mananhō   95

mazdāe ashahyācā yōi zazeñtī vanhāu sravahī.   96

30. 11

hyat tā urvātā sashathā yā mazdāe dadāt mashyāenhō   97

hvīticā ēneitī hyatcā daregēm dregvōdebyō rashō   98

savacā ashavabyō at aipī tāis anhaitī ushtā.   99

Then, (the saved man) shall obtain for thee, O Mazdâh (mindful), with the help of Vohu Manah (good disposition), the
Xshathra (power) realm.   89

Which will be the fulfillment (of the world's destiny,) and this
will be obtained by those, who shall deliver the Druj, into-the-
two-hands of Asha (justice)   90

III. Zarathushtra Hopes for Universal Conversion
by Choice between Eternal Bliss and Woe.

XXX.—9

And may we be those who shall make life progressive (M) or
purposeful (B) !   91

Assemble together, along with Asha (justice), O Ahuras Mazdâh
(lords mindfuls) and come hither   92

So that here where our thoughts formerly developed (separately),
they may now mature together, (fuse, or culminate) and become
wisdom.   93

XXX.—10

Then shall the success of the Druj break down,   94

And all those who shall be attaining a good renown   96

Shall obtain their reward, meeting at the good dwelling of Vohu
Manah, (good disposition), Mazdâh, (mindful), and Asha,
(justice).   95

XXX.—11

When, O you Mortals, you have familiarized yourselves with these
commandments of Mazdâh (mindful) (about the twin Mentalities), (which mean)   97

Prosperity as opposed to adversity, and the length of the suffering
of the Drujists, as contrasted with the useful progress of the
Ashaists;   98

(When, I repeat, you have fully realized the significance of this
contrast, I feel quite sure none of) you all, will (hesitate or delay to) enter into the desired abode of praise.   99

YASNA 31

31. 1

Tā vê urvātā mareñtō agushtā vacāe sêñghāmahī   100

aēibyō yōi urvātāis drūjō ashahyā gaēthāe vīmereñcaitē   101

atcīt aēibyō vahishtā yōi zarazdāe anhen mazdāi.   102

31. 2

yezī āis nōit urvānē advāe aibī-dereshtā vahyāe   103

at vāe vīspêñg āyōi yathā ratūm ahurō vaēdā   104

mazdāe ayāe asayāe yā ashāt hacā jvāmahī.   105

31. 3

yam dāe mainyū āthrācā ashācā cōis rānōibyā xshnūtem   106

hyat urvatem cazdōññhvadebyō tat nê mazdā vīdvanōi
   vaocā   107

hizvā thwahyā āenhō yā jvañtō vīspêñg vāurayā.   108

HYMN 31
Prayers for Enlightenment
and Exhortations to Partisanship.

I. Practical Introduction : Enlightenment Claimed
As no more than Justice to Zarathushtra.

XXXI.—1

Minding these your commands, (O Gods), let us pronounce
   speeches   100

Unheeded by those who would, by the commands of Druj, destroy
   the substance of Asha (justice),   101

But most acceptable to them who will trust in Mazdâh (mindful).

XXXI.—2

But since the preferable path is not always obvious   103

Therefore, as (heaven) appointed arbiter and judge over both
   parties,   104

Will I go to you, that we may live in accordance with Asha
   (justice).   105

XXXI —3

In order that I may cause all men to choose aright, (I pray thee)
   O Ahura Mazdâh (lord mindful), with the tongue of thy mouth
   to tell   108

(1) What satisfaction, taught through Asha (justice), thou wilt
   give to both contending Parties, through Mentality and
   fire;   106

(2) What is thy command for the enlightened, that we may understand (that command).   107

XXXI.—4

(And this command is), that as far as Asha (justice) and the
   other Ahuras Mazdâh (lords mindfuls) are willing to be invoked   109

Through Ashay (compensation) and Armaiti (love) and the best
   Manah (disposition),   110

31. 4

yadā ashem zevīm anhen mazdāescā ahurāenhŏ   109

ashicā ārmaitī vahishtā ishasā mananhā   110

maibyō xshathrem aojōñghvat yehyā veredā vanaēmā
drujem.   111

31. 5

tat mōi vīcidyāi vaocā hyat mōi ashā dātā vahyō   112

vīduyē vohū mananhā mēñcā daidyāi yehyā-mā ereshis   113

tācīt mazdā ahurā yā nōit vā anhat anhaitī vā.   114

31. 6

ahmāi anhat vahishtem yê mōi vīdvāe vaocāt haithīm   115

mathrem yim haurvatātō ashahyā ameretātascā   116

mazdāi avat xshathrem hyat hōi vohū vaxshat mananhā;   117

31. 7

yastā mañtā pouruyō raocēbīs rōithwen hvāthrā;   118

hvō xrathwā damis ashem; yā dārayat vahishtem manō;   119

tā mazdā mainyū uxshyō yê ā nūrêmcīt ahurā hāmō.   120

So far shall I seek for myself the Xshathra (power of realm) by
the vigorous increase whereof, we may defeat the Druj. 111

XXXI.—5

Tell me, O Ahura Mazdâh (lord mindful) what is not to occur,
and what is to occur, 114

In order that I may distinguish that, what (ever success therein)
You may have given me, through Asha (justice) was the better
thing, 112

In (2) order that I may understand it through Vohu Manah (good
disposition) and (3) may ponder-over this (so that by understanding it fully) I may gather therefrom a reward. 113

II. First Call for Enlightenment, and Answer from Within.
1. Call.

XXXI.—6

(This is the best reward of life: namely), that Xshathra (realm)
which (the man who receives it) may for his (own concurrent
advantage) increase for Mazdâh (the mindful one), through
Vohu Manah (good disposition); 117

May this best (reward) be granted to him who after having discovered for himself, (the right solution to these following
problems that distress me), will tell me sincerely 115

(1) Asha (justice) 's mystic word (which is the secret) of Haurvatat (health) and Ameretat (immortality). 116

XXXI.—7

(2) Whether Mazdâh (mindful) was the first one to fill the glories
(of heaven) with lights (of stars or flames), 118

(3) Whether Mazdâh (mindful) through understanding created
Asha (justice), and (4) whether Asha (justice) will maintain
the best activity of Vohu Manah (good disposition), 119

(5) Whether Mazdâh (mindful) shall cause these (Asha and
Vohu Manah) to prosper through the (Holy) Mentality, which
is ever the same until the present time. 120

31. 8

at thwā méñghī pourvīm mazdā yezīm stōi manaṇhā   121

vaṇhêus patarêm manaṇhō hyat thwā hêm cashmainī
    héñgraben   122

haithīm ashahyā damīm aṇhêus ahurem shyaothanaēshū 123

31. 9

thwōi as ārmaitīs thwê ā gêus tashā as xratūs   124

manyêus mazdā ahurā hyat ahyāi dadāe patham   125

vāstryāt vā āitē ye vā nōit aṇhat vāstryō   126

31. 10

at hī ayāe fravaretā vāstrīm ahyāi fshuyañtem   127

ahurem ashavanem vaṇhêus fshêñghīm manaṇhō   128

nōit mazdā avāstryō davascinā humeretōis baxshtā.   129

2. Answer.

XXXI.—8

Whereupon, when Zarathushtra with his (own) eye (by looking at nature) and through (his) mind by puzzling out its significance, comprehended Mazdâh (mindful) and Manah (disposition),   122

Then Zarathushtra understood that Mazdâh (mindful) was (1)
ꞔ both the first and youngest of creation (2) and the father of Vohu Manah (good disposition);   121

(3) The genuine creator of Asha (justice) and (4) the (ruling) lord in the deeds of life;   123

XXXI—9

(5) That, O Mazdâh Ahura (mindful lord), to thee belongs both Armaiti and the Shaper of the Bovine (creation) which was part of) the understanding of the (holy) Mentality.   124

(6) That when for (the cow) thou didst ordain a path (of freedom of will, following which)   125

She might repudiate the herdsman, and go to abide with the nomad   126

XXXI.—10

Then she chose for herself from among the two (possible) lords, (the herdsman or nomad) the herdsman who would follow her,   127

(Namely), the Ashaist, (who feels-that-it-is-his-mission-to-see-to-it-that-all-things-that-belong to Vohu Manah (good-disposition) prosper, and who-in-return-is-prospered-by-him,   128

(Whereas) the nomad shall not get a share of Vohu Manah (good disposition)'s favorable-report (at the judgment, as in the verse 14) even though he should urge for it (so long as he will not herd cattle).   129

31. 11

hya*t* ne mazdā paourvīm gaēthāescā tashō daēnāescā   130

thwā mana*n*hā xratūscā hya*t* astvañtem da*d*āe ushtanem 131

hya*t shy*aothanācā se*ñ*ghascā yathrā varenē*ñ*g vasāe dāyetē. 132

31. 12

athrā vācem baraitī mithahvacāe vā *e*resvacāe vā   133

vīdvā*e* vā *e*vīdvā*e* vā ahyā zeredācā mana*n*hācā   134

ānus-haxs ārmaitīs mainyū pe*r*esāitē yathrā maēthā.   135

31. 13

yā frasā āvīs*hy*ā yā vā mazdā peresāitē tayā   136

ye vā kase̱us aēna*n*hō ā mazisht*a*m ayamaitē būjem   137

tā cashmē*ñ*g thwisrā hārō aibī ashā aibī vaēnahī vīspā. 138

31. 14

tā-thwā pe*r*esā ahurā yā-zī āitī je*ñ*ghaticā   139

yāe ishudō dadeñtē dāthran*a*m hacā ashāunō   140

yāescā mazdā dre*g*vōde*b*yō yathā tā*e* a*n*hen hē*ñ*keretā hya*t*. 141

XXXI.—11

(7) That at first thou, O Mazdâh (mindful) with thy mind and
understanding,   130

(a) Thou didst shape substance and spirits, and (b) didst establish
body and life,   131

And (c) deeds and doctrines whereby men who exercised their
faculties of choice might develop convictions.   132

III. Second Call for Enlightenment.
1. Introduction.

XXXI.—12

(Amidst such sublime issues) vulgar men who speak either falsely
or justly, the Expert-knower or the ignorant.   133

Each (according to the fancy of his heart and mind, dares to
raise his (impudent) voice   134

Where Armaiti (love) counsels sucessively with the spirits who
yet are wavering.   135

XXXI.—13

O Mazdâh (mindful), thou with Asha (justice), keepest a watch,
with thy watchful gleaming eyes,   138

(1) Over all these (men who ask) questions openly or furtively;
and   136

(2) (Over all officials who) inflict the greatest penance for even a
small transgression.   137

2. The Second Call.

XXXI.—14

O Ahura Mazdâh (lord mindful), I ask thee about these conditions, present and future—   139

(Namely), (1) what compensations will be given to satisfy the
claims of the Ashaist,   140

(And what compensations shall be enforced) from the Drujist:—
How shall both stand at the time of awarding the compensations?   141

31. 15

peresā avat yā mainis yê dregvāitē xshathrem hunāitī   142

dus-shyaothanāi ahurā yê nōit jyōtūm hanare vīnastī   143

vāstryehyā aēnanhō pasêus vīrāatcā adrujyañtō.   144

31. 16

peresā avat yathā hvō yê hudānus demanahyā xshathrem   145

shōithrahyā vā dahyêus vā ashā fradathāi asperezatā   146

thwāvas mazdā ahurā yadā hvō anhat yā-shyaothanascā.147

31. 17

kadārêm ashavā vā dregvāe yā verenvaitē mazyō?   148

vīdvāê vīdushē mraotū mā evīdvāe aipī-dêbāvayat   149

zdī-nê mazdā ahurā vanhêus fradaxshtā mananhō!   150

31. 18

mā-cis at vê dregvatō mathrascā gūshtā sāsnāescā   151

āzī demānem vīsen vā shōithrem vā dahyūm vā ādāt   152

dushitācā marakaēcā athā īs sāzdūm snaithishā!   153

XXXI.—15

(2) O Ahura (lord) I ask thee what shall be the punishments (a)
    of those who encourage the dominion of the Drujist,   142
(b) of those who cannot make their living   143
    Without violence to cattle and to men devoted to herding
    them.   144

XXXI.—16

(3) O Mazdâh Ahura, (mindful lord) I ask thee whether the well-
    disposed man who may strive   145
To improve the houses, the villages, the clans and the provinces,
    through Asha (justice)   146
Whether (a) he may (at all) become a being like unto Thee; (b)
    if so, when shall he arise (unto this likeness) and (c) what
    (deeds) he shall do (to become such).   147

XXXI.—17

(4) (Tell me O lord), which is the more important object of
    choice—that of the Ashaist or that of the Drujist?   148
Do thou who art the Expert-knower inform me who would become
    one, and do not permit the ignorant man to continue deluding
    (such as me who would like to learn)   149
O Ahura Mazdâh, be Thou to us an instructor of Vohu Manah
    (good disposition)!   150

IV. The Partisan Close: Choose Sides, Take Zarathushtra's Word

XXXI.—18

Therefore O well disposed believer, hearken not to the mystic-
    words or teachings of any of the Drujists,   151
For these would reduce house, village, clan or province, to misfor-
    tune or death;   152
Therefore, rather oppose them with the weapon!   153

31. 15

peresā ava*t* yā mainis y*ê* dregvāitē xshathrem hunāitī   142

dus-*sh*yaothanāi ahurā y*ê* nōi*t* jyōtūm hana*re* vīnastī   143

vāstryehyā aēna*n*hō pas*ê*us vīrāa*t*cā adrujyañtō.   144

31. 16

pe*re*sā ava*t* yathā hvō y*ê* hudānus *de*manahyā xshathrem   145

shōithrahyā vā da*h*y*ê*us vā ashā fradathāi asperezatā   146

thwāva*s* mazdā ahurā yadā hvō a*n*ha*t* yā-*sh*yaothanascā.   147

31. 17

kadār*ê*m ashavā vā dre*g*vāe yā verenvaitē mazyō?   148

vīdvā*ê* vīdushē mraotū mā *e*vīdvāe aipī-d*ê*bāvaya*t*   149

zdī-n*ê* mazdā ahurā va*n*h*ê*us fradaxshtā mana*n*hō!   150

31. 18

mā-cis a*t* v*ê* dregvatō *m*athrascā gūshtā sāsnāescā   151

āzī demānem vīsen vā shōithrem vā da*h*yūm vā ādā*t*   152

dushitācā marakaēcā athā īs sāzdūm snaithishā!   153

XXXI.—15

(2) O Ahura (lord) I ask thee what shall be the punishments (a)
of those who encourage the dominion of the Drujist,   142
(b) of those who cannot make their living   143
Without violence to cattle and to men devoted to herding
them.   144

XXXI.—16

(3) O Mazdâh Ahura, (mindful lord) I ask thee whether the well-
disposed man who may strive   145
To improve the houses, the villages, the clans and the provinces,
through Asha (justice)   146
Whether (a) he may (at all) become a being like unto Thee; (b)
if so, when shall he arise (unto this likeness) and (c) what
(deeds) he shall do (to become such).   147

XXXI.—17

(4) (Tell me O lord), which is the more important object of
choice—that of the Ashaist or that of the Drujist?   148
Do thou who art the Expert-knower inform me who would become
one, and do not permit the ignorant man to continue deluding
(such as me who would like to learn)   149
) Ahura Mazdâh, be Thou to us an instructor of Vohu Manah
(good disposition)!   150

V. The Partisan Close: Choose Sides, Take Zarathushtra's Word

XXXI.—18

Therefore O well disposed believer, hearken not to the mystic-
words or teachings of any of the Drujists,   151
For these would reduce house, village, clan or province, to misfortune or death;   152
Therefore, rather oppose them with the weapon!   153

31. 19

gūshtā yê mañtā ashem ahūmbis vīdvāe ahurā   154

erezuxdāi vacanham xshayamnō hizvō vasō   155

thwā āthrā suxrā mazdā vanhāu vīdātā ranayāe.   156

31. 20

yê āyat ashavanem divamnem hōi aparem xshyō   157

daregêm āyū temanhō dushvarethêm avaētās vacō   158

têm vā ahūm dregvañtō shyaothanāis hvāis daēnā naēshat! 159

31. 21

mazdāe dadāt ahurō haurvatō ameretātascā   160

būrōis ā ashahyācā hvāpaithyāt xshathrahyā sarō   161

vanhêus vazdvarê mananhō yê hōi mainyū shyaothanāiscā
urvathō.   162

31.22

cithrā ī hudāenhē yathanā vaēdemnāi mananhā   163

vohū hvō xshathrā ashem vacanhā shyaothanācā haptī   164

hvō tōi mazdā ahurā vāzishtō anhaitī astis.   165

XXXI.—19

But hearken to him who thought out Asha, (justice); that is,
    Zarathushtra who is the life healing Expert-knower;   154
Him who is able to vindicate his tongue's speeches at will, (at the
    Latter Day)   155
(When) O Ahura Mazdâh, (lord-mindful), with thy red (fire)
    the good (compensations) of the two contending parties are to
    be distributed; (with thy red fire, produced by the two good
    rubbing sticks).   156

XXXI—20

Destruction, lasting darkness, bad food, and imprecations   158
Shall at the (Latter Day) be kept away from whomsoever identifies
    himself with the Ashaists,   157
(Beware) O Drujists: (it is to) that sort of existence that your
    (evil) spirit may lead you!   159

XXXI.—21

From the resources of his innate glory, Ahura Mazdâh (lord mind-
    ful) shall grant sustained communion   160
And fulness of Haurvatat, (health) and Ameretat, (immortality,
    and of Asha, (justice) and of Xshathra, (power) and Vohu
    Manah (good disposition)   161
To whomsoever is a friend (to Ahura Mazdâh, (lord mindful) in
    mind and deeds.   162

XXXI.—22

The man who is well-disposed, (understands) this as clearly as
    does Mazdâh (mindful) who knows with the (divine) Manah,
    (disposition).   163
(It is this well-disposed man) who holds Asha (justice) in
    union with the good Xshathra (political power), through his
    speech and deeds.   164
(It is this well-disposed man) who is the most prospering compan-
    ion to thee, O Ahura Mazdâh (lord mindful.)   165

YASNA 32

32. 1

Ahyācā *h*vaētus yāsa*t* ahyā verezênem ma*t* airyamnā   166

ahyā daēvā mahmī manōi. ahurahyā urvāzemā mazdā*e*   167

thwōi dūtā*en*hō āe*n*hāmā têñg dārayō yōi vā*e* daibisheñtī   168

32. 2

aēibyō mazdā*e* ahurō sāremnō vohū mana*n*hā   169

xshathrā*t* hacā paitī-mrao*t* ashā hus-haxā *h*vênvātā: 170

'speñta*m* vê ārmaitīm va*n*uhīm varemaidī hā-nê a*n*ha*t*.'   171

32. 3

a*t* yūs daēvā vīspāe*n*hō akā*t* mana*n*hō stā cithrem   172

yascā vā*e* mas yazaitē drūjascā pairimatōiscā   173

*sh*yaoma*m* aipī daibitānā yāis a*s*rūdūm būmyā*e* haptaithē.   174

HYMN 32

At a Parley,
Vituperation *of the* Rival Prophet Grehma.

I. Public Self-consecration, and its Acceptance.

XXXII.—1

(All three classes) : The kinsman-lord, the worker and the priestly

  peer shall, O Daeva, (in spite of You)   166

Pray for the joys of Ahura Mazdâh (lord mindful) according to

  my conceptions, (says Zoroaster).   167

(The three classes answer:) May we be thy messengers, to repel

  those who hostilely decive You (O divine beings).   168

XXXII.—2

To them replied Ahura Mazdâh, (lord mindful), who is in com-

  munion with Vohu Manah (good disposition,)   169

By Xshathra, (power), with the gloriously sunny, well-befriend-

  ing Asha, (justice),   170

"We have accepted (this) your holy, good, submissive confession

  (which we name Armaiti) ; she shall be Ours."   171

II. Zarathushtra Vituperates his Rival Grehma to the Daevas.

XXXII.—3

(Zarathushtra to the Daevas) : But you O Daevas are all as a

  seed (descended from) the Bad Mind,   172

And whatever mortal man will dare to reverence you, he shall be

  considered as belonging to the Druj (party), for he is proud,

  (the opposite of Armaiti (love,) ;   173

For you have become notorious, event to the seventh (region) of

  the earth, as being long since preceded by (the evil reputation

  of) your deeds.   174

32. 4

yā*t* yūstā framīmathā yā ma*sh*yā acishtā dañtō   175

vaxsheñtē daēvō-zushtā va*nh*êus sīzdyamnā mana*nh*ō   176

mazdā*e* ahurahyā xratêus na*s*yañtō ashāa*t*cā;   177

32. 5

tā debenaotā mashīm hujyātōis ameretātascā   178

hya*t* vā*e* akā mana*nh*ā yéñg daēvéñg akascā mainyus   179

akā s*h*yaothanem vaca*nh*ā yā fracina*s* dregvañtem xshayō.   180

32. 6

pourū-aēnā*e* *ê*nāxshtā yāis s*r*āvahyeitī yezī tāis athā   181

hātā-marānē ahurā vahishtā vōistā mana*nh*ā   182

thwahmī v*ê* mazdā xshathrōi ashāicā s*êñ*ghō vīda*m*.   183

32. 7

aēsham aēna*nh*a*m* naēcī*t* vīdvā*e* aojōi hādrōyā   184

yā jōyā s*êñ*ghaitē yāis s*r*āvī *h*vaēnā aya*nh*ā   185

yaēsha*m* tū ahurā irixtem mazdā vaēdishtō ahī.   186

XXXII.—4

Since it is due to you that the worst behaving men are called
daeva-darlings 175
And are excluded from Vohu Manah (good disposition's) (fellowship in the congregation) 176
Perishing away from Asha (justice) and from the understanding
of Mazdâh Ahura (mindful lord); 177

XXXII.—5

Therefore, you will defraud man of good life (here) and immortality (beyond) 178
Because with evil mind and bad speech (he, Grehma, verse 12) of
the evil Mentality, 179
Advises the deeds with which he causes you, who arc Dacvas, and
the Drujist (man afore mentioned,) to perish. 180

XXXII—6

(Grehma) has (so far) succeeded in perpetrating the many violences through which he has become notorious; 181
'(But) whether he shall (continue this success, here on earth) thou
alone knowest through thy Vohu Manah (good disposition) O
Ahura (lord); 182
(But of this I am sure: that) in thy Xshathra (realm) O Mazdâh
(mindful), Your doctrinal decision shall be given for Asha
(justice). 183

XXXII.—7

The Expert-knower is not to commit any of these deeds of violence, whose (fatal) end, thou, O Ahura Mazdâh best
knowest. 184
(He is not to commit any of them, even if tempted to do so)
through a (well intentioned, misguided) desire for (proper)
gain; 186
(For it was) such (a desire that) led (Grehma) to become notorious through his glittering sword of violence . 185

32. 8

aēsham aēna*n*ham vīva*n*hushō srāvī yimascī*t*   187

yê ma*sh*yêñg cixshnushō ahmākêñg gāus bagā *hv*āremnō 188

aēsha*m*cī*t* ā ahmī thwahmī mazdā vīcithōi aipī!   189

32. 9

dus-*sast*is sravā*e* mōreñda*t* hvō jyātê*u*s *sêñ*ghanā*i*s xratūm 190

apō mā.ĭshtīm apayañtā be*rexdam* hāitīm va*n*hêus mana*n*hō 191

ᵗā ux*d*ā manyê*u*s mahyā mazdā ashāicā yūshmaibyā *gereze*. 192

32. 10

hvō mā-nā *srav*ā*e* mōreñda*t* yê acishtem vaēna*n*hē aogedā 193

gam ashibyā hvarecā yascā dāthêñg d*reg*vatō dadā*t*   194

yascā vāstrā vīvāpa*t* yascā vadarê vōiz*d*a*t* ashāunē.   195

32. 11

taēcī*t* mā mōreñden jyōtūm yōi d*reg*vatō mazibīs cikōiter*es* 196

a*n*uhīscā a*n*hvascā apayeitī raēxena*n*hō vaēdem   197

yōi vahishtā*t* ashāunō mazdā rār*es*hya*n* mana*n*hō.   198

32. 12

yā rāe*n*hayen srava*n*hā vahishtā*t* *sh*yaothanā*t* maretānō 199

aēibyō mazdā*e* akā mrao*t* yōi gêus mōreñden urvāxs-uxtī
    jyōtūm   200

yāis gerêhmā ashā*t* varatā karapā xshathremcā īshana*m*
    drujem.   201

XXXII.—8

As is (well) known, (there was) among these (committers) of violence a certain Yima (son) of Vivahvant,   187

Who in order to satisfy our men, gave pieces of beef to be devoured.   188

I (certainly) expect to be (divided) from these (sinners) in thy discriminating-judgment, O Mazdâh (mindful)!   189

XXXII —9

The prophet of evil, Grehma, with his pronouncements will destroy the words (which form) the understanding of life,   190

By hindering my wealth, the prized possession of Vohu Manah (good disposition).   191

With these uttered expressions (of my thought (as a complaint) I appeal to thee, O Mazdâh (mindful), through Asha (justice).

XXXII.—10

(It is Grehma) who destroys (the effect of) my words, and who (1) preaches that   193

The cattle and the sun are the worst objects to behold, and (2) who makes Drujists out of clever ʻ(believers),   194

And (3) who destroys the cultivated lands, and (4) raises the weapon against the Ashaist.   195

XXXII.—11

His followers would destroy my life. They have had many consultations with the Drujists, so as   196

(1) To deprive the (Ashaist) masters and the mistresses of the possession of their inheritance, and   197

(2) To cause the Ashaists to apostacize from the Best Mind, O Mazdâh (mindful),   198

XXXII —12

(3) And by their speeches, to cause men to apostacize from their best deeds.   199

Mazdâh (mindful) spoke: "Bad are ye (1) who destroy the life of cattle with cries of joy,   200

And who (2) to Asha prefer Grehma, Karpa and the power favorable to the Druj."   201

32. 13

yā xshathrā gerêhmō hīshasat acishtahyā demānē manaṇhō 202

aṇhêus maraxtārō ahyā yaēcā mazdā jīgerezat kāmē   203

thwahyā maṭhrānō dūtīm yê-īs pāt daresāt ashahyā.   204

32. 14

ahyā gerêhmō ā-hōithōi nī kāvayascīt xratūs nī dadat   205

varecāe hīcā fraidivā hyat vīseñtā dregvañtem avō   206

hyatcā gāus jaidyāi mraoī yê dūraoshem saocayat avō.   207

32. 15

anāis ā vī-nênāsā yā karapōtāescā kevītāescā   208

avāis aibī yêñg daiñtī nōit jyātêus xshayamnêñg vasō   209

tōi ābyā bairyāeñtē vaṇhêus ā-demānē manaṇhō.   210

32. 16

hamêm tat vahishtācīt yê ushuruyê syascīt dahmahyā   211

xshayas mazdā ahurā yehyā-mā aithīscīt dvaēthā   212

hyat aēnaṇhē dregvatō êeānū ishyêñg aṇhayā.   213

XXXII.—13

Through which Xshathra (power) of the above Asha (justice),
  Grehma will be degraded to hell, the dwelling of the Worst
  Mind,   202

(Where dwell) the destroyers of this life; and (then) O Mazdâh
  (mindful) he will complain, being moved by a desire   203

For the message of thy prophet, who (then) (however) will keep
  him from beholding Asha (justice).   204

XXXII.—14

Grehma (1) (plans) the subjection of this (Asha, justice);
  (2) long since he supports both the Kavayas and the powerful
  (Drujists) through his plans,   205

Which raises help unto the Drujist;   206

And (3) (he cries that) the cow is to be killed; and (4) he will
  burn (the Ashaist) who-repels-death from her (by being) of
  help to her.   207

III. Zarathushtra will Exult in Executing this Final Judgment.

XXXII.—15

But through these Ashaists, I will expel both the Karapans and
  Kavayites   208

Who will not permit the Ashaists to rule their lives as they wish
  (by the divine law of cattle herding)   209

Which (Ashaists) I pray will be borne (to heaven) the (dwelling
  of Vohu Manah (good disposition) by the twins (Haurvatat and
  Ameretat.)   210

XXXII —16

All this is from that Best (divinity) who is teaching in the wide
  light (of the stars) (or of the altar-flame, (M)   211

Thou, O Mazdâh Ahura (mindful-lord), controllest whomsoever
  threatens me with destruction,   212

So that I may encourage the beloved (believers) by setting limits
  to the violence of the Druj, by (the words of) my mouth. 213

YASNA 33

33. 1

Yathāis ithā vareshaitē yā dātā anhêus paouruyehyā   214

ratūs shyaothanā razishtā dregvataēcā hyatcā ashāunē   215

yehyācā hêmemyāsaitē mithahyā yācā hōi ārezvā.   216

33. 2

at yê akem dregvāitē vacanhā vā at vā mananhā   217

zastōibyā vā vareshaitī vanhāu vā cōithaitē astīm   218

tōi vārāi rādeñtī ahurahyā zaoshē mazdāe.   219

33. 3

yê ashāunē vahishtō hvaētū vā at vā verezênyō   220

airyamnā vā ahurā vīdas vā thwaxshanhā gavōi   221

at hvō ashahyā anhat vanhêuscā vāstrē mananhō.   222

.HYMN 33

High-priestly Prayer for
Acceptance, Conversion, *and* Paradise.

(Apparently belonging to the Close of the former Hymn, on)
Zarathushtra's Exultation on Executing the Final Judgment.

XXXIII.—1

In accordance with these laws of the first life   214
The judge will enact, the most just decisions for the Drujist, as
    well as the Ashaist,   215
And for the man who combines the false and just actions (B)
    (and do whatever may suit the needs of the false and the just,
    (M)   216

XXXIII.—2

But whoever (1) by speech, word or deed do harm to the Drujist,
Or (2) converts one to the good (i. e., either injures or converts)
    or (3) instructs a fellow believer,   218
They (are those who are thereby) working for the (divine) will,
    and for the pleasure of Ahura Mazdâh (lord mindful) in the
    (great work of the) preparation.   219

XXXIII.—3

Whoever, through being a gentleman-by-birth, is best (in-
    clined) to the Ashaist, or which herd-laborer,   220
Or an expert peer, or is zealous for the cattle O Ahura (lord),
Surely he will come to be on the pasturage of Asha (justice) and
    Vohu Manah (good disposition).   ,   222

33. 4

yê thwa*t* mazdā asrushtīm akemcā manō yazāi apā   223

*h*vaētêuscā tarêmaitīm verezêna*h*yācā nazdisht*am* drujem   224

airyamanascā nadeñtō gêuscā vāstrā*t* acishtem mañtūm   225

33. 5

yastē vīspê-mazishtem *s*eraoshem zbayā ava*n*hānē   226

apānō daregō-jyāitīm ā-xshathrem va*n*héus mana*n*hō   227

ashā*t* ā *e*rezūs pathō yaēshū mazdā*e* ahurō shaētī   228

33.ˉ6

yê zaotā ashā *e*rezūs hvō manyêus ā vahishtā*t* kayā   229

ȧhmā*t* avā mana*n*hā yā verezyeidyāi mañtā vāstryā   230

tā-tōi izyāi ahurā mazdā darshtōiscā hêm-parshtōiscā.   231

I. Prayer for Acceptation.

XXXIII.—4

I, who, by praying, would, O Ahura Mazdâh (lord mindful) conjure away (1) disobedience and badness from (what the opponents think of) thee,   223

And (2) contrariness from the gentleman, and (3) the neighborhood of the Drujist from the group of laboring men,   224

And (4) cursing from the peer, and (5) poor farmers (fodder)
(M) from the pasturage of the cattle;   225

XXXIII.—5

I who will invoke Sraosha (obedience) as the greatest of all
· (divinities) for help (to man)   226

Having reached (1) long life, (2) the realm of Vohu Manah
(good disposition)   227

And (3) the Asha (justice) straightened paths, on which Ahura
Mazdâh (lord mindful) dwells;   228

XXXIII.—6

I who, as priest (coming) through Asha (justice) from the Best
(Mind) desire (to walk) the just (paths) of the Bounteous
Mentality   229

Going (from us) (the Ashaist's priests) towards the pastures
which advisory-managers ought to work through the (Vohu)
Manah (disposition).   230

(For these two objects) I wish, O Ahura Mazâh (lord mindful)
to consult together (both the Best (Mind) and the Bounteous
Mentality) visibly.   231

XXXIII.—7

Come hither to me O you Best (divinities) ; come here personally,
O Mazdâh (mindful)   232

Visibly, with Asha (justice), and Vohu Manah (good disposi-

33. 7

ā-mā āidūm-vahishtā ā-*hv*aithyācā mazdā daresha*t*cā   232

ashā vohū mana*n*hā yā *s*ruyē par*ê* magāunō,   233

āvis-nā*e* añtar*e* hêñtū nema*hv*aitīs cithrā*e* rātayō.   234

33. 8

frō-mōi fravōizdūm ar*e*thā tā yā vohū *s*hyavāi mana*n*hā   235

ya*s*nem mazdā xshmāvatō a*t* vā ashā *s*taomyā vacā*e*   236

kātā v*ê* ameretāescā utayūitī haurvatā*s* draonō.   237

33. 9

a*t* tōi mazdā t*ê*m mainyūm ashaoxshayañtā*e* saredyayā*e* 238

*hv*āthrā maēthā mayā vahishtā bar*e*tū mana*n*hā   239

ayā*e* arōi hākur*e*nem yayā*e* haciñtē urva*n*ō.   240

33. 10

vīspā*e*-stōi hujītayō yā*e*-zī āe*n*har*ê* yā*e*scā heñtī   241

yā*e*scā mazdā bavaiñtī thwahmī hīs zaoshē ābaxshōhvā   242

vohū uxshyā mana*n*hā xshathrā ashācā ushtā tanūm.   243

tion); inform me how I may be heard before (M) or outside
of (B) the Magians; (and, for this purpose)   233
Let reverent services of worship be (performed) clearly and
' manifestly among us.   234

II. Prayer for General Conversion.

XXXIII.—8

O do Thou regard (1) the interests which I am advancing
through Vohu Manah (good disposition),   235
(2) The hymn, O Mazdâh (mindful) (addressed to) one-like-
You and (3) my grateful communions with Asha (justice), 236
And give me Your-twin enduring possessions of Ameretat (immortality) and Haurvatat (health).   237

XXXIII —9

But let me O Mazdâh (mindful) bring the (holy) Mentality of
these two (divine) companions who prosper (the) Ashaist
(just) life   238
Unto the comfortable dwellings, with me, who have the best
Manah (best disposition),   239
In thus arousing the support of these two (divinities) whose souls
are accompanying each other.   240

XXXIII.—10

Distribute, O Mazdâh, from thy delight, all the pleasures of life,
Which were, and are, and are yet becoming;   242
And cause my-body to grow as-I-wish, with Vohu Manah (good
disposition,) Xshathra (power,) and Asha (justice.)   243

33. 11

yê *s*evishtō ahurō mazdāescā ārmaitiscā   244

ashemcā frāda*t*-gaēthem manascā vohū xshathremcā   245

sraotā-mōi, mere*z*dātā-mōi ādāi kahyāicī*t* paitī!   246

33. 12

us-mōi uzāreshvā ahurā ārmaitī tevīshīm da*s*vā   247

*s*pênishtā mainyū mazdā va*n*huyā zavō ādā   248

ashā hazō êmava*t* vohū mana*n*hā *f*eseratūm!   249

33. 13

ra*f*ed*r*āi vourucashānē dōishī-mōi yā-*v*ê abifrā   250

tā xshathrahyā ahurā yā va*n*hêus ashis mana*n*hō   251

frō *s*peñtā ārmaitē ashā daēnā*e* fradaxshayā!   252

33. 14

a*t* rāt*am* zarathushtrō tanvascī*t* hvahy*āe* ushtanem   253

dadāitī paurvatātem mana*n*hascā va*n*hêus mazdāi   254

*s*hyaothanahyā ashāi yācā ux*d*a*h*yācā *s*eraoshem xshathremcā.   255

III. Prayer for Paradise.

XXXIII.—11

(Thou) (Asha) who art the strongest Ahura of Mazdâh (lord of mindful) and Armaiti (love),   244

Prospering, as if they were earthly substance, Asha, (justice) and Vohu Manah, (good disposition) and Xshathra (power), 245

Hear me, pity me, when to every man (shall come) retribution!

XXXIII.—12

Arise up to me, O Ahura Mazdâh, (lord mindful) grant me (1) through Armaiti (love), vitality;   247

(2) Through the most bounteous Mentality, grant me strength; (3) through good Ada (retribution),   248

And through Asha (justice) (grant me) powerful might, (4) and through Vohu Manah (good disposition) (grant) compensation.   249

XXXIII.—13

In order to grant me support, O thou wide glancing (divinity,) show me (that) the incomparable (riches)   250

Of thy realm, O Ahura (lord), (are) the compensations of Vohu Manah, (good disposition);   251

O bounteous Armaiti, (love) instruct the spirits through Asha, (justice).   252

XXXIII.—14

But, O Ahura Mazdâh (lord mindful), Zarathushtra offers as an oblation his own body,   253

And the first fruits of Vohu Manah (good disposition),   254

And the Sraosha (obedience) and Xshathra (power) of his deeds and uttered words, through Asha (justice).   255

YASNA 34

34. 1

Yā *sh*yaothanā, yā vaca*n*hā, yā ya*s*nā ame*r*etatātem   256

ashemcā taēibyō dāe*n*hā mazdā xshathremcā haurvatātō 257

aēsh*am* tōi ahurā *ê*hmā pourutemāis dastē,   258

34. 2

a*t*cā ī-tōi mana*n*hā mainyuscā va*n*hus vīspā dātā   259

speñta*h*yācā ne*r*es *sh*yaothanā yehyā urvā ashā hacaitē 260

pairigaēthē xshmāvatō vahmē mazdā garōbīs stūt*am*!   261

34. 3

a*t* tōi mya*z*dem ahurā nema*n*hā ashāicā dāmā   262

gaēthā*e* vīspā*e* ā-xshathrōi yā*e* vohū thraoshtā mana*n*hā   263

ārōi-zī hudāe*n*hō vīspāis mazdā xshmāvasū savō!   264

HYMN 34

Congregational Prayer for Protection *and* Instruction.

I. Congregational Prayer for Protection and Instruction.

XXXIV—1

Among the foremost (of thy worshippers) we offer to thee, O
Ahura Mazdâh mindful lord, through the mind of the good
Mentality,   258

XXXIV—2

All the deeds, speeches and hymns   259
Through which (deeds, speeches and hymns)   256
Thou shalt bestow Ameretat, (immortality) Asha, (justice)
Xshathra, (power) and Haurvatat, (health)   257
And we bear the praises of thy grateful people, with a bounteous-
ness, such as would gratefully follow along the paths of Asha,
(justice)   260
(Even) into the outer realms (of-the-heavenly-presence) of a
(divinity) such as You, O Ahura Mazdâh (lord mindful)! 261

XXXIV—3

But to thee, O Ahura Mazdâh (lord mindful) and to Asha, (justice) we shall with reverence offer the oblation   262
(That) you with Vohu Manah (good disposition) may cause all
substantial beings which are in the Xshathra (realm) to mature
(into perfection B),   263
Seeing that the perfecting of the beneficent man is at all times
valuable in (the sight of) One-like-You.   264

34. 4

at tōi ātrêm ahurā aojōnhvañtem ashā usêmahī   265

asīshtīm êmavañtem stōi rapañtē cithrā-avanhem   266

at mazdā daibishyañtē zastāishtāis dereshtā-aēnanhem.   267

34. 5

kat vê xshathrem kā īshtīs shyaothanāi mazdā yathā vā
hahmī   268

ashā vohū mananhā thrāyōidyāi drigūm yūshmākem   269

parê-vāe vīspāis parê vaoxemā daēvāiscā xrafstrāis
mashyāiscā.   270

34. 6

yezī athā stā haithīm mazdā ashā vohū mananhā   271

at tat mōi daxshtem dātā ahyā anhêus vīspā maēthā   272

yathā vāe yazemnascā urvāidyāe stavas ayēnī paitī.   273

34. 7

kuthrā tōi aredrā mazdā yōi vanhêus vaēdenā mananhō 274

sênghūs raēxenāe aspêñcīt sādrācīt caxrayō usheurū?   275

naēcīm têm anyêm yūshmat vaēdā ashā athā-nāe thrāzdūm! 276

XXXIV.—4

We wish O Mazdâh, (lord mindful) that thy fire, whose strength
is Asha, (justice)   265

May be a promised (swift, M) powerful, clear, delightful help for
supporting the land or the people;   266

But (that it may be) for the enemies a visible, suggestive and
practical token of harm.   267

XXXIV.—5

Have You (enough) Xshathra (power)? Have You (enough)
Wealth? O Ahura Mazdâh (lord mindful), for the deeds
which I (urge) You (to do, namely),   268

With Asha, (justice) and Vohu Manah (good disposition), to protect Your poor?   269

Through (our preaching among) the daevic-enemies, savages, and
and doomed-men, we will declare You to all foreigners.   270

XXXIV.—6

Since You therefore actually have the above powers, O Ahura
Mazdâh (lord mindful), with Asha (justice) and Vohu Manah
(good disposition),   271

Therefore grant me as token thereof, a change for better now in
this life,   272

So that I may the more approach You with greater joy and adoration.   273

XXXIV.—7

(O Lord, listen to me who wish to ask thee about certain people)

Are they faithful to thee, O Ahura Mazdâh, (lord mindful), who,
though they know of Vohu Manah, (good dispostion),   274

Turn the difficulties of traditionally-inherited doctrine unto their
own advantage, by sophistries?   275

As for me, I know none other but You, O Asha! therefore protect
us.   \   276

34. 8

tāis zī-nāe *sh*yaothanāis byeñtē yaēshū a*s* pairī pourubyō
ithyejō   277

hya*t* a*s* aojyā*e* nāidyā*e*nhem thwahyā mazdā *a*stā urvātahyā 278

yōi nōi*t* a*sh*em mainyañtā aēibyō dūirē vohū a*s* manō! 279

34. 9

yōi speñt*a*m ārmaitīm thwahyā mazdā berexd*a*m vīdushō 280

dus-*sh*yaothanā avazaza*t* va*n*hê*u*s *e*vistī mana*n*hō   281

aēibyō mas ashā *s*yazda*t* yava*t* ahma*t* aurunā xrafstrā.   282

34. 10

ahyā va*n*hê*u*s mana*n*hō *sh*yaothanā vaoca*t* gereb*a*m
huxratus   283

speñt*a*mcā ārmaitīm d*a*mīm vīdvā*e* hith*a*m ashahyā   284

tācā vīspā ahurā thwahmī mazdā xshathrōi ā vōyathrā! 285

34. 11

a*t* tōi ubē haurvāescā *h*varethāi ā ameretatāescā   286

va*n*hê*u*s xshathrā mana*n*hō ashā ma*t* ārmaitis vaxsht   287

utayūitī tevīshī tāis ā mazdâ vīdvaēsh*a*m thwōi ahī !   288

XXXIV.—8

With such specious deeds, under which lurk danger for many,
they are intimidating us; especially   277

Me, who am the weaker, for (Bendva) is strong with hate of thy
commands, O Mazdâh, (mindful).   278

But those who think not of Asha, (justice) they are surely distant
from Vohu Manah (good disposition)!   279

XXXIV.—9

Those evil doers who drive away bounteous Armaiti, (love) so
highly prized by the Expert-knower O Mazdâh (mindful)   280

Because they have no share of Vohu Manah (good disposition)

Are shunned by the man endowed by Asha, (justice) as much as
the savages are shunned by us.   282

XXXIV —10

The clever Expert-knower will say he holds (1) to the deeds of
Vohu Manah, (good disposition)   283

And (2) to the bounteous creator Armaiti (love) the associate
(wife?) of Asha (justice)   284

And (3) to all thy hopes (that are to be realized) in thy Xshathra
(power), O Ahura Mazdâh, (lord mindful)!   285

XXXIV.—11

Thus for (that Expert-knower) both Haurvatat (health) and
Ameretat (immortality) (serve) for food   ·   286

And Armaiti ever has caused the-two enduring and vital (divinities just mentioned,) to grow through the Xsathra (power) of
Vohu Manah (good disposition) and through Asha (justice);

Thus, O Mazdâh (mindful), thou blessest the opponents of thy
enemies!   288

XXXIV.—12

What is Thy decree? What is Thy wish? What praise, what
hymn (wouldst thou have me raise to Thee?)   289

34. 12

kat tōi rāzarê? kat vashī? kat vā stūtō? kat vā yasnahyā? 289

srūidyāi mazdā frāvaocā yā vīdāyāt ashīs rāshnam 290

sīshā-nāe ashā pathō vanhêus hvaētêñg mananhō. 291

34. 13

têm advānem ahurā yêm mōi mraos vanhêus mananhō 292

daēnāe saoshyañtam yā hū-karetā ashācīt urvāxshat 293

hyat civishtā hudābyō mīzdem mazdā yehyā tū dathrem. 294

34. 14

tat zī mazdā vairīm astvaitē ushtānāi dātā 295

vanhêus shyaothanā mananhō yōi zī gêus verezênê azyāe 296

xshmākam hucistīm ahurā xratêus ashā frādō verezênā. 297

34. 15

mazdā at mōi vahishtā sravāescā shyaothanācā vaocā 298

tā-tū vohū mananhā ashācā ishudem stūtō 299

xshmākā xshathrā ahurā ferashêm vasnā haithyêm dāe
  ahūm! 300

(In order) that we may hear it, do thou, O Ahura Mazdâh, (lord
    mindful), reveal what compensation thou wilt grant (as a re-
    ward) for keeping Thy observances.   290

Teach us, O Asha (1) the passable paths of Vohu Manah, (good
    disposition)   291

XXXIV.—13

'And (2) the way of Vohu Manah (good disposition, (a) of which
    thou toldst me,   292

(b) Which is well formed by Asha, (justice) (c) on which the
    spirits of the Saviors progress;   293

(d) Which thou, O Mazdâh (mindful) hast assigned for the
    clever, as one of the compensations which are at thy disposal.

II. Zarathushtra Closes with a Prayer
for Congregation and Humanity.

XXXIV.—14

Which 'choice' (compensation) O Ahura Mazdâh (lord mindful)
    give (1) to my corporeal life   295

Through the action of Vohu Manah (good dispositions); and
    (2) to whomsoever belongs to-the-groups-of-those-who-labor-
    at-herding calving (cows);   296

(For your compensations consist of) good wisdom of the under-
    standing, which causes prosperity-for-the-caste-of-laboring-men.

XXXIV.—15

O Ahura Mazdâh, (lord mindful), with Vohu Manah (good dispo-
    sition), and with Asha (justice), inform me of   298

The best teachings and deeds and speeches, and what praise of ours
    You claim as Your due.   299

Through Xsthathra (power) grant that, according to Your will
    humanity may be progressive.   300

Gatba Ushtavaiti

YASNA 43

43. 1

Ushtā ahmāi, yahmāi, ushtā kahmāicī*t*! 301

vasê-xshay*as* mazdā*e* dāyā*t* ahurō 302

utayūitī tevīshīm, ga*t*-tōi vasemī! 303

ashem deredyāi ta*t* mōi dāe, ārmaitē, 304

rāyō ashīs va*nh*êus gaēm mana*nh*ō! 305

43. 2

a*t*cā ahmāi vīspan*a*m vahishtem 306

*h*vāthrōyā nā *h*vāthrem daidītā. 307

thwā cīcīthwā spênishtā mainyū mazdā, 308

yā dā*e* ashā va*nh*êus māyā*e* māna*nh*ō 309

vīspā ayār*ê* dareg*ō*jyātōis urvāda*nh*ā! 310

HYMN 43

The Interior Call *of* Zarathushtra

I. Prayer for fulfilment of Human Aspirations

43.1

Success to Me, to You, and to Whosoever will!   301
May AHURA Mazdah (mindful lord) who rules at will over
  all things, grant   2
(That) both Enduringness and Vitality (health and immortality) may come to thee (O Believer)! Of Thee, O Lord,
  do I desire this!   3
As to me, grant me that I maintain my hold on Asha (justice)! And do Thou, O Armaiti (love), grant me   4
Riches, Compensations, and the life of Vohu Manah (good
  disposition)!   5

43.2

Yea, Vohu Manah (good disposition) will give the best of
  all things to this Zarathushtra;   306
According to his wish, He will give him the comfort of
  heaven.   7
O Mazdah (mindful), through Thy most (bounteous mentality) Spenta Mainyu reveal   8
All these blissful mysteries of Vohu Manah (good disposition) which Thou givest through Asha (justice)   9
With all the joys that are long and vital on every day!   10

43. 3

aṭ hvō vaṇhêus vahyō nā aibī-jamyāṭ   311

yê nāe erezūs çavaṇhō pathō çīshōiṭ   312

ahyā aṇhêus açtvatō manaṇhaççā,   313

haithyêñg āçtīs yêñg ā-shaētī ahurō,   314

aredrō thwāvaç huzêñtuse çpeñtō mazdā !   315

43. 4

aṭ thwā mêñghāi taxmemcā çpeñtem mazdā   316

hyaṭ tā zaçtā yā-tū hafshī avāe   317

yāe dāe ashīs dregvāitē ashāunaēcā,   318

thwahyā garemā āthrō ashā-aojaṇhō,   319

hyaṭ mōi vaṇhêus hazê jimaṭ manaṇhō.   320

43. 5

çpeñtem aṭ thwā mazdā mêñghī, ahurā,   321

hyaṭ thwā aṇhêus zaṭhōi dareçem paourvīm.   322

hyaṭ dāe skyaothanā mīzdavan yācā uxdā   323

akêm akāi vaṇuhīm ashīm vaṇhaovē   324

thwā hunarā dāmōis urvaēçē apêmē.   325

43.3

May he (Zarathushtra) who, like Thee, O Mazdah (mind-
ful), is faithful, well-informed, and bounteous,   315
Who would teach us the just paths of profit—namely,   12
Those of the good life (both) corporeal and mental, that
lead to   13
The real worlds where dwells (the lord) AHURA;   14
May he (Zarathushtra) arrive to What-is-better-than-
good!   11

43.4

In order that I may receive the power of Vohu Manah
(good disposition)   320
I would , in Thee, O AHURA Mazdah (mindful lord), acknowledge heroism and bounteousness,   16
(1) Through the Hand in which thou holdest   17
The Compensation to be given to Drujist and Ashaist, 18
And (2) through the glow of thy (judgment) Fire, whose
vigor is Asha (justice).   19

II. Reminiscences of Six Earlier Visionary Experiences.
VISION I. At Beginning, Mazdah plans Rewards and Punishments.

43.5

I acknowledged thee, O AHURA Mazdah (mindful lord), as
the bounteous divinity when   321
(1) At the beginning, I beheld Thee at the birth of life 22
(2) When Thou didst establish (proper) Compensations for
deeds and words :   23
A bad (compensation) for the bad, and a good compensation for the good ;   24
(Which is to occur,) with Thy skill, at the last crisis of
of creation ;   25

43. 6

yahmī speñtā thwā mainyū urvaēsē jasō   326

mazdā xshathrā ahmī vohū manaṇhā   327

yehyā shyaothanāis gaēthāe ashā frādeñtē   328

aēibyō ratūs sēñghaitī ārmaitis   329

thwahyā xratêus yêm naēcis dābayeitī.   330

43. 7

speñtem at thwā mazdā mêñghī ahurā   331

hyat mā vohū pairī-jasat manaṇhā   332

peresatcā mā, cis ahī? kahyā ahī?   333

kathā ayārê daxshārā ferasayāi dīshā   334

aibī thwāhū gaēthāhū tanushicā?   335

43. 8

at hōi aojī zarathushtrō paourvīm: 336

haithyō dvaēshāe hyat isōyā dregvāite,   337

at ashāune rafenō hyêm aojōñghvat,   338

hyat ābūshtīs vasase xshathrahyā dyā   339

yavat ā thwā mazdā stāumī ufyācā !   340

43.6

At which crisis come Thou, O Mazdah (mindful), with
    Thy Spenta Mainyu (bounteous mentality),   326
With Xshathra (power), Vohu Manah (good disposition),
    and Asha (justice),   27
Through whose deeds are prospered the human-estates 28
For which Armaiti (love) formulates judgments   29
Of (mindful) Mazdah's understanding which no one ever
    deceives.   30

VISION II. Establishment of Orthodoxy.

43.7

I recognized Thee, O ahura Mazdah (mindful lord), as
    the bounteous (divinity), through the answer with which
    I was inspired   331
When, with (good disposition) Vohu Manah, (some man)
    came around to me, and asked,   32
'Who art thou? To what divinity belongest thou?   33
With what (divine) token wilt thou appoint the Day-for-
    questioning   34
About thy substance and thyself ?'   35

43.8

Therefore I, Zarathushtra, said to him at first: 336
"I would wish to be a genuine enemy to the Drujist,   37
But a vigorous support for the Ashaist,   38
So that I may plan for the developments of the now lim-
    ited Xshathra (coming kingdom)   39
(With) as-much-(zeal)-as I am now praising and lauding
    Thee, O Mazdah (mindful)!   40

43.9

speñtem a*t* thwā mazdā meñghī ahurā · 341

hya*t* mā vohū pairī-jasa*t* mana*n*hā. · 342

ahyā fera*s*em, 'kahmāi vīvīduyē vashī?' · 343

a*t* ā thwahmāi āthrē rāt*a*m *n*ema*n*hō · 344

ashahyā-mā yava*t* isāi manyāi! · 345

43. 10

a*t* tū mōi dāis ashem hya*t* mā zaozaomī! · 346

'ārmaitī hacimnō ī*t* ārem, · 347

peresācā nā*e* yā tōi ēhmā parshtā · 348

parshtêm zī thwā yathanā ta*t* êmavat*a*m; · 349

hya*t* thwā xshay*as* -aēshem dyā*t* êmavañtem?' 350

43. 11

speñtem a*t* thwā mazdā meñghī ahurā · 351

hya*t* mā vohū pairī-jasa*t* mana*n*hā · 352

hya*t* xshmā ux*d*āis dīdai*n*ghē paourvīm: · 353

'sādrā-mōi *sas* mash*y*aēshū zaraz-dāitis · 354

ta*t* v̌erezyeidyāi hya*t* mōi mraotā vahishtem?' 355

VISION III. Theophany of ASHA
43.9

I recognized Thee, O AHURA Mazdah (mindful lord), as
the bounteous (divinity)   341

When, with good disposition) Vohu Manah, (some man)
came-around to me, and asked (a question).   42

To his question, "What cause dost thou intend to adopt?"

I, (Zarathushtra), answered, "At each oblation of reverence
brought to Thy sacrificial fire (O Lord)   44

I will, to the extent of my ability, fix my mind on Asha
(justice)!   45

43.10

"But, (O God), show me the Asha (justice) whom I invoke !"   346

(Mazdah speaks:) "In company with Armaiti (love), and
Asha (justice) I have come,   47

For thy question was as the question of powerful (men) 49

When some ruler insists on having his mighty powerful
wish (granted by) thee.   50

Now ask Us what thou hast to ask Us !"   48

VISION IV. The Sincere shall be Supported.
43.11

I recognized Thee, O AHURA Mazdah (mindful lord), as
the bounteous (divinity)   351

When (1) I was first instructed in Your utterances;   52

And when with (good disposition) Vohu Manah, (some
man) came-around to me, (and asked),   53

'Will the doing of that which You have told me is the
Best (to do)   54

Arouse trouble among men for me?"   55

43. 12

hya*t*cā mōi mraos: 'ashem jas*ō* frāxshnenē!'   356

a*t* tū-mōi nōi*t* asrushtā pairyaog*z*ā: 357

'uzeredyāi parā hya*t* mōi ā-jima*t*   358

seraoshō ashī ma*z*ā-rayā hacimnō   359

yā vī ashīs rānōibyō savōi vīdāyā*t*!'   360

43. 13

spe*ñ*tem a*t* thwā mazdā mē*ñ*ghī ahurā   361

hya*t* mā vohū pairī-jasa*t* mana*n*hā   362

arethā vōizdyāi kāmahyā tê*m*: 'mōi dātā   363

daregahyā yāus yê*m* vāe naēcīs dāresht itē   364

vairyāe stōis yā thwahmī xshathrōi vācī!'   365

43. 14

hya*t* nā fryāi vaēdamnō isvā daidī*t*   366

maibyō mazdā tavā rafenō frāxshnenem   367

hya*t* thwā xshathrā ashā*t* hacā frashtā   368

uzereidyāi azê*m* saredanāe sê*ñ*ghahyā   369

ma*t* tāis vīspāis yōi-tōi mathrāe mare*ñ*tī.   370

43.12

And at the same time, when Thou toldst me to answer
    him, "Depend on Asha (justice) for support !"   356
Then to me (Zarathushtra,) who was not disobedient, Thou
    utteredst the command: 57
"Thou hadst better arouse (thy prophecy) before the com-
    ing   58
Of Sraosha (obedience) together with the rich Ashay (com-
    pensation),   59
Who will distribute to both contending Parties compens-
    ations for their profit."   60

VISION V. Demand for Help to Execute God's Judgments.

43.13

I recognized Thee, O AHURA Mazdah (mindful lord), as
    the bounteous (divinity)   361
When, with (good disposition) Vohu Manah, (some man)
    came-around   62
To learn the details of my desire :   63
"Give me the inalienable gift of long enjoyment   64
Of the desired existence which is said to be in Thy
    Xshathra (realm)."   65

43.14

Just as a wealthy man, according to his knowledge or abil-
    ity gives to a friend,   366
Do Thou, O AHURA Mazdah (mindful lord), give to me
    those Thy provisions of support,   67
Inasmuch as Thou endowedst me with Asha (justice), so
    that I might stand forth   68
With all those who remember Thy mystic Word   70
To arouse (those who may become) church-organizers of Thy
    teachings.   69

43. 15

speñtem a*t* thwā mazdā mḗñghī ahurā   371

hya*t* mā vohū pairī-jasa*t* mana*n*hā   372

daxsha*t* us*h*yāi tushnā maitis vahishtā: 373

'nōit nā pourūs dre*g*vatō *h*yā*t* cixshnushō   374

a*t* tōi vīspḗñg añgrḗñg ashāunō ādarê.'   375

43. 16

a*t* ahurā hvō mainyūm zarathushtrō   376

vereñtē mazdā yastē ciscā spênishtō   377

astva*t* ashem *h*yā*t* ushtānā aojōñghva*t*   378

*h*vḗñg daresōi xshathrōi *h*yā*t* ārmaitis   379

ashīm *sh*yaothanāis vohū daidī*t* mana*n*hā.   380

VISION VI. Mission of Orthodoxy—Armaiti Aligns the Parties.

43.15

I recognized Thee, O AHURA Mazdah (mindful lord), as
the bounteous (divinity)   371
When, with (good disposition) Vohu Manah, (some man)
came around (to ask me a question).   72
Then the best Tushnamatay (silent devotion) inspired me
to proclaim (to him)   73
"A (man as) important (as an Ashaist) should not curry favor with a Drujist,   74
For (it is the duty) of the Ashaist (to consider) all (Drujists
as) hostile."   75

43.16

Yea, O AHURA Mazdah (mindful lord), inasmuch as Zara-
thushtra chooses the (bounteous Mentality) Mainyu of
Mazdah (mindful),   376
He (Zarathustra) teaches that each most bounteous (man)
should to himself attach Asha (justice)   77
By living in a vigorous corporeal manner.   78
May Armaiti (love) (be found) in the Xshathra (realm)
that ever beholds the Sun;   79
Where, we pray, may Armaiti (love), with Vohu Manah
(good disposition), to all grant a Compensation, through
the instrumentality of the deeds they may have performed!   80

YASNA 44

44. 1

Ta*t* thwā peresā *eres*-mōi vaocā ahurā!   381

nema*n*hō ā yathā nem*ê* xshmāvatō?   382

mazdā fryāi thwāva*s* sa*h*yā*t* mavaitē   383

a*t* n*ê* ashā fryā dazdyāi hākurenā   384

yathā-n*ê* ā vohū jima*t* mana*n*hā?   385

44. 2

ta*t* thwā peresā *eres*-mōi vaocā ahurā!   386

kathā a*n*hêus vahishtahyā paourvīm?   387

kāth*ê* sūidyāi y*ê*-ī paitishā*t*   388

hvō zī ashā spentō irixtem vīspōibyō   389

hārō mainyū ahūmbis urvathō mazdā?   390

HYMN 44

Oracular Consultation as to Advisability of Conversion by War.

I. Questions about Theology.

44.1

O AHURA Mazdah (mindful lord), this I ask of Thee:
speak to me truly !   381
How should I pray, when I wish to pray to One-like-You?
May One-like-You, O Mazdah (mindful), who is friendly,
teach one-like-me?   83
And may You give us supporting-aids through the friendly
Asha (justice),   84
And tell us how You may come to us with Vohu Manah
(good disposition?)   85

44.2

O AHURA Mazdah (mindful lord), this I ask of Thee:
speak to me truly !   386
1, Whether at the beginning of the best life   87
The retributions will be of profit to their recipients ?   88
And 2, whether He 1, who is bounteous to all through
Asha (justice), and 2, who watches the End   89
Through His (mentality) Mainyu,—(whether) He is the
life-healing Friend (of the people, M) ?   90

44. 3

tat thwā peresā eres-mōi vaocā anurā!   391

kasnā zathā patā ashahyā pouruyō?   392

kasnā hvēñg starēmcā dāt advānem?   393

kē yā māe uxshyeitī nerefsaitī thwat?   394

tācīt mazdā vasemī anyācā vīduyē!   395

44. 4

tat thwā peresā eres-mōi vaocā ahurā!   396

kasnā deretā zamcā adē nabāescā   397

avapastōis? kē apō urvarāescā?   398

kē vātāi dvanmaibyascā yaoget āsū?   399

kasnā vanhēus mazdā damis mananhō?   400

44. 5

tat thwā peresā eres-mōi vaocā ahurā!   401

kē hvāpāe raocāescā dāt temāescā?   402

kē hvāpāe hvafnemcā dāt zaēmācā?   403

kē yā ushāe arēm-pithwā xshapācā   404

yāe manaothrīs cazdōñghvañtem arethahyā?   405

44.3

O AHURA Mazdah (mindful lord), this I ask of Thee:
   speak to me truly!   391

Who was the first father of Asha (justice) by (giving) birth
   (to Him)?   92

Who established the sun(lit day)s and the star (glistering
   sphere) and the (Milky) Way?   93

Who, apart from Thee, established (the law) by which the
   moon waxes and wanes?   94

These and other things would I like to know!   95

44.4

O AHURA Mazdah (mindful lord), this I ask of Thee:
   speak to me truly!   396

Who was from beneath sustaining the earth and the clouds
So-that-they-would-not-fall-down?   Who made the waters
   and the plants?   98

Who yoked the-two-swift-ones (thunder and lightning?)
   to the wind and to the clouds?   99

Who is the creator of Vohu Manah?   400

44.5

O AHURA Mazdah (mindful lord), this I ask of Thee:
   speak to me truly!   401

Who produced well-made lights and darkness?   2

Who produced sleep, well-induced through laborious
   waking?   3

Who produced the dawns and the noon through the contrast with the night   4

Whose daily changes (act) for the enlightened believers (as)
   monitors of their interests?   5

44. 6

ta*t* thwā peresā *e*res-mōi vaocā ahurā !   406

yā fravaxshyā yezī tā athā haithyā?   407

a*sh*em *sh*yaothanāis de*b*azaitī ārmaitis   408

taibyō xshathrem vohū cina*s* mana*n*hā   409

kaēibyō azīm rānyō-*sk*eretīm *g*a*m* tashō?   410

44. 7

ta*t* thwā *p*eresā *e*res-mōi vaocā ahurā!   411

kê be*r*ex*dam* tāsht xshathrā ma*t* ārmaitīm?   412

kê uzemêm cōre*t* vyānayā puthrem pithrē?   413

azêm tāis thwā fraxshnī avāmī mazdā   414

speñtā mainyū vīspana*m* dātārem!   415

44. 8

ta*t* thwā peresā *e*res-mōi vaocā ahurā!   416

meñdaidyāi yā-tōi mazdā ādishtis   417

yācā vohū ux*d*ā frashī mana*n*hā   418

yācā ashā a*n*hêus arêm vaēdyāi   419

kā-m*ê* urvā vohū urvāsha*t* āgema*t* tā?   420

44.6

O AHURA Mazdah (mindful lord), this I ask of Thee:
    speak to me truly!   406

Is the message I am about to proclaim genuine?   7

Does Armaiti (love) support Asha (justice) through
    deeds?   8

Dost Thou with Vohu Manah (good disposition) destine
    the Xshathra (realm) for these (believers)?   9

For whom but these (believers) didst Thou shape the for-
    tune-bringing cattle?   10

44.7

O AHURA Mazdah (mindful lord), this I ask of Thee:
    speak to me truly!   411

Who shaped prized Armaiti (love) with Xshathra (power)?

                                             12

Who, by guidance (education, M), rendered sons reverent
    to their fathers?   13

(It is) I who strive to learn-to-recognize Thee   14

Through the (bounteous Mentality) Spenta Mainyu as
    Giver of all (good things)!   15

44.8

O AHURA Mazdah (mindful lord), this I ask of Thee:
    speak to me truly!   416

(I would like) to know (1) what (sort) of a purpose (is
    Thine), that I may be mindful of it;   17

(2) What are Thy utterances, about which I asked through
    the aid of Vohu Manah (good disposition);   18

(3) The proper knowledge of life through Asha (justice) 19

(4) How shall my soul, encouraged by bliss, arrive at that
    good reward?   20

44. 9

tat thwā peresā eres-mōi vaocā ahurā!   421

kathā-mōi yam yaos daēnam yaos dānē   422

yam hudānāus paitise sahyāt xshathrahyā   423

ereshvā xshathrā thwāvas asīshtīs mazdā   424

hademōi ashā vohucā shyas mananhā?   425

44. 10

tat thwā peresā eres-mōi vaocā ahurā!   426

tam daēnam yā hātam vahishtā   427

yā-mōi gaēthāe ashā frādōit hacêmnā   428

ārmatōis uxdāis shyaothanā eres daidyat   429

mahyāe cistōis thwā īshtīs usên mazdā?   430

44. 11

tat thwā peresā eres-mōi vaocā ahurā?   431

kathā tếñg-ā vījêmyāt ārmaitis   432

yaēibyō mazdā thwōi vashyetē daēnā   433

azêm tōi āis pouruyō fravōividē   434

vīspêñg anyêñg manyêus spasyā dvaēshanhā!   435

44.9

O AHURA Mazdah (mindful lord), this I ask of Thee:
  speak to me truly!   421
How may I accomplish the sanctification of those spirits 22
To whom Thou, the well-disposed Master of the Coming
  (Kingdom) Xshathra,   23
Hast pronounced promises about its genuine blessings, 24
Promising that those spirits shall dwell in the same Dwell-
  ing with Asha (justice) and Vohu Manah (good dispos-
  ition)?   25

44.10

O AHURA Mazdah (mindful lord), this I ask of thee:
  speak to me truly!   426
(How) will (such a promise) properly nurture (1) (good)
  deeds,   29
—Which are the best qualities of these my followers' spirits—together with (2) utterances of humility?   27
(How) will (the promise) cause my (followers') settlements
  to prosper through Asha (justice)?   28
The aspirations of my mystic wisdom shall wish for Thy
  (second birth, SEE 48.5), O Mazdah (mindful)!   30

44.11

O AHURA Mazdah (mindful lord), this I ask of Thee:
  speak to me truly!   431
How will Armaiti (love) actually, in deeds, extend over
  those (persons)   32
To whom Thy spirit (religion?) was announced (as a doctrine)?   33
On account of whom I first was elected (acknowledged,M)
  (and whom I love);   34
All others I look upon with hostility of mentality!   35

44. 12

taʈ thwā peresā eres-mōi vaocā ahurā!   436

kê ashavā yāis peresāi dregvāe vā?   437

katārêm ā añgrō vā hvō vā añgrō   438

yê-mā dregvāe thwā savā paitī-eretē   439

cyanhaʈ hvō nōiʈ ayêm añgrō manyetē?   440

44. 13

taʈ thwā peresā eres-mōi vaocā ahurā!   441

kathā drujem nīs ahmaʈ ā nīs nāshāmā?   442

têñg-ā avā yōi asrushtōis perenāenhō   443

nōiʈ ashahyā ādīvyeiñtī hacêmnā   444

nōiʈ frasayā vanhêus cāxnarê mananhō.   445

44. 14

taʈ thwā peresā eres-mōi vaocā ahurā!   446

kathā ashāi drujêm dyam zastayō   447

nī hīm merazdyāi thwahyā mathrāis sêñghahyā   448

êmavaitīm sinam dāvōi dregvasū   449

ā-is dvafshêñg mazdā anāshē astascā.   450

II. Questions about Propaganda by War.
44.12

O AHURA Mazdah (mindful lord), this I ask of Thee:
    speak to me truly!   436
How shall I, from among those whom I am addressing,
    tell the Ashaist from the Drujist?   37
To which of these two is the Enemy of life (opposed)? 38
Or shall I take it for granted that whoever opposes Thy
    profit is an enemy and a Drujist?   39
What is the real condition of affairs with him (the Druj-
    ist)? Shall he not be considered an enemy?   40

44.13

O AHURA Mazdah (mindful lord), this I ask of Thee:
    speak to me truly!   441
How may we drive off from us the Drujist?   42
I exclaim, "Down with those who, being full of disobed-
    ience,   43
(1) Do not strive to be together with Asha (justice),   44
(2) Nor desire to understand the problems of Vohu Ma-
    nah (good disposition)."   45

44.14

O AHURA Mazdah (mindful lord), this I ask of Thee:
    speak to me truly!   446
How may I deliver the Druj into the hands of Asha (jus-
    tice)?   47
That I may smite them down (according to the promises,
    OR, through the power) of Thy Words of (Thy) doc-
    trines,   48
So that (even) within (OR, among) the Drujists (I) may
    accomplish powerful destruction,   49
That those torturers and haters may perish.   50

44. 15

tat thwā peresā eres-mōi vaocā ahurā!   451

yezī ahyā ashā pōi mat xshayehī   452

hyat hêm spādā anaocanhā jamaētē   453

avāis urvātāis yā-tū mazdā dīderezō   454

kuthrā ayāe kahmāi vananam dadāe?   455

44. 16

tat thwā peresā eres-mōi vaocā ahurā!   56

kê verethrem-jā thwā pōi señghā yōi heñtī?   457

cithrā mōi dam ahūmbis ratūm cīzdī   458

at hvō vohū seraoshō jañtū mananhā   459

mazdā ahmāi yahmāi vashī kahmāicīt?   460

44. 17

tat thwā peresā eres-mōi vaocā ahurā !   461

kathā mazdā zarem carānī hacā xshmat   462

āsketīm xshmākam hyatcā mōi hyāt vāxs aēshō   463

sarōi būzdyāi haurvātā ameretātā   464

avā mathrā yê rāthemō   ashāt hacā?   465

44.15

O AHURA Mazdah (mindful lord), this I ask of Thee:
   speak to me truly!   451
(Tell me) whether, in order to protect me, Thou hast tak-
   en control of this (opposition)?   52
Whenever the two hostile armies shall meet,   53
By those commands of righteousness which Thou shalt
   maintain,   54
To which of the two Parties wilt Thou give victory?   55

44.16

O AHURA Mazdah (mindful lord), this I ask of Thee:
   speak to me truly!   456
(Tell me) who comes victoriously with Thy doctrines to
   protect those who are existent?   57
(Do Thou who art) life-healing, clearly designate to me an
   established judge;   58
To him, whosoever he be, to whom Thou wishest (to give
   this appointment as judge),   60
To him may (then) Sraosha (obedience), with Vohu Manah (good disposition), then come?   59

44.17

O AHURA Mazdah (mindful lord), this I ask of Thee:
   speak to me truly!   461
How shall I carry out the object inspired by You,   62
(Namely,) my attachment to You, in order that (1) my
   speech may grow mighty, and   63
(2) That by that word of mine the adherent of Asha (justice)   64
May in-the-future commune with Haurvatat (health), and
   Ameretat (immortality)?   65

44. 18

tat thwā peresā eres-mōi vaocā ahurā!   466

kathā ashā tat mīzdem hanānī   467

dasā aspāe arshnavaitīs ushtremcā   468

hyat mōi mazdā apivaitī haurvātā   469

ameretātā yathā hī taēibyō dāenhā?   470

44. 19

tat thwā peresā eres-mōi vaocā ahurā !   471

yastat mīzdem haneñtē nōit dāitī   472

yê-īt ahmāi erezuxdā nā dāitə   473

kā-têm ahyā mainis anhat pouruyē   474

vīdvāe avam yā-īm anhat apêmā?   475

44. 20

cithenā mazdā huxshathrā daēvā āenharê   476

at īt peresā yōi pishyeiñtī aēibyō kam   477

yāis gam karapā usixscā aēshemāi dātā   478

yācā kavā anmênē urūdōyatā   479

nōit hīm mīzên ashā vāstrem frādainghē!   480

44.18

O AHURA Mazdah (mindful lord), this I ask of Thee:
speak to me truly !   466

How shall I earn through Asha (justice) that compensation   67

Which was announced to me, on account of Haurvatat
(health) and Ameretat (immortality)   69

(Namely,) ten mares with stallions, and a camel   68

(So that) I might-in-the-future impart the mystic Word of
these twin divinities to those adherents of Asha (justice)?

44.19

O AHURA Mazdah (mindful lord), this I ask of Thee:
speak to me truly !   471

(How shall be punished) he who does not give (the above)
compensation to (me who earned it,)   72

(To me) who (earned it) by uttering just teachings?   73

I know what punishment will overtake him at the Last
(Day);   74

But (tell) me what punishment will overtake him here in
this first (life)?   75

44.20

(O People, you might as well obey me, as I shall let you
judge for yourselves :)

Have you prospered under the rule of the Daevas ?   476

(As umpires between us) I shall ask those for the sake of
whose feeding   77

The Karapas and the Uxic give up the Cattle to Aeshma
(fury and rapine),   78

For whom the Kavays have made (the Cattle) lament
exceedingly,   79

Instead of, through Asha (justice), prospering pasturage,
so as to care for (the Cattle).   80

YASNA 45

45. 1

A*t* fravaxshyā! nū gūshōdūm, nū *s*raotā	481
yaēcā asnā*t*, yaēcā dūrā*t* ishathā	482
nū īm vīspā cithrê zī mazdāe*n*hōdūm	483
nōi*t* daibitīm dus-*s*astis ahūm me*ra*shyā*t*	484
akā varanā d*re*gvāe hizvāe ̕āveretō.	485

45. 2

a*t* fravaxshyā! a*n*hêus mainyū pouruyē	486
yayāe spanyāe ūitī mrava*t* yêm añgrem:	487
nōi*t* nā manāe, nōi*t* sêñghā, nōi*t* xratavō,	488
naēdā varanā, nōi*t* ux*d*ā, naēdā *s*hyaothanā,	489
noi*t* daēnāe, nōi*t* urva*n*ō hacaiñtē!	490

45. 3

a*t* fravaxshyā a*n*hêus ahyā pourvīm	491
yā mōi vīdvāe ̕ mazdāe vaoca*t* ahurō:	492
'yōi īm vê nōi*t* ithā mathrem varesheñtī	493
yathā īm mênāicā vaocacā	494
aēibyō a*n*hêus avōi a*n*ha*t* apêmem !'	495

HYMN 45
Repeated Sermon on Dualiʃm
Teaching Agriculture aʃ *the* Road to Paradise

I. Repeated Exhortation to the Faithful
To Open their Ears to the Mystery.

45.1

Now will I speak out: listen and hear,	481
You who, from far and near, have come-to-seek (my word) ;	82
Now (I exhort you) clearly to impress on your memory (the evil teacher) and his faults ; (for)	83
No longer shall the evil Teacher—druj that he is !—destroy the second life,	84
In (the speech of) his tongue misleading to the evil life.	85

II. The Doctrinal Dualistic Foundation of Partisanship

45.2

Now will I speak out: At the beginning of life	486
The holier (Mentality) said to the (opposing Mentality who was) more hostile,	87
"Neither our thoughts, doctrines, plans,	88
Beliefs, utterances, deeds,	89
Individualities, nor souls agree."	90

III. The Good Spirit Teaches the Best Word of Agriculture.

45.3

Now will I spea kout! Of that (which) at the beginning of life	491
The knowing AHURA Mazdah (mindful lord) said :	92
"Those who do not practise the Word,	93
As I consider and declare it,	94
They shall have woe at the end of life."	95

45. 4

a*t* fravaxshyā·a*n*hêus ahyā vahishte*m* :   496

ashā*t* hacā mazdā vaēdā yê īm dā*t*,   467

patarêm va*n*hêus va*r*ezayañtō mana*n*hō,   498

a*t* hōi dugedā hus*h*yaothanā ārmaitis,   499

nōi*t* diw*z*aidyāi vīspā-hishas ahurō.   500

45. 5

a*t* fravaxshyā hya*t* mōi mrao*t* speñtōtemō   501

vacê srūidyāi hya*t* maretaēibyō vahishte*m* :   502

yōi mōi ahmāi *s*eraoshem d*a*n cayascā   503

upā-jimen haurvātā ameretātā   504

va*n*hêus manyêus *s*hyaothanāis mazdā*e* ahurō! 505

45. 6

a*t* fravaxshyā vīspan*a*m mazishte*m*   506

*s*tava*s* ashā yê hudā*e* yōi heñtī   507

speñtā mainyū *s*raotū mazdā*e* ahurō   508

yehyā vahmē vohū frashī mana*n*hā   509

ahyā xratū frō-mā *s*āstū vahishtā!   510

45.4

Now will I speak out (what is) the best of life: 496

Through Asha (justice), O Mazdah (mindful), have I discovered (1) Thee, who hast created Him (Asha);   97

(2) That Mazdah (mindful) is the Father of the working
Vohu Manah (good disposition);   98

(3) And that Armaiti (love), who produces good deeds, is
His daughter;   99

(4) And that the all-detecting AHURA (lord) is not to be
deceived.   500

45.5

Now will I, who am the Utterer of this Word which is the
best for mortal men to hear,   501

Speak out what the most bounteous AHURA Mazdah (mindful lord) said to me :   2

"Those who, for (the attainment of) this (mystic manthric
Word) grant Me their obedience,   3

They shall come up with Haurvatat (health), and Ameretat (immortality),   4

With the deeds of the good (Mentality) Mainyu."   5

IV. By Rewards and Punishments will Ahura Mazdah
Vindicate Zarathushtra as Judge.

45.6

Now will I speak out about the greatest (Being) of all   506

Through Asha (justice) praising Mazdah (mindful), who
blesses all existent (beings) !   7

Let AHURA Mazdah (mindful lord) hear, through Spenta
Mainyu (the bounteous Mentality), (the fact)   8

That I consulted Vohu Manah (good disposition) (as to)
how I should adore (Mazdah, mindful),   9

Through whose (Mazdah's) understanding, may He, Vohu Manah, teach me the best (teachings ?) !   10

45. 7

yehyā savā ishāeñtī rāda*n*hō   511

yōi-zī jvā āe*n*harecā bvañticā   512

ameretāitī ashāunō urvā aēshō   513

utayūtā yā nera*s* sādrā dregvatō   514

tācā xshathrā mazdāe d*a*mis ahurō.   515

45. 8

têm nê *s*taotāis nema*n*hō ā vīvareshō   516

nū-zī*t* cashmainī vyādare*s*em   517

va*n*hêus manyêus *sh*yaothanahyā ux*dah*yācā   518

vīdus ashā yêm mazd*a*m ahurem   519

a*t* hōi vahmêñg demānē garō nidāmā!   520

45. 9

têm nê vohū ma*t* mana*n*hā cixshnushō   521

yê-nê usên cōre*t* spêncā aspêncā   522

mazdāe xshathrā verezênyāe dyā*t* ahurō   523

pasūs vīrêñg ahmākêñg fradathāi ā   524

va*n*hêus ashā haoz*a*thwā*t* ā mana*n*hō!   525

45.7

Let the Preparers (for the conversion of the world), both
those who were, and (those who) are (yet) becoming 512
Wish for the profits of the Compensations ;   11
The successful soul of the Ashaist (abiding) in Ameretat
(immortality)   13
With enduringness; (while) the Drujists shall endure griefs
And all this AHURA Mazdah (the mindful lord) creates
through Xshathra (the coming of the kingdom).   15

45.8

Thou-shalt-seek-to-win (Mazdah, mindful) with such prai-
ses of reverence (as) for instance (this psalm:)   516
'With my (own) eyes shall I now behold (the heaven) 17
Of the good Mentality of word and deed;   18
Having, through Asha (justice), known AHURA Mazdah
(the mindful lord),   19
To whom let us, in heaven, set down adorations for the fil-
ling of the (dwelling of praise, paradise) Garodman." 20

45.9

Him (Mazdah), along with Vohu Manah (good disposition), shalt thou seek-to-satisfy for us,   521
(Because it is) He who, by His will, makes our fortune or
misfortune.   22
May AHURA Mazdah (the mindful lord) through his Xshathra (realm)   23
Grant, for the group of herdsmen, prospering of our cattle
and men   24
By the proficiency of Vohu Manah (good disposition),
through Asha (justice).   25

45. 10

têm nê yasnāis ārmatōis mimagzō	526
yê anmênī mazdāe srāvī ahurō	527
hyat mōi ashā vohucā cōisht mananhā	528
xshathrōi hōi haurvātā ameretātā	529
ahmāi stōi dan tevīshī utayūitī.	530

45.'11

yastā daēvêñg aparō mashyascā	531
tarê-mastā yōi īm tarê-manyañtā	532
anyêñg ahmāt yê hōi arêm manyātā	533
saoshyañtō dêñg patōis speñtā daēnā	534
urvathō, barātā, patā vä, mazdā ahurā!	535

45.10

-How shalt thou, (O individual believer), with hymns of
　Armaiti (love), magnify　　　　　　　　　　　　526
Him who is reputed to be AHURA Mazdah (the mindful
　lord) for eternity ;　　　　　　　　　　　　　27
Since through Asha (justice), and Vohu Manah (good dis-
　position), He has (promised us)　　　　　　　　28
That in His Xshathra (realm) we shall obtain Haurvatat
　(health) and Ameretat (immortality) ;　　　　　29
-But we shall obtain that His (heavenly) dwelling through
　vitality and enduringness.　　　　　　　　　　30

V. Supporting the Prophet is therefore the Chief Duty.

45.11

Whoever, therefore, in the future scorns (1) the Daevas 531
And (2) the men who scorn him (Zarathushtra),　　32
And all others (luke-warm neutrals) except whoever is de-
　voted to him (Zarathushtra),　　　　　　　　33
Shall be considered, by the bounteous individuality of (Za-
　rathushtra, who is) Savior and Master-of-the-house　34
As his Friend, Brother, or Father,—O AHURA Mazdah
　(mindful lord) !　　　　　　　　　　　　　35

YASNA 46

46. 1

Kām nemōi zam? kuthrā nemōi ayenī?	536
pairī *hv*aētêus airyamanascā dadaitī,	537
nōi*t* mā xshnāus yā vereznā hêcā,	538
naēdā da*h*yêus yōi sāstārō dregva*ñ*tō;	539
kathā thwā mazdā xshnaoshāi ahurā?	450

46. 2

vaēdā ta*t* yā ahmī mazdā anaēshō!	541
mā kamnafshvā hya*t*cā kamnānā ahmī	542
gerezōi tōi ā-ī*t* avaēnā ahurā	543
ra*f*edrm cagvā*e* hya*t* fryō fryāi daidī*t*;	544
āxsō va*n*hêus ashā īshtīm mana*n*hō!	545

HYMN 46

War Preliminaries *of*
Heart-*s*earchings *and* Encouragement.

I. Failure in Conversion, and Demand on Mazdah for Vindication

46.1

Toward what earth shall I turn to flee?   Whither shall I
turn to escape?   536
The groups of the herdsmen do not offer me the satisfaction of support;   38
Nobody offers me (gifts) on the part of gentleman or of
peer;   37
Neither do those who are princes of the land (favor me)
because of the Drujist;   39
How shall I ever please Thee (by successful establishment
of Thy cult), O AHURA Mazdah (mindful lord)?   40

46.2

I know, O AHURA Mazdah (mindful lord), the reason why
I am so (despised as to be) impotent—   541
It is only because I possess so few flocks and followers! 42
I complain of this to Thee! Investigate this complaint, 43
And then support me as friendship would dictate!   44
But I specially ask instruction (as to how to attain) through
Asha (justice) the possession of Vohu Manah (good
disposition)!   ·45

46. 3

kadā mazdā yōi uxshānō asn*a*m   546

a*n*hêus daretḥrāi frō ashahyā frāreñtē   547

verezdāis sêñghāis saos*h*yañt*a*m xratavō?   548

kaēībyō ūthāi vohū jima*t* mana*n*hā?   549

maibyō thwā *sastrāi* verenē ahurā!   550

46. 4

a*t* têñg dregvā*e* yêñg ashahyā vazdrêñg pā*t*   551

gā*e* frōretōis shōithrahyā vā da*h*yêus vā   552

du*z*azōbā*e* ha*s* *h*vāis *sh*yaothanāis ahêmustō   553

yastêm xshathrā*t* mazdā mōitha*t* jyātêus vā   554

*h*vō têñg frō-gā*e* pathmêñg hucistōis carā*t*.   555

46. 5

yê vā xshay*as* ad*as* drītā ayañtem   556

urvātōis vā huzêñtus mithrōibyō vā   557

rashnā jv*as* yê ashavā dregvañtem   558

vīcirō h*as* ta*t* frō *h*vaētavē mruyā*t*   559

uzūithyōi īm mazdā xrūnyā*t* ahurā!   560

46.3

When, O AHURA Mazdah (mindful lord) will those 'bully'
    (glorious) days arrive   546

When humanity's life will attain (the blessings) of Asha
    (justice)   47

Through the growing teachings of saviors (who will be
    men) of understanding?   48

(Who are they) to whom (Zarathushtra) will come with
    (good disposition) Vohu Manah to help?   49

For myself I choose (this mission), to fulfil (it), with Thy
    (aid), O AHURA (lord)!   50

46.4

But the Drujist is restraining those who are a-prospering of
    Asha (justice)   551

To prosper (the interests) of the cattle, or of the village,
    or of the province;   52

Being notorious, repulsive through his own deeds,   53

(So much so, that) who(ever) may despatch him from the
    (realm) Xshathra of life,   54

He will (1) be doing the community a service, and (2) be
    going-on, on the progressing paths of good teachings. 55

II. Rules How to Treat Converts.

46.5

Whatever well-informed person may have managed to with-
    hold an Ashaist or Drujist   556

From keeping his vows or engagements (that are evil),   57

So as to come to a decision to live according to the divine
    observances,   58

That (above well-informed person) should give-due-public-
    notice (of that conversion) to some gentleman   59

(So that this gentleman might from then on) protect-the-
    convert from further maltreatment, O AHURA Mazdah
    (mindful lord)!   60

46. 6

at yastêm nōit nā isemnō āyāt   561

drūjō hvō dāman haithyā gāt   562

hvō zī dregvāe yê dregvāitē vahishtō   563

hvō ashavā yahmāi ashavā fryō   564

hyat daēnāe paouruyāe dāe ahurā!   565

46. 7

kêm-nā mazdā mavaitē pāyūm dadāt   566

hyat mā dregvāe dīdareshatā aēnanhē?   567

anyêm thwahmāt āthrascā mananhascā   568

yayāe shyaothanāis ashem thraoshtā ahurā   569

tam mōi dastvam daēnayāi frāvaocā.   570

46. 8

yê vā mōi yāe gaēthāe dazdē aēnanhē   571

nōit ahyā-mā āthris shyaothanāis frōsyāt   572

paityaoget tā ahmāi jasōit dvaēshanhā   573

tanvêm ā yā īm hujyātōis pāyāt   574

nōit duzjyātōis kācīt mazdā dvaēshanhā!   575

46.6

But whoever, when thus warned of the convert('s conver-
sion), shall not go (to his side) to stand-up-for-him, 561
He shall-be-banished-to the genuine Houses of the Druj
(he will be accounted a genuine Druj),   62
(Just as) a Drujist is most attractive to the Drujist,   63
(While) the Ashaist is dear to whomsoever is an Ashaist 64
Since (the time when) Thou createdst the first spirits,
O AHURA Mazdah (mindful lord)!   65

III. Actual Struggle to Protect Converts (from Bendva?)

46.7

Whom, O Mazdah (mindful), wilt Thou commission as
guardian for one-like-me,   566
Whenever the Drujist prepares to commit violence against
me?   67
Unless he be some one of divine power like Thee, such as
Thy Fire and Manah (mind),   68
Through the deeds of both of whom Asha (justice) is
ripened for the consummation, O AHURA (lord):   69
This is the teaching I propose to proclaim to human
spirits.   70

46.8

May not misfortune attain me through the deeds   571
Of any one who intends-to-commit-violence against my
substance !   72
Rather, may his deeds (1) with hostility rebound on his
own body,   73
(2) And restrain him from good life, O Mazdah (mindful),
(3) And, with hostility, fail to restrain him from the bad-
life !   75

46. 9

kê hvō yê-mā aredrō cōitha*t* pouruyō   576

yathā thwā zevīshtīm uzemōhī   577

*sh*yaothanōi *s*peñtem ahurem ashavanem ?   578

yā-tōi ashā yā ashāi gêus tashā mrao*t*   579

isheñtī mā tā tōi vohū mana*n*hā.   580

46. 10

yê vā mōi nā genā vā mazdā ahurā   581

dāyā*t* a*n*hêus yā-tū vōistā vahishtā   582

ashīm ashāi vohū xshathrem mana*n*hā   583

y*a*scā haxshāi xshmāvat*a*m vahmāi ā   584

frō-tāis vīspāis cinvatō frafrā peretūm.   585

IV. Zarathushtra is the First Prophet;
Obedience to him Gains Paradise.

46.9

Who is that faithful (believer) who will be the first one 576
To teach me (by object lesson) to consider Thee the most
   helpful (divinity), 77
And the most bounteous lord (as) judge over deeds? 78
(On the contrary,) the believers are, with the aid of Vohu
   Manah (good disposition), seeking (to hear) from me 79
What Asha (justice) uttered to Thee, and what the Shaper
   of the Cattle uttered to Asha (justice). 80

46.10

(O AHURA Mazdah, mindful lord, grant) Xshathra (the
   power of the coming kingdom) through Vohu Manah
   (good disposition) as a Compensation to doers-of-right;
   (namely,) 583
Whatever any man or woman may contribute or give to
   me, (do Thou, O Lord, reward with) 81
What (spiritual gifts) Thou, O AHURA Mazdah (mindful
   lord), knowest to be best for life (OR, people); 82
And I will also urge these (rewarded people) to adoration
   of such-as-You 84
(When) I precede all of these (rewarded contributors) on
   to the Sifter's Bridge of Judgment. 85

46. 11

xshathrāis yūjén karapanō kāvayascà 586

akāis *sh*yaothanāis ahūm mereñgeidyāi mashīm 587

yêñg *hvê* urvā *hv*aēcā xraoda*t* daēnā 588

hya*t* aibī-*gemen* yathrā cinvatō *peretus* 589

yavōi vīspāi drūjō demānāi astayō! 590

46. 12

hya*t* u*s* ashā naptyaēshū nafshucā 591

tūrahyā uzjén fryānahyā aojyaēshū 592

ārmatōis gaēthā*e* frādō thwaxsha*nh*ā 593

a*t* īs vohū hê*m* aibī-mōist mana*nh*ā 594

aēibyō raf*e*drāi mazdā*e sast*ē ahurō. 595

46. 13

yê spitāmem zarathushtrem rāda*nh*ā 596

maretaēshū xshnāus hvō-nā *ferasrū*idyāi *erejw*ō 597

a*t* hōi mazdā*e* ahūm dadā*t* ahūrō 598

ahmāi gaēthā*e* vohū frāda*t* mana*nh*ā 599

tê*m* vê ashā mêhmaidī hus-haxāim. 600

46.11

Through their political power, the Karapans will join the
Kavays   586
In destroying the (second) life of men through evil-deeds;
(Fools! whereas) their own souls and spirits shall terrify
them   88
When they shall come to the Sifter's Bridge of Judgment!
As (fit) companions shall they be admitted to the Home
of the Druj forever!   90

46.12

When, through the (help) of Asha (justice) among the vigorous (closer) relatives and (more distant) relatives   591
Of the Friendly Turas, there shall arise   92
Such-as-will, with zeal, prosper the substance of Armaiti
(love);   93
Then shall AHURA Mazdah (the mindful lord), with the aid
of Vohu Manah (good disposition),   94
In-the-consummation, give support to these (Friendly Turas).   95

46.13

Whoever satisfies Spitama Zarathushtra through preparations (for him)   596
Among men, (1) he is worthy to be heard of;   97
(2) And besides, he shall be given life (OR, people) by (the
mindful lord) AHURA Mazdah;   98
(3) And shall have his substance prospered through Vohu
Manah (good disposition);   99
(4) And he shall be considered well-befriended with Asha
(justice).   600

46. 14

zarathushtrā kastē ashavā urvathō	601
mazōi magāi kê vā ferasrūidyāi vashtī	602
a*t* hvō kavā vīshtāspō yāhī	603
yêñgstū mazdā hademōi minas ahurā	604
têñg zbayā va*n*hêus ux*d*āis mana*n*hō!	605

46. 15

haēca*t*-aspā vaxshyā vê spitamāe*n*hō	606
hya*t* dāthêñg vīcayathā adāth*a*scā:	607

—   —   —   —   —   —

tāis yūs *sh*yaothanāis ashem xshmaibyā daduyē	608
yāis dātāis paouruyāis ahurahyā.	609

46. 16

*f*erashaoshtrā athrā-tū are*d*rāis idī	610
hvō-gvā tāis yêñg u*s*vahī ushtā-stōi	611
yathrā ashā hacaintē ārmaitis,	612
yathrā va*n*hêus mana*n*hō īshtā xshathr*em*,	613
yathrā mazdāe vare*d*ema*m* shaēitī ahurō.	614

V. Praise for the Supporters of his Cause.
46.14

(Would you like to know) who is (one of these, namely,)
   a friendly Ashaist?   601

(One) who would like to be-heard-from-for-the-Magian-
   Cause along with Zarathushtra   2

In the crisis (of political establishment)? (It is) Kavay
   Vishtaspa!   3

(He is,) O AHURA Mazdah (mindful lord), (one of those)
   whom Thou wilt (surely) unite (to Thyself) in Thy
   same Abode (of Praise, Garodman);   4

Them (from among the people) am I inviting with utterances of Vohu Manah (good disposition)!   5

46.16

O Frashaoshtra Hvogva, go thou with the faithful to   610

Where we both desire to be, (namely), with those-who-are-
   Beloved ;   11

Where Armaiti (love's well-being) follows along with Asha
   (justice),   12

Where are found the treasures of Vohu Manah (good disposition),   13

And where (the mindful lord) AHURA Mazdah dwells and
   prospers the Xshathra (kingdom).   14

VI. Partisanship with Zarathushtra Essential to Gain Paradise.
46.15

I will inform you, O you (clansmen of) Haechataspa, and
   of Spitama,   606

How to sift the Clever from the Foolish :   7

—   —   —   —   —   —   —   —   (MISSING ?)

With these deeds you maintain for yourselves Asha (justice)   8

Through the first decrees of (the lord) AHURA.   9

46. 17

yathrā vê afshmānī sêñghānī   615

nōi*t* anafshm*a*m dêjāmāspā hvō-gvā   616

hadā vêstā vahmêñg *s*eraoshā rāda*n*hō   617

yê vīcinao*t* dāthemcā adāthemcā   618

dañgrā mañtū ashā mazdāe ahurō!   619

46. 18

yê maibyā yaos ahmāi asc*īt* vahishtā   620

ma*h*yā*e* ishtōis vohū cōishem mana*n*hā   621

*a*stêñg ahmāi yê nā*e a*stāi daidītā   622

mazdā ashā xshmākem vārem xshnaoshemnō   623

ta*t* mōi xratêus mana*n*hascā vīcithem.   624

46. 19

yê-mōi ashā*t* haithīm hacā var*e*shaitī   625

zarathushtrāi hya*t* vasnā ferashōtemem   626

ahyāi mī*z*dem hanêñtê parāhūm   627

manê-vistāis ma*t* vīspāis gāvā azī   628

tācī*t* mōi *s*as tvêm mazdā vaēdishtō!   629

46.17

So that in (this) place of trouble, O Jamaspa Hvogva, 615

I am uttering for (all of) you utterances, not of indifferent matters, 616

But praises of the Preparer (Zarathushtra himself), who-will-have-stood-for-you together with Sraosha (obedience)

Who shall sift the Clever from the Fools 18

Through Asha (justice), his clever advisory-manager, O AHURA Mazdah (mindful lord)! 19

ALTERNATES for lines 615-617:

Where I shall mention your misfortunes only, so as to arouse Mazdah's pity, B.

Where I shall sing in metred, not unmetred lines, M.

46.18

This is the sifting-conclusion of my understanding, and of my mind: 624

'Whoever to me concedes the best our age (affords in the way of recognition or contributions), to him would-I-by-teaching (promise) 20

The best (treasures) of my wealth, with the Vohu Manah (good disposition); 21

But I will oppose hate to those-who-hate us, 22

(And in doing so, I consider), O Mazdah (mindful), that I am, through Asha (justice), satisfying Your Will.' 23

46.19

Whoever, through the inspiration of Asha (justice) may genuinely cooperate with me, Zarathushtra, 625

(Doing those deeds) which suit my will, 26

(These deeds) will earn for him future Compensation, 27

And with all (other) expected (rewards in Paradise), a pair of calving cows (on the 'pasture of Asha'? SEE 33.3) 28

And mayest Thou, O Mazdah (mindful), effect these (promises) (to those) whom (they) best (suit)! 29

Spentamainyush Gatha.

YASNA 47

47. 1

Speñtā mainyū vahishtācā manaɴhā   630

hacā ashā*t* s*h*yaothanācā vacaɴhācā   631

ahmāi d*a*n haurvātā ameretātā   632

mazdā*e* xshathrā ārmaitī ahurō.   633

47. 2

ahyā manyêus spênishtahyā vahisht*e*m   634

hizvā ux*d*āis vaɴhêus êeānū manaɴhō   635

ārmatōis zastōibyā s*h*yaothanā verezya*t*   636

ōyā cistī: 'hvō patā ashahyā mazdā*e*.'   637

47. 3

ahyā manyêus tvêm ahī tā speñtō   638

yê ahmāi g*a*m rānyō-skeretīm hêm-tasha*t*   639

a*t* hōi vāstrāi rāmā-dā*e* ārmaitīm   640

hya*t* hêm vohū mazdā hême-frashtā manaɴhā!   641

HYMN 47

Song *of the* Spirit as Inspirer *of* War.

47.1

With Spenta Mainyu (the bounteous Mentality), and with
the best Manah (disposition),   630
With the Xshathra (power), and Armaiti (love), AHURA
Mazdah (the mindful lord)   33
Gives Haurvatat (health) and Ameretat (immortality)   32
For the deeds and speeches caused by Asha (justice).   31

47.2

Mazdah (mindful) **is the Father of Asha** (justice)! With
this doctrinal thought   634
(Zarathushtra (1) declares) the best (treasure) of the most
(Bounteous Mentality) Spenta Mainyu   35
With utterances through the tongue in the mouth of (good
disposition) Vohu Manah;   36
And (2) works the deeds of Armaiti (love) with-both-his-
hands.   37

47.3

Thou art the bounteous (father) of this Mentality,   638
Who hast shaped (1) the fortune-bringing Cow for this
(Zarathushtra),   39
And (2) peace-bringing Armaiti (love) as her pasture,   40
When (the Mentality) consulted with Vohu Manah (good
disposition), O Mazdah (mindful)!   41

47. 4

ahmā*t* manyêus rāres*h*yeiñtī dregvañtō   642

mazdā speñtā*t* nōi*t* ithā ashāunō;   643

kasêuscī*t* nā ashāunē kāthē a*n*ha*t*   644

isvācī*t* h*as* paraos akō dregvāitē.   645

47. 5

tācā speñtā mainyū mazdā ahurā   646

ashāunē cōis yā-zī cīcā vahishtā   647

hana*re* thwahmā*t* zaoshā*t* dregvā*e* baxshaitī   648

ahyā *sh*yaothanāis akā*t* ās*h*y*as* mana*n*hō?   649

47. 6

tā dā*e* speñtā mainyū mazdā ahurā   650

āthrā va*n*hāu vīdāitīm rānōibyā   651

ārmatōis deba*zan*hā asha*h*yācā   652

hā-zī pourūs isheñtō vāurāitē!   653

47.4

The Drujists have apostacised from this bounteous (Fa-
    ther) of the Mentality (namely, Thyself),   642
O Mazdah (mindful)! But not thus the Ashaists; (for) 43
Though a man be no more than poor, yet should he, to
    the best of his ability, entertain the Ashaists;   44
(And, in addition,) if a man is powerful, he should effect
    evil for the Drujists.   45

47.5

And through that (Bounteous Mentality) Spenta Mainyu,
    O AHURA Mazdah (mindful lord),   46
Mayest Thou teach to the Ashaist what (doctrines and
    deeds) are the best;   47
But shall the Drujist, (who) lacks Thy good pleasure, 48
And dwells with the deeds of the Aka Manah (bad dispo-
    sition) have-a-share of this (best reward)?   49

47.6

Mayest Thou, O AHURA Mazdah (mindful lord), give that
    (Best) thro' (Bounteous Mentality) Spenta Mainyu 650
(At) a distribution to both contending (Parties) by means
    (1) of the good Fire,   51
(2) And by the support of Armaiti (love) and Asha (jus-
    tice),   52
(I feel sure that) this (distribution of the Best) will cause
    many who desire (the Best) to choose conversion (to it)!

YASNA 48

48. 1

Yezī adāis ashā drujem vēñnhaitī   654

hya*t* *a*sashutā yā daibitānā fraoxtā   655

ameretāitī daēvāiscā ma*s*hyāiscā   656

a*t* tōi *s*avāis vahmem vaxsha*t* ahurā.   657

48. 2

vaōcā-mōi yā tvêm vīdvā*e* ahurā !   658

parā hya*t* mā yā mēñg perethā jimaitī   659

ka*t* ashavā mazdā vēñgha*t* dregvañtem ?   660

hā-zī a*n*hêus va*n*uhī vistā ākeretis !   661

48. 3

a*t* vaēdemnāi vahishtā sāsnan*a*m   662

y*a*m hudā*e* sāstī ashā ahurō   663

speñtō vīdvā*e* yaēcī*t* gūzrā sēñghāe*n*hō   664

thwāv*a*s mazdā va*n*hêus xrathwā mana*n*hō.   665

HYMN 48
Incoherent Appeal for Champions *and* Defenders

I. Hope for Rewards in This Life.
48.1

When (Zarathushtra) shall overcome the Druj by retributions through Asha (justice), 654

When he arrives at what long since was announced 55

Through (the fate of) Daevas and the 'Doomed' (unbelievers), in (the realm of) Immortality, 56

Then, O AHURA (lord), (Zarathushtra) will, with profits,
prosper (the faithful believer who) prays to Thee. 57

48.2

Speak to me, O AHURA (lord)! For Thou art an Expert-
knower! 658

Will the Ashaist overcome the Drujist (in this world) 60

Before the-beginning-of the Compensations (which) Thou
hast thought out? 59

That would be a good Message to the world! 61

II. Punishment for Opposers and Waverers.
48.3

But, for an Expert-knower, (that) is the best of teachings 62

Which the beneficent AHURA (lord) is-teaching, with Asha
(justice). 63

The Expert-knower who is one-like-Thee, O Mazdah
(mindful), through the understanding of Vohu Manah
(good disposition), 64

Knows bounteous secrets which-are-expressed-in-the-doc-
trines. 65

48. 4

yê dā*t* manō vahyō mazdā a*sh*yascā   666

hvō daēn*am sh*yaothanācā vaca*n*hācā   667

ahyā za*o*shêñg ushtis varenêñg hacaitē   668

thwahmī xratā*e* apêmem nanā a*n*ha*t*?   669

48. 5

huxshathrā xshêñt*am* mā-nê duse-xshathrā xshêñtā   670

va*n*huyā*e* cistōis *sh*yaothanāis ārmaitē   671

yao*z*dā*e* ma*sh*yāi aipī *z*athem vahishtā   672

gavōi ve*r*ezyāt*am* t*am* nê *h*varethāi fshuyō.   673

48. 6

hā-zī-nê hushōithemā hā-nê utayūitīm   674

dā*t* tevīshīm va*n*hêūs mana*n*hō berexdē   675

a*t* a*h*yāi ashā mazdā*e* urvarā*e* vaxsha*t*   676

ahurō a*n*hêus zathōi paouruyehyā.   677

48.4

Whoever, O Mazdah (mindful), exercises his mind (now)
through the better, (and then again) through the worse
(meditations),   666

Who(ever) exercises his spirit with such uncertain deed and
word,   67

Who(ever) follows the delights, wishes, and convictions of
such uncertainty,—   68

Shall he, in Thy estimation, at last be separated from those
who have done Thy Will (or, who are worthy of being
in several places; or, of becoming confused)?   69

III. Right of Believers to Present Comfort.

48.5

May not bad rulers rule over us! (Rather,) may good
rulers rule   670

With deeds (inspired by) good doctrinal thoughts, O Armaiti (love), (Thou) Best One!   71

(Who), for (1) mortal men, dost perfect an additional-or-
later-or-especial-birth,   72

But (2) for the Cattle (perfecting) that pasturage which
should fatten It for our food.   73

48.6

O Armaiti (love), prized by (men of good disposition)
Vohu Manah!   674

For (1) men, She produced good dwelling, enduringness,
and vitality;   75

But for (2) that (Cattle), AHURA Mazdah (the mindful lord)
with Asha (justice), caused plants to grow   76

At the birth of the first life.   77

48. 7

nī aēshemō nī dyātam paitī remem paitī syōzdūm   678

nōit ā vanhêus mananhō dīdragzōduyē   679

ashā vyam yehyā hithāus nā speñtō   680

at hōi dāmam thwahmī ā-dam ahurā.   681

48. 8

kā-tōi vanhêus mazdā xshathrahyā īshtis?   682

kā-tōi ashōis thwahyāe maibyō ahurā?   683

kā-thwōi ashā ākāe aredrêñg ishyā?   684

vanhêus manyêus shyaothananam javarō!   685

48. 9

kadā vaēdā yezī cahyā xshayathā   686

mazdā ashā yehyā-inā āithis dvaēthā?   687

eres-mōi erezūcam vanhêus vafus mananhō   688

vīdyāt saoshyas yathā hōi ashis anhat?   689

48.7

Let Aeshma (fury of rapine) be put down; oppose cruelty!

Ye who wish-to-assure-yourselves of the reward of Vohu
Manah (good disposition),   679

Through Asha (justice), to whose bond would wish to belong the bounteous man   80

Who shall abide in Thy Dwelling, O AHURA (lord)!   81

IV. Uncertainty Here and Hereafter.

48.8

O AHURA Mazdah (mindful lord), is the wealth of Thy
good Xshathra (realm) (meant for me?)   682

Is (the wealth) of Thy Compensation (meant) for me? 83

Will Thy (realm and Compensation) please the faithful
(believer) when it shall have been made manifest through
Asha (justice)?   84

(This would indeed be) an incitation (M) OR, weighing-off
(B) of the deeds of the good Mentality!   85

48.9

When may I know, O AHURA Mazdah (mindful lord),
whether Thou rulest through Asha (justice),   686

Over-every-one from whom destruction threatens me? 87

It is no-more-than right that Thou shouldst tell me, in
just words, the decrees of Vohu Manah (good disposition),   88

For (I Zarathushtra who am) the Savior would-like-to-know
how his (my) compensation shall be given to him (me)?

48. 10

kadā mazdā manarōis narō vīseñtē? 690

kadā ajên mūthrem ahyā magahyā? 691

yā añgrayā karapanō urūpayeiñtī 692

yāca xratū duse-xshathrā da*h*yun*a*m. 693

48. 11

kadā mazdā ashā ma*t* ārmaitis 694

jima*t* xshathrā husheitis vāstravaitī ? 695

kōi d*r*egvōdebīs xrūrāis rām*a*m dāeñtē? 696

kêñg ā va*n*hêus jima*t* mana*n*hō cistis? 697

48. 12

a*t* tōi a*n*hen saos*h*yañtō da*h*yun*a*m 698

yōi xshnūm vohū mana*n*hā hacāeñtē 699

s*h*yaothanāis ashā thwahyā mazdā sêñghahyā 700

tōi-zī dātā hamaēstārō aēshem mahyā! 701

V. Nobles must resign Luxury, enforce Security, gain Salvation.

48.10

When, O AHURA Mazdah (mindful lord), will men gain
knowledge of the Message?   690
When will they expel the dregs of this (Haoma) intoxica-
tion?   91
Whereby is-practised-deceit by (1) the hostile Karapans 92
And (2) the bad land-rulers (who are) in (the position to)
understand.   93

48.11

When, O Mazdah (mindful), will Armaiti (love) with
Asha (justice), and Xshathra (power),   694
And Good-Dwelling, come (Ye to us, and eventuate) in a
pastoral realm?   95
Who will give us peace through bloody (slaughter) of the
Drujists?   96
Unto whom will the doctrinal-thought of Vohu Manah
(good disposition) enter (and with him abide)?   97

48.12

But these are the Saviors of lands, O Mazdah (mindful),
Who, with Vohu Manah (good disposition) and Asha
(justice),   699
Strive to satisfy Thy teachings-or-doctrines through deeds,
They become conquerors of Aeshma (fury of rapine)! 701

YASNA 49

49. 1

Aᵗ mā yavā bêñdvō pafrē mazishtō   702

yê duserethrīs cixshnushā ashā mazdā   703

vaⁿuhī ādā gaidī mōi ā-mōi arapā   604

ahyā vohū aoshō vīdā manaⁿhā!   705

49. 2

aᵗ ahyā-mā bêñdvahyā mānayeitī   706

ᵗkaēshō dregvāe daibitā ashāᵗ rāreshō   707

nōiᵗ speñtam dōresht ahmāi stōi ārmaitīs   708

naēdā vohū mazdā frashtā manaⁿhā.   709

49. 3

aᵗcā ahmāi varenāi mazdā nidātem   710

ashem sūidyāi ᵗkaēshāi rāshayeⁿghē druxs   711

tā vaⁿhêus sarê izyāi manaⁿhō   712

añtarê vīspêñg dregvatō haxmêñg añtarê mruyē   713

HYMN 49

Zarathushtra, Defeated by Bendva, Appeal*s* for Defender*s*.

- I. Zarathushtra Utters Imprecations on his Successful Opponent.

49.1

Ever has Bendva hindered me, (and proved himself the)
greater (of us two)   702

When I, O Mazdah (mindful), through Asha (justice),
was trying to satisfy the misled (crowds) !   3

(O mindful Mazdah), come to my support with Thy good
Ada (retribution),   4

And with the Vohu Manah (good disposition) (through
whom) Thou (fore)knowest the (impending) destruction
of that (Bendva).   5

49.2

But that Bendva's teacher (Grehma, that) apostate from
Asha (justice),   706

That Druj, has long hindered me ;   7

He fails to insist on having with him the bounteous
Armaiti (love),   8

Neither, O Mazdah (mindful), does he counsel with Vohu
Manah (good disposition).   9

49.3

In our belief, Asha (justice) is set down as the means to
profit ;   710

While, on the contrary, in their teaching, the Lie-of-the-
Druj is set down as the means to harm ;   11

Consequently, I zealously-insist-on communion with Vohu
Manah (good disposition),   12

And on 'swearing-off' (renouncing) all association with the
Druj   13

49. 4

yōi dus-xrathwā aēshemem vareden rāmemcā 714

*hv*āis hizubīs fshuyasū afshuyañtō 715

yaēsh*am* nōi*t* hvarshtāis *vas* du*z*varshtā 716

tōi daēvê*ñg dan* yā dre*g*vatō daēnā. 717

49. 5

a*t* hvō mazdā ī*z*ācā ā*zū*itiscā 718

y*ê* daēn*am* vohū sārshtā mana*n*hā 719

ārmatōis kasci*t* ashā hu*z*ê*ñ*tus 720

tāiscā vīspāis thwahmī xshathrōi ahurā! 721

49. 6

frō vā*e* fraē*shy*ā mazdā ashemcā mrūitē ·722

yā v*ê* xratêus xshmākahyā ā-mana*n*hā 723

*er*es vīcidyāi yathā-ī srāvayaēmā 724

tam daēn*am* yā xshmāvatō ahurā! 725

49.4

Who, through perverted principles, increase fury-of-rapine
    (Aeshma) and cruelty   714
Among the herd-prosperers, by their tongues' conversation,
    themselves not being herd-prosperers;   15
Whose own crimes they do not overcome with good works;
These may (yet) establish the divinities of the Daevas,
    through the spirits of the Drujists.   17
(OR, Away with them into the Dwelling of the Daevas! B)

49.5

May zeal and fat food (reward) him   718
Who, in spirit, communes with Vohu Manah (good dispo-
    sition),   19
Because he is well-informed about Armaiti (love) through
    Asha (justice);   20
I judge all these belong into Thy realm, O Mazdah
    (mindful)!   21

II. Frashaoshtra is Urged to Become Defender.

49.6

O AHURA Mazdah (mindful lord), I beg You and Asha
    (justice) to declare   722
Your wisdom's (double) purposes in connection with 23
The proper solution of the problem   24
How to obtain a (ready) hearing for the spirit of One-like-
    You!   25

49. 7

tatcā vohū mazdā sraotū mananhā!　　　726

sraotū ashā gūshahvā-tū ahurā!　　　727

kê airyamā, kê hvaētus dātāis anhat　　　728

yê verezênāi vanuhīm dāt frasastīm?　　　729

49. 8

ferashaoshtrāi urvāzishtam ashahyā dāe　　　730

sarêm tat thwā mazdā yāsā ahurā,　　　731

maibyācā yam vanhāu thwahmī ā-xshathrōi　　　732

yavōi vīspāi fraēshtāenhō āenhāmā!　　　733

49. 9

sraotū sāsnāe fshéñghyō suyē tashtō,　　　734

nōit eres-vacāe sarêm didas dregvātā,　　　735

hyat daēnāe vahishtē yūjén mīzdē　　　736

ashā yuxtā yāhī dejāmāspā!　　　737

49.7

Hear, O Vohu Manah (good disposition)!   Hear, O Asha
(justice)!   726

Hearken Thou, O AHURA Mazdah (mindful lord)!   27

What peer, what gentleman (whose influence would enforce
regulations) will initiate regulations   28

Whose observance would earn a good reputation for the
group-of-those-who-labor-at-herding-cattle?   29

49.8

I beg of Thee, O AHURA Mazdah (mindful lord) to grant

(1) To Frashaoshtra the most blissful communion with
Asha (justice);   731

And (2) to me, to attain the Good in the Xshathra (realm)

While (3) both-of-us-wish-to-be Thy messengers for ever-
in-the-age.   33

49.9

Let the Prosperer (Ashaist believer) who was shaped (OR
formed) to profit the world, listen to the teachings! 734

Let not him who (utters OR, possesses) the just Words
have any communion with the Drujists ;   35

Let the spirits (occupied in search) of the best Compensation join together ;   36

Let both the man (Zarathushtra) and Jamaspa unite with
Asha (justice) !   37

49. 10

tatcā mazdā thwahmī ādɑm nipāenhē   738

manō vohū urunascā ashāunɑm   739

nemascā yā ārmaitis īzācā   740

mazā xshathrā vazdɑnhā avêmīrā!   741

49. 11

at dusexshathrêñg, dus-shyaothanêñg, duzvacɑnhō   742

duzdaēnêñg dus-manɑnhō dregvatō   743

akāis hvarethāis paitī urvɑnō paityeiñtī   744

drūjō demānē haithyā ɑnhen astayō!   745

49. 12

kat tōi ashā zbayeñtē avɑnhō   746

zarathushtrāi? kat tōi vohū manɑnhā?   747

yê-vê staotāis mazdā frīnāi ahurā   748

avat yāsɑs hyat vê īshtā vahishtem!   749

49.10

Whereupon, O AHURA Mazdah (mindful lord), Zarathush-
  tra will commit to Thy Dwelling   738
(As treasury of merit of the 'mindful' divinity, the memory
  of) the good thoughts, souls, and adorations,   39
With the zeal and (loving) Armaiti-devotions of the
  Ashaists,   40
All of which, O (great ruler) Xshathra, mayest Thou
  guard with enduring energy (B; DOUBTFUL, M).   41

49.11

(But, on the other hand, for the evil man), the (psycho-
  pompic) souls, (carrying) foods, will go to meet   742
The bad administration, bad deeds, bad speeches,   43
And bad spirits of the evil-minded Drujists;   44
(Who) will be genuine (worthy and accepted) companions
  (to the inmates) of the Dwelling of the Druj !   45

49.12

O Asha (justice) ! What sort of help hast Thou for me,
  Zarathushtra, who am calling to Thee?   46
With Vohu Manah (good disposition), what help hast
  Thou perhaps for me?   47
O AHURA Mazdah, with praises do I sue for Thy friend-
  ship,   48
Praying for whatever is best among Your compensating
  rewards !   49

YASNA 50

50. 1

Ka*t* mōi urvā isē cahyā ava*n*hō   750

kê-mōi pasêus kê-mê-nā-thrātā vistō   751

anyō ashā*t* thwa*t*cā mazdā ahurā?   752

azdā zūtā vahishtāa*t*cā mana*n*hō?   753

50. 2

kathā mazdā rānyō-ske*r*etīm g*a*m ishasōi*t*   754

yê-hīm ahmāi vāstravaitīm s*t*ōi usyā*t*?   755

*e*rezejīs ashā pourushū hvar*ê* pis*h*yasū   756

ākāstêñg mā nishasyā dāthêm dāhvā.   757

HYMN 50

Ordination *of* Discipleʃ
To Form New Settlementʃ

I. How to Form New Settlements.

50.1

Except Thy Asha (justice) or Thy Vohu Manah (good
   disposition), O AHURA Mazdah (mindful lord),   750
Whom may I, with certainty, invoke   51
To protect my cattle and myself ?   52
On what help may my soul count?   53

50.2

How, O Mazdah (mindful), might (a man) seek (possession of) a fortune-bringing cow,   54
If he desire both (1) her and (2) the pasture?   55
By living justly among the many men who appreciate the
   comforts (OR, agricultural benefits) of the sun;   56
By settling open lands (OR, bad lands, as yet belonging to
   the bad Drujists) to be acquired OR, settled-down 'as a
   clever man' would do, cleverly; OR, which may be given
   as gifts.   57

The text is in a hopeless condition. This interpretation is as faithful
as possible, yet is partially suggested by the context. It possesses the
merit of agreeing with the practical interests of that civilization.

50. 3

atcīt ahmāi mazdā ashā anhaitī   758

yam hōi xshathrā vohucā cōisht mananhā   759

yê-nā ashōis aojanhā varedayaētā   760

yam nazdishtam gaētham dregvāe baxshaitī.   761

50. 4

at vāe yazāi stavas mazdā ahurā   762

hadā ashā vahishtācā mananhā   763

xshathrācā yā īshō stāenhat ā-paithī   764

ākāe aredrēñg demānē garō seraoshānē!   765

50.5

ārōi-zī xshmā mazdā ashā ahurā   766

hyat yūshmākāi mathrānē vaorāzathā   767

aibī-dereshtā āvīshyā avanhā   768

zastāishtā yā-nāe hvāthrē dāyat!   769

50.3

But through Asha (justice) shall (legal right), O AHURA
   Mazdah (mindful lord), be (the portion of) this (pioneer);   758

(Getting possession) of what (settlements) the good (teaching, or teacher, Zarathushtra) taught him (to take possession of) with (wit) Vohu Manah and (good management
   or power) Xshathra;   59

And who, through the vigor of compensation (by paying
   an equivalent), (may acquire)   60

The nearest estate which the (nomadic) Drujists may (yet)
   share (for some time).   61

II. These Settlers are to Act as Missionaries.

50.4

Thereupon, when the Wisher (for a recently settled home)
   stands upon the path leading to the (above-mentioned)
   open (OR, bad, lands), then   765

I (Zarathushtra) will hear (these) faithful (home-seekers)
   (going) to (their new) dwelling (which, when occupied,
   will be full) of (grateful) praise;   64

And I, (Zarathushtra), praising You, O AHURA Mazdah
   (mindful lord) with Asha (justice) and the best (disposition) Manah, and Xshathra (power),   63

Will, (for this joyful information about new settlements)
   worship You!   62

50.5

As You (also) have rejoiced with-and-for-Your-prophet's
   (joy),   767

Therefore, O Mazdah AHURA (mindful lord), I have,
   through Asha (justice), aroused myself,   66

On-account-of Your visible and manifest help,   68

50. 6

yê mathrā vācem mazdā baraitī	770
urvathō ashā nemaṇhā zarathushtrō	771
dātā xratêus hizvō raithīm stōi	772
mahyā rāzêñg vohū sāhīt manaṇhā!	773

50. 7

at vê yaojā zevīshtyêñg aurvatō	774
jayāis perethūs vahmahyā yūshmākahyā	775
mazdā ashā ugrêñg vohū manaṇhā	776
yāis azāthā mahmāi hyātā avaṇhē!	777

50. 8

mat vāe padāis yā frasrūtā izayāe	778
pairijasāi mazdā ustānazastō!	779
at vāe ashā aredrahyācā nemaṇhā!	780
at vāe vaṇhêus manaṇhō hunaretātā!	781

Through hand-sought (labor), which restores us (the faithful) to (prosperous) well-being (from the destitution consequent on the furious rapine of the Drujists)!   69

50.6

(I) Zarathushtra, (1) (who) through reverence am the friend
of Asha (justice),   771
And (2) who give direction(s) to the settlements through
my tongue,—   72
(I pray), O Mazdah (mindful), that (the Wisher-Settler)
may (also) raise up his speech in a word (as I do),   70
And with (the aid of) Vohu Manah (good disposition)
may teach the commands of my understanding!   73

50.7

(By thus enlisting missionaries) for You, O Mazdah (mindful), with Asha (justice) and Vohu Manah (good disposition),   776
I-will-yoke-on speedy runners, thick-set and strong,   74
With spurs of adoration of You,   75
Through which (runners) may You (and Your cause) drive
on (to progress) : and might You aid me (too, last, but
not least)!   77

50.8

With these Verses, which are famous as (verses) of zeal, 78
I will, with stretched-out hands, encompass You, O Maz-
dah (mindful)!   779
You also, O Asha (justice), with the reverence of the
faithful!   80
You also, (all Ye divinities), with the full ability of Vohu
Manah (good disposition)!   81

50. 9

tāis vāe yasnāis paitī stavas ayenī   782

mazdā ashā vanhêus shyaothanāis mananhō   783

yadā ashōis mahyāe vasê xshayā   784

at hudānāus ishayas gerezdā hyêm.   785

50. 10

at yā vareshā yācā pairī āis shyaothanā   786

yācā vohū cashmam arejat mananhā   787

raocāe hvêñg asnam uxshā aēurus   788

xshmākāi ashā vahmāi mazdā ahurā!   789

50. 11

at vê staotā aojāi mazdā anhācā!   790

yavat ashā tavācā isāicā!   791

dātā anhêus aredat vohū mananhā   792

haithyāvareshtam hyat vasnā ferashōtemem?   793

III. But Zarathushtra Remains the Only Mediator.

50.9

I will come towards You, O Mazdah (mindful), and Asha
(justice),   782
Praising (1) with these hymns, and with the deeds of (good
disposition) Vohu Manah;   83
And when I shall rule-at-will over my Compensation, 84
Then shall I become recipient (thereof), caring for that of
the well-disposed (faithful believer).   85

50.10

Thus, (1) whatever deeds I may have done before,   786
And (2) whatever (objects) interest the eye through Vohu
Manah (good disposition), (still they are as nothing
when compared to)   87
The lights (of the sky), the sun, the dawn ('the shimmer-
ing bull of days');   88
All these, O AHURA Mazdah (mindful lord), and Asha
(justice), exist for Your adoration!   89

50.11

I will preach that I am Your praise-singer, O Mazdah
(mindful)!   790
And-may-I-be-this, O Asha (justice), as far as I am able,
and can!   91
May the Creator-of-life, through the help of Vohu Manah
(good disposition),   92
Prosper whatever genuine work is most suitable to His
Will!   93

Vobuksbatbra Gatba

YASNA 51

51. 1

Vohū xshathrem vairīm bāgem aibī-bairishtem   794

vīdīshemnāis īzācīt ashā añtare-caraitī   795

shyaothanāis mazdā vahishtem tat nê nūcīt vareshānē!   796

51.2

tā-vê mazdā paourvīm ahurā ashāi yecā   797

taibyācā ārmaitē dōishā-mōi ishtōis xshathrem   798

xshmākem vohū manaṇhā vahmāi dāidī savaṇhō!   799

51.3

ā-vê gêushā hêmyañtū yōi vê shyaothanāis sāreñtē   800

ahurā ashā-hizvāe uxdāis vaṇhêus manaṇhō   801

yaēsham tū pouruyō mazda fradaxshtā ahī!   802

HYMN 51

Proclamation *of the* Kingdom.

I. The Children of the Kingdom.

51.1

Asha (justice) will procure the good Xshathra (realm),
  which is a 'choice' and most productive destiny,   794
For those who, with zeal, through their deeds, practice the
  best (doctrines),   95
O (mindful) Mazdah ! (Grant that) I may effect (carry into
  execution, realize) that (realm) !   96

51.2

First of all, O ahura Mazdah (mindful lord), assure me
  the Xshathra (realm) of Compensation,   797
And then Thine, O Asha (justice) ! and Thine, O Armaiti
  (love) !   98
Through Vohu Manah (good disposition), oh do You
  grant profit to the worshipper of You !   99

51.3

Thou, O Mazdah (mindful), art the first Teacher of those
  who   802
With their deeds, and in their tongue, commune with the
  utterances of Vohu Manah (good disposition);   801
May they attract (the attention of) Your ears, O ahura
  Mazdah (mindful lord), and O Asha (justice) !   800

51. 4

kuthrā ārōis āf*ser*atus? kuthrā me*rez*dikā axshta*t*? 803

kuthrā yasō *hy*ên ashem? kū *sp*eñtā ārmaitis? 804

kuthrā manō vahishtem? kuthrā thwā xshathrā mazdā? 805

51. 5

vīspā-tā *peresas* yathā ashā*t* hacā *gam* vīda*t* 806

vāstryō *shy*aothanāis *ereshvō has* huxratus nema*n*hā 807

y*ê* dāthaēibyō *eres*-ratūm xshay*as* ashivā*e* cistā? 808

51. 6

y*ê* vahyō va*n*h*ê*us dazdē yascā hōi vārāi rāda*t* 809

ahurō xshathrā mazdā*e* a*t* ahmāi akā*t* a*shy*ō 810

y*ê* hōi nōi*t* vīdāitī apêmē a*n*h*ê*us urvaēsē. 811

(Well) mayest thou ask all these (following questions:) 806

51.4

Where are the Compensations for griefs? Where may we
    find pity? 803
Where may (men) attain Asha (justice)? Where may a
    man establish the bounteous Armaiti (love)? 4
Where (may he establish) the best (disposition) Manah?
    Where, O Mazdah (mindful), (may He establish) Thy
    Xshathra (realm)? 5

51.5

Where may the Pasturer, having become a just man
    through his deeds, acquire cattle? 806
Will he (succeed in) doing so if, being of good under-
    standing, he reverently prays to 7
Him who is a just Judge, ruling over both Compen-
    sations for the benefit of the 'clever' (believers)? 8

51.6

(The mindful lord) AHURA Mazdah (is He) who, at the last
    crisis of life, through His (power) Xshathra, dis-
    tributes 810
(1) What is better-than-good to any one who prepares (the
    world) for His Will, 9
But (2) what is worse-than-bad to (every one) who does not
    distribute (contributions to Zarathushtra, SEE 44.19, or
    46.1, 10, 18). 11

51. 7

dāidī-mōi yê gam tashō apascā urvarāescā   812

ameretātā haurvātā spênishtā mainyū mazdā   813

tevīshī utayūitī manaᵣhā vohū sêñᵣhē.   814

51. 8

aᵗ zī tōi vaxshyā mazdā vīdushē zī-nā mruyāᵗ   815

hyaᵗ akōyā dregvāitē ushtā yê ashem dādrē   816

hvō zī maᵗhrā shyātō yê vīdushē mravaitī.   817

51. 9

yam xshnūtem rānōibyā dāe thwā āthrā suxrā mazdā   818

ayaᵣhā xshustā aibī ahvāhū daxshtem dāvōi   819

rāshayeᵣghē dregvañtem savayō ashavanem.   820

51.7

O Mazdah (mindful), (Thou who art the) Fashioner of the
  Bovine (creation), the waters and the plants!   812
Through the most (bounteous Mentality) Spenta Mainyu,
  grant me Ameretat (immortality) and Haurvatat (health)
Which are full-of-vitality, and are, through Vohu Manah
  (good disposition), enduring in the holy doctrines.   14

II. Opposition to the Prophet is Enmity to Humanity.

51.8

I shall speak for Thee, O Mazdah (mindful), about what
  (1) is threatened against the Drujist, and (2) what is
  wished-for (and promised) to him-who maintains Asha
  (justice).   816
(I shall speak thus because it is proper) to speak to the (intelligent man, referred to as the) Expert-knower;   15
(And besides, the prophet) rejoices through the Word
  which is told to the Expert-knower.   17

51.9

And do Thou, O Mazdah (mindful), within (the nature of)
  both contending Parties, set satisfaction, as a token (of
  the accuracy of my prophecy of the Judgment by) 819
The metal, molten through Thy red fire (which, as a sifter,
  shall)   18
Harm the Drujist, (but) profit the Ashaist.   20

51. 10

at yĕ mā-nā marexshaitē anyāthā ahmāt mazdā   821

hvō dāmōis drūjō hunus tā duzdāe yōi heñtī   822

maibyō zbayā ashem vanhuyā ashī gat tē.   823

51. 11

kĕ urvathō spitamāi zarathushtrāi nā mazdā?   824

kĕ vā ashā āfrashtā? kā speñtā ārmaitis?   825

kĕ vā vanhêus mananhō acistā magāi ereshvō?   826

51. 12

nōit tā-īm xshnāus vaēpyō kevīnō peretō zemō   827

zarathushtrem spitāmem hyat ahmī urūraost ashtō   828

hyat hōi īm caratascā aoderescā zōishenū vāzā.   829

51.10

(Wherefore I am fearless; even those who would kill me
    here are only bringing me closer to my reward)
Whereas, he who would wish to kill me, not considering
    this coming event, O (mindful) Mazdah,   821
He (punishes himself by becoming) malicious towards the
    creatures that are existent, (and thereby becomes) a son
    of the Druj (and will therefore share their fate),   22
While I, (even though killed) will, for myself, call Asha
    (justice), that He may come with a good Compensation.

51.11

(Such being the fate of my enemies, I would like to know)
    O (mindful) Mazdah, who is a friend to Spitama Zara-
    thushtra?   824
(Is it not he) who has consulted with Asha (justice)? What
    (is) bounteous Armaiti (love)?   25
Or who, as a just (supporter) for the Magian Cause, show-
    ed himself to be considerate of Vohu Manah (good dis-
    positon) ?   26

51.12

(Returning to my enemies,) not very much did (Kik,) that
    pederast (or, vulgar fellow) of the Kavay-tribe ingratiate
    himself with me   827
When at the bridge (or passage) of (the) earth (a mountain
    pass?) he refused hospitality (1) to Zarathushtra Spitama
And (2) to both (the oxen?) shivering with cold, whom he
    (Zarathushtra) was driving along (all uncertain).   29

51. 13

tā dregvatō maredaitī daēnā *erezāus* haithīm   830

yehyā urvā xraodaitī cinvatō *peretāe* ākāe.   831

hvāis shyaothanāis hizvascā ashahyā *nasvāe* pathō.   832

51. 14

nōi*t* urvāthā dātōibyascā karapanō vāstrā*t* arêm   833

gavōi ārōis āsêñdā *hvāis shyaothanāiscā* sêñghāiscā   834

yê-īs sêñghō apêmem drūjō demānē ādā*t*!   835

51. 15

hya*t* mī*zd*em zarathushtrō magavabyō cōisht parā   836

garō demānē ahurō mazdā*e* jasa*t* pouruyō   837

tā vê vohū mana*n*hā ashāicā savāis civīshī.   838

51.13

Thus the spirit of the Druj destroys the genuine (reward)
    of the straight (path);   830
And his soul trembles at the Bridge of the Sifting which
    will make manifest (his deeds),   31
    (Giving access to the other world, M)
And through his deeds, and (through whose evil words of
    their) tongue, the Druj have perished from the path of
    Asha (justice).   32

51.14

(Even) the friend(ly disposed) Karapans do not cultivate
    their pasture properly by the proper rules;   833
They effect, by their deeds and doctrines, griefs for the
    Bovine (creation);   34
Which doctrine will at last bring (the Karapans) into the
    Dwelling of the Druj!   35

51.15

(On the contrary, when) Ahura Mazdah (the mindful lord)
    shall, as first-comer, come into Garodman (the Dwelling
    of Praise).   537
I, Zarathushtra, expect, through (having produced) profits
    for Asha (justice), and through Vohu Manah (good dis-
    position),   38
The Compensation which I taught to the Magians.   36

51. 16

tam kavā vīshtāspō magahyā xshathrā nasat   839

vanhêus padebīs mananhō yam cistīm ashā mañtā   840

speñtō mazdāe ahurō athā-nê sazdyāi ushtā.   841

51. 17

berexdam mōi ferashaoshtrō hvō-gvā daēdōisht kehrpêm   842

daēnayāi vanhuyāi yam hōi ishyam dātū   843

xshayas mazdāe ahurō ashahyā āzdyāi gerezdīm !   844

51. 18

tam cistīm dêjāmāspō hvō-gvō ishtōis hvarenāe   845

ashā vereñtē tat xshathrem mananhō vanuhīs vīdō   846

tat mōi dāidī ahurā hyat mazdā rapên tavā!   847

51. 19

hvō tat nā maidyōi-māenhā spitamā ahmāi dazdē   848

daēnayā vaēdemnō yê ahūm ishasas aibī   849

mazdāe dātā mraot gayehyā shyaothanāis vahyō.   850

III. Supporters of the Prophet are Heroes and Saints.

51.16

But Kava Vishtaspa attained (more than) these (both rewards); together with the rule over the Magian tribe, 839

Through Asha (justice) as advisory-manager, and through
the Verses of (good disposition) Vohu Manah, he attained Chisti (SOPHIA, or wisdom) ;   40

Thus, for us (the faithful) is AHURA Mazdah (the mindful
lord) bounteous-at-wish.   41

51.17

Frashaoshtra Hvogva has shown (and promised) to me (as
wife his daughter's) prized body.   842

(Now,) in-order-that I may attain (to be) the recipient of
Asha (justice), may the ruling AHURA Mazdah (mindful
lord)   44

Grant (to me) her desired (body) for the benefit of her
good spirit (that she may be saved through me as husband, SEE 53.3) !   43

51.18

May Jamaspa Hvogva, glorious with riches, choosing this
Chisti (SOPHIA, wisdom, daughter of Zarathushtra, whom
he marries in Yasna 53)   845

Through Asha (justice) (also) partake in that Xshathra
(realm) of (the good disposition) Vohu Manah ;   46

May AHURA Mazdah (the mindful lord) grant to me that
they may find support with Thee (Ahura Mazdah) ! 47

51.19

O Maidyomangha-Spitama ! He (Zarathushtra) who has
given that (prize of verse 18, his daughter Chisti) to this
(Jamaspa),   848

Who, as having known through his spirit the (first) life, is
wishing again the (the second),   49

51. 20

taṭ vê-nê hazaoshāenhō vīspāenhō daidyāi savō   851

ashem vohu manaɴhā uxdā yāis ārmaitis   852

yazemnāenhō nemaɴhā mazdāe rafedrem cagedō.   853

51. 21

ārmatōis nā speñtō hvō cistī uxdāis shyaothanā   854

daēnā ashem spênvaṭ vohū xshathrem manaɴhā   855

mazdāe dadāṭ ahurō têm vaɴuhīm yāsā ashīm.   856

51. 22

yehya mōi ashāṭ hacā vahishtem yesnē paitī   857

vaēdā mazdāe ahurō yōi āeɴharecā heñticā   858

ta yazāi hvāis nāmenīs pairicā jasāi vañtā!   859

Says that thou (hast) the better (part) of life, having (prac-
ticed) the decrees of (mindful) Mazdah through thy
deeds.   50

51.20

That (better part which is) a profit of yours, all (you like-
willed four leaders of the four preceding verses 15-19,
Vishtaspa, Frashaoshtra, Jamaspa, and Maidyomangha),
(I repeat, that better part induces you) to give (utter-
ance to)   851

Utterances with which Armaiti (love), with Vohu Manah
(good disposition) being worshipped with reverence,   52

Will grant Asha (justice) as a support of Mazdah (mind-
ful).   53

51.21

I desire a good Compensation (such as) this : to grow
bounteous through the influence of Armaiti (love);   856

Such a person is prospering Asha (justice) with his doctrinal (thought SOPHIA, wisdom) through his utterances,
deeds, and spirit ;   54

(To such a person) will (the mindful lord) AHURA Mazdah
through Vohu Manah (good disposition), grant the
Xshathra (realm or power).   55

51.22

If (the mindful lord) Mazdah AHURA knows among (any
of the men) who were, and who (yet) are (living,   858

Any persons) to whom because of their hymns the best
(reward) from Asha (justice, is) yet (to come),   57

These (men, like the above-mentioned four heroes), even
by their names will I worship (publicly and individually);
and into their presence will I enter with praise !   59

Vahishtoishti Gatha

YASNA 53

53. 1

Vahishtā īshtis srāvī zarathushtrahē 860

spitāmahyā yezī hōi dāt āyaptā 861

ashāt hacā ahurō mazdāe yavōi vīspāi ā hva*n*hevīm 862

yaēcā hōi daben sas*h*eñcā daēnayāe va*n*huyāe ux*d*ā shyaothanācā. 863

53. 2

a*t*cā hōi scañtū mana*n*hā ux*d*āis shyaothanāiscā 864

xshnūm mazdāe vahmāi ā fraore*t* yasnascā 865

kavacā vīshtāspō zarathushtris spitāmō ferashaoshtrascā 866

dāenhō erezūs pathō *y*am daēnam ahurō saos*h*yañtō dadā*t*. 867

53. 3

têmcā-tū pourucistā haēca*t*-aspānā 868

spitāmī yezivī dug*e*dram zarathushtrahē 869

va*n*hêus paityāstêm mana*n*hō ashahyā mazdāescā taibyō dā*t*
sarem 870

athā hêm ferashvā thwā xrathwā spênishtā ārmatōis
hudānvareshvā. 871

HYMN 53

Zarathushtra Gives his Daughter
To Secure a Champion.

I. Marriage Ceremony.

53.1

The best riches that have been heard of are those of Zarathushtra,   860

Since (the mindful lord) AHURA Mazdah grants to him by
Asha (justice)   61

For all eternity (1) felicities, (2) a good life, and (3) (the
conversion of) those who deceived him ;   62

(And Zarathushtra prays that his followers) may learn to
formulate-correctly the utterances and deeds of the good
spirit-of-religion.   63

53.2

And may Vishtaspa and (Maidyomangha) the Zarathushtrian son of-the-Spitama-family, and Frashaoshtra,   866

Establish the straightly just paths of the spirits for whom
(the lord) AHURA has appointed Saviors   67

Who strive through utterances and deeds (inspired by
Vohu) Manah (good disposition)   64

To utter cheerfully hymns for the adoration of (the mindful) Mazdah (in order to give him) satisfaction.   65

53.3

O Pouruchista, daughter of Haechataspa,   868

Thou youngest of the daughters of Zarathushtra,   69

(Zarathushtra) gives to thee this (Jamaspa as a husband
who will) impress (on thee) communion with Vohu Manah (good disposition), Asha (justice), and Mazdah
(mindful);   70

So take counsel with thy understanding (so that it may become) most bounteous (when it has become full) of well-
disposed Armaiti (love).   71

53. 4

têm zī vê speredānī varānī yā fedrōi vīdā*t*   872

paithyaēcā vāstryaēibyō a*t*cā *h*vaētaovē   873

ashāunī ashavabyō mana*n*hō va*n*hêus *h*vênva*t* ha*n*hus mêm
bêedus   874

mazdā*e* dadā*t* ahurō daēnayāi va*n*huyāi yavōi vīspāi ā.   875

53. 5

sā*h*vênī vazyamnābyō kainibyō mraomī   876

xshmaibyācā vademnō mêñcā-ī ma*z*dazdūm   877

vaēdōdūm daēnābīs abyastā ahūm yê va*n*hêus mana*n*hō   878

ashā vê anyō ainīm vīvêñghatū ta*t* zī hōi hushênem a*n*ha*t*.   879

53. 6

ithā-ī haithyā narō athā jênayō   880

drūjō hacā rāthemō yême spashuthā frāidīm   881

drūjō āyesē hōis pithā tanvō parā vayū-beredubyō dus-*h*varethêm nasa*t* *h*vāthrem   882

dregvōde*b*yō dêjī*t*-aretaēibyō   anāis ā manahīm ahūm
mereñgeduyē.   883

53.4

(The bride speaks:) Him will I emulate ! (The bridegroom
   speaks:) (Her) will I choose   872
Who-shall-generously-distribute-service to father, husband,
   pasturer, gentleman, Ashaist and pagan !   73
(The bride speaks:) The sunlit fruit of (good disposition)
   Vohu Manah shall be mine (I shall have a child? M)74
(The bridegroom speaks:) May (the mindful lord) AHURA
   Mazdah grant it to (thy) good spirit for all eternity ! 75

53.5

(Zarathushtra speaks:) I utter admonitions to those who
   are being married, and to maidens ;   876
(That which) I am counseling to you, you should heed, remember, and realize,   77
Through spirit(ual precepts) striving for the life of (good
   disposition) Vohu Manah,   78
Vying with each other in Asha (justice), and spiritual precepts: thus shall you be happy !   79

53.6

Thus shall you be genuine men and women (husband and
   wife?)   880
For, can you discover any advantage in belonging to the
   party of the Drujists?   I
For what the Drujists desire shall be kept away from their
   bodies: AHURA Mazdah (the mindful lord) shall present
   bad food to those who (then shall be) crying 'woe',
   and shall withdraw comfort from the law-scorning Druj; 2
Thereby (with these other contrasting actions) you destroy
   the spiritual life (for yourselves).   3

53. 7

atcā vê mīzdem anhat ahyā magahyā 884

yavat āzus zarazdishtō būnōi haxtayāe 885

paracā mraocas aorācā yathrā mainyus dregvatō anasat parā 886

ivīzayathā magêm têm at vê vayōi anhaitī apêmem vacō. 887

53. 8

anāis ā duzvareshnanhō dafshnyā hêñtū 888

zahyācā vīspāenhō xraoseñtam upā 889

huxshathrāis jêneram xrūneramcā rāmamcā āis dadātū shyeitibyō vīzibyō 890

īratū īs dvafshō hvō derezā merethyāus mazishtō moshucā astū. 891

53. 9

duzvarenāis vaēshō rāstī tōi narepīs rajīs 892

aēshasā dêjīt-aretā peshō-tanvō 893

kū ashavā ahurō yê īs jyātêus hêmithyāt vasê-itōiscā 894

tat mazdā tavā xshathrem yā erezejyōi dāhī drigaovē vahyō? 895

53.7

But to you (the newly-married pair) shall be (granted) the
Compensation of the Magian Cause 884

In-the-measure-that most hearty zeal (therefor) be rooted
in your body; 5

But if you dismiss (abandon) the Magian Cause, you shall
at the last cry 'woe!' 6

When the spirits of the Druj dodge downwards, and disappear! 7

II. The Bride-groom is Goaded to Conversion by the Sword.

53.8

Thereby let all the malefactors be deluded through Causes
other (than the Magian) 888

Through whose good rulers peace shall be given to the
dwellings and villages; 90

(On the contrary, let the malefactors through whom are effected) murder and bloody deed, let them all be abandoned, and cry upwards in vain; 89

Let the greatest torture attack those captives of destruction—and let that occur soon, too! 91

53.9

(Vagabond nomads) shall reach the Place of Decay with
the Malefactors who, being law-scorning, and, as to their
bodies, doomed, 892

Are seeking to degrade the worthy (Magians). 93

Where is the (Ashaist) lord who will deprive them of freedom and of life, 94

(And establish) the (Kingdom) Xshathra, by which,
O (mindful) Mazdah, Thou shalt give, to the Poor
man, who lives justly, that Better (part)? 95

PART III

Higher Criticism
of the Gathas.

Higher Criticism of the Gathas

Chapter I

Why Gathic Criticism is Inevitable.

I. Higher Criticism Universal, even if Unconscious.

The clear understanding of any book presupposes a grasp of the principles of interpretation. A novelist is not expected to be as accurate as a geographer, nor a poet as a sociologist or theologian. With most books this preliminary attitude of the reader is so obvious that the question of interpretation is never raised or even mooted. Nevertheless it exists, for many books have, from time to time, been misunderstood, and hence have caused misunderstandings—exploded literary jokes, still deceiving the unwary, generation after generation.

The question of interpretation has been raised principally in connection with the most important books, such as the Bible, Homer, or the Hindu epics. It might well, therefore, be applied to the Gâthas which form the nucleus of a historical religion which has survived several millenniums. But the study of the Gâthas is nowadays less of a problem of orthodoxy, than one of comparative religion by such as do not profess their dogmatic authority. On this latter account, indeed, application of the canons of interpretation to them might seem a need less burning, were it not that they present some very real special difficulties which are set forth at length in this chapter, and which compel the application of the methods of the 'higher criticism.'

It is granted that it is most unfortunate that we have to judge of our facts before making deductions from them; it would seem to destroy all hopes of attaining results that are objective. But this misfortune is common to most inquiries. Even so certain a study as the differential calculus rests on an illogical basis—namely, that one would ever reach a limit by approaching it by infinitesimal quantities. We must therefore resign ourselves to unavoidable human limitations, and make the best of them.

II. Special Gathic Difficulties Demanding Interpretation.

The special Gâthic difficulties which demand interpretation or higher criticism may be distinguished as difficulties of

1, The works themselves, their language, author, and condition—*Internal.*

2, Their date, and traditional orthodox interpretation—*Mazdean*

3, Their bearing on the development of Christianity—*Christian*

4, Modern conditions of thought—*Modern.*

1. Internal Causes of the Extraordinary Difficulties of Interpreting the Gathas.

1 Great wealth of forms for a single case of the same class. Justi mentions ten forms for the accusative plural of nouns of the first â-class.

2 Conversely, many particular forms are found repeated in different cases. For instance, o could be found as termination in some one of the declensions for every case except dative or ablative singular. This source of uncertainty is of vital dogmatic importance in the case of the termination â which occurs in the vocative and instrumental singular, and nominative and accusative plural of the first declension, so that it is always uncertain whether Asha is addressed as an independent being, or only as an instrument of the Supreme.

3 The uncertainty of many tenses, as to whether they should be interpreted in the definite *conjunctive* mood, or in the indefinite *injunctive* mood, which may mean either past, present or future.

4 Justi mentions a number of cases where scholars have claimed that case-forms are interchanged.

5 In the later periods, grammatical degeneration set in, resulting in chaos; this may account for some of the hopeless passages.

6 Syntax, at best, is scanty, allowing of different interpretations.

7 As in other languages, so here words have several meanings, so that the same words are interpreted *life* or *people*, and *religion* or *individuality*. This opens the way for great uncertainties and differences of opinion, some of which may never be settled authoritatively.

8 The great number of apparently synonymous words whose distinctive shades of meaning seem to be hopelessly lost for reasons both internal and external. Internally, many of them occur only once, so that we are deprived of internal comparative assistance, while

9 The lack of contemporary writings deprives us of external guides to interpretation.

10 The difficulties of Avestan writing are great in themselves, for the letters are both numerous and difficult to form and to distinguish both in enunciation and representation.

11 The natural vicissitudes incident to the repeated copying of the manuscripts must have led to many errors and changes, which would explain many of the variant readings given by Geldner.

12 The political vicissitudes of the Persian race and the Mazdean religion were so extreme as to lead to the hopeless destruction of all but the fragments we possess, which, themselves, must have been affected by the persecutions.

13 The evident literary manipulation of the Gâthas, whose order is not logical or topical, but mechanical, apparently according to the numbers of the lines of the stanzas, which are 3 in Yasna 28-34; 5 lines in Y 43-46; 4 lines in Y 47-50; 3 lines in Y 51; and 5 lines again in Y 53.

14 There are places and words generally given up as hopelessly insoluble or corrupt. Among such passages are perhaps 46.17;

50.2; 51.12, 17, 18. One'most important line in 46.15 is omitted. Difficult are javar in 48.8; dahyā in 48.10; beedus in 53.4, and yaême in 53.6.

15 The clearly expressed desire of certain scholars to keep the text of the Gâthas, as much as possible, from the public. One scholar who had begun the text in Roman transcription, stopped off short, and purposely continued it in the difficult Avestan characters. Are they trying to monopolize the subject?

16 The personal animosities of the chief scholars have led them to ignore each other. This has hindered the progress of the comparative commentary method to so fatal an extent that the one goes out of his way to announce that his interpretation of 29.6; 30,7,8,10; 34.4 and 44.7 is so certain as to be unquestioned, whereas the other has a differing rendering.

17 The mutual uncharitableness of the scholars which does not stop short of quoting other interpretations, while suppressing the names of their authors, to whom, however, unworthy motives are ascribed.

18 The frank disregard of case-forms by the most prominent translators, even after they have formally announced that they will not even consider the interpretation of any man who does so.

19 Perhaps the chief internal difficulty is the interpretation of the divine names. Should they be considered as personal divinities or as the psychological faculties of the believer? Bartholomæ's statement of the problem (G d A.vii) is useful:

"According as *ameretāt* indicates the divinity or the abstract idea, the word has been rendered *Ameretat* or *immortality*. It is, however, quite impossible to decide with certainty everywhere; for the poet himself did not hold to a firm delimitation between the abstract idea and the divinity. Only on this assumption can we understand that the divinity usually named *Vohu Manah* (i.e., Good Mind) is also occasionally referred to as *Vahishta Manah* (i.e., Best Mind), or even *Thy* (i.e., Mazdah's) Manah (mind). Consequently it is necessary, when such divinities are named, ever to keep in our consciousness, what the name really signifies; and conversely, when these abstract ideas are named, that they present themselves to the bard also as divinities; only thus do we approach his meaning."

But who will or can decide where the bard intended the divinity, and where the concept?

2. Mazdean or External Difficulties of Interpreting the Gathas.

The mere fact that the Gâthas are embedded in the scriptures of the Mazdeans is proof that their orthodox traditions, developed in their later commentaries, have established a theological canon of interpretation, even if the Pahlavi translation, Neryosangh's Sanskrit text, and the later manuscripts, for the first time assembled by Mills, were not to be considered. But of course, these later Mazdean ecclesiastical interpretations are of no soteriological interest to us. On the contrary, they are serious hindrances to us who wish to arrive at the significance of the Gâthas in themselves, before Zarathushtra's personal prayers and praises were erected into doctrines and ritual.

The hindrance to correct interpretation of the Gâthas by these Mazdean ecclesiastical commentaries cannot be fully or sufficiently realized until we recall the Reformation when a century-long war and persecution were necessary to divorce well-meaning humanity from similar ecclesiastical interpretations. Moreover every assured result of modern criticism has been achieved by a fresh re-statement of ancient problems, and studious avoidance of ecclesiastical interpretation. The same general rules must obtain in the Gâthic field; hence we must consider Pahlavi and ecclesiastical interpretations as obstacles rather than guides.

3. Christian Difficulties of Interpreting the Gathas.

Comparative Religion, as well as the History of Christianity, are vitally interested in discovering the real nature of the Persian religion before the days of Cyrus *the Messiah of the Lord* (Isaiah 45.1), of his friendliness to the Jews, and his liberating them for the express purpose of reestablishing their national worship. Enmity between them is incredible; the only question possible is the extent to which the friendship and interaction went. Unfortunately, this question has not been argued dispassionately, because Catholic, Protestant, Jewish and Parsee confessional interests are involved. Each seeks the facts that will aid his cause, and by conducting his enquiry suitably, finds them. Evidently confusion will not cease until the whole subject is removed from partisan associations.

4. MODERN CAUSES OF DIFFICULTIES.

The mental and moral attitude of the reader must ever be considered in the attempt at a correct understanding of a writing. Hence we must not fail to recall and reckon with that shallowness of many unemployed, irresponsible, but socially prominent persons (most frequently females) whose good intentions have led them to forget the 'shorter and uglier word' expressive of statements denying diseases, and that 'mysticism' *may at times be, and frequently is* no more than a cheap and lazy haziness. The publican who, because he is seeking absolute truth, goes through the world with despair gnawing at heart, is no doubt dearer to the God who endowed man with intelligence. But these well-intentioned 'mystics' are in the majority, and, no doubt, will be antagonized by the *apparent* materialism and scepticism of this honest effort to discover the primitive beliefs which alone Zarathushtra could have had so early in the evolution of the race—the only alternative being to deny evolution to something better, and to turn around from the future to the past, looking on it as the mirror of *one's own self*, usually.

III. Guides of Interpretation.

Have we any compass on our adventurous voyage of discovery? Have we any quadrant, any log, any sounding-line, any anchor?

Our guides should be
1, Precautionary measures preventive of self-delusion;
2, History and ethnology as the *frames* within which
3, Comparative Religion may aid us to recognize and marshal
4, Whatever definite facts, however few or faint, we may possess.

1 PRECAUTIONARY GUIDES AGAINST SELF-DECEIT.

We will be considerably helped in our self-analysis by scrutinizing the development of the recognized criticism of other ancient scriptures. To begin with, we must

(a) Throw by the board all those familiar theological notions and later Mazdean legends, readmitting them, if at all, only one by one, and that on due proof. We will therefore begin by rejecting all ideas of archangels (*M 122*), theology (*M 173*), saints (*M 183*), millennium (*M 174*), primeval world (*M 82, 80*), covenant (*B 1109*), book-keeping and weighing (*B, G dA, 122*), and open-laying (*B 309*), among all other Mazdean and Hebrew notions.

(b) Neither must we explicitly draw conclusions which may indeed be inferentially implied in our documents. The history of religions shows that the self-conscious drawing of logical conclusions from generally accepted statements has generally required centuries. This applies especially to Zarathushtra's eschatology which the Mazdeans later reduced to a very logical system, of which he himself may have been entirely unconscious even though he used language which may be interpreted best by those very Mazdean deductions.

(c) We must avoid methods that are *Procrustean*—that is, to cut up the facts to suit some theory of ours, or to find a unity where none was intended. In the recognised criticism of ancient scriptures, as long as every line had to be tortured into absolute agreement with every other, no progress was made; and not until the individuality of the several component parts was acknowledged, was the larger harmony of the whole discovered. Who would want to listen to a harp all the strings of which were tuned to the same pitch? Even in the Gâthas we must expect to find developments of belief by the same person, and interpolations by others; we must be prepared to differentiate later from earlier parts; we must not shrink from studying pre-Zoroastrian religion in order to learn the significance and extent of his innovations.

2 COMPARATIVE RELIGION ILLUSTRATES GATHIC PROBLEMS.

We may confidently appeal to Comparative Religion for the preliminary presumptive solution of one of the special Gâthic difficulties: how far we should translate the divine names into moral conceptions and psychological functions, or whether we should consider that they represent pre-Zoroastrian divinities, no doubt moulded and transformed?

Comparative Religion teaches us to distinguish, in the eternal spiral of religious progress, two contrasting moments: tradition and innovation. But the sane man, who is both aspiring and conservative, attempts to combine these stand-points by reading enlightened morality into traditional divine names or formulas become incomprehensible or misunderstood—an attitude known as *euhemerism*. On the other hand the reformer, either too ignorant to know that absolute truth is unattainable, and that the peculiar charm of what to him seems truth really consists merely in its being *his own opinion;* or that he is so unfortunate as to live at some time of particular stress—in both cases the reformer destroys what he does not understand, and establishes a moral religion in the guise of reform (partial) or innovation (entire). Now where did Zarathushtra stand—was he a Euhemerist, a reformer, or an innovator?

He was no innovator, for he frequently infers the preexistence of some of the cults. Our question, therefore, narrows itself down to which is most likely to have been the original interpretation of the Gâthas, the moral Euhemeristic, or the objective polytheistic? But we may ask, was any Euhemerism ever original?

Surely not, for interpretation presumes the preexistence of its facts. We may therefore conclude that the objective polytheistic interpretation of the Gâthic divine names may have been the more original. This would seem all the more likely in that it would yield a solid basis from which to distinguish the two great efforts of Zarathushtra against polytheism:

1 To superimpose a supreme monotheistic divinity, Mazdâh;

2 To spiritualize away euhemeristically the earlier gods wherever convenient or advisable.

Our problem receives a strong illustration from Greek religion. Euhemerus and the Stoics found moral mysteries in the questionable Homeric stories about the divinities. Fortunately for us, this occurred within comparatively historical times so that we may assert without much fear of contradiction that to Homer himself those childish stories appeared as objective as they no doubt seemed to his childish contemporaries. In the matter of the origin of religious ideas, we should therefore not seek any *original spiritual idea*, but rather some ethnological or historical fact, with which, at times, its spiritual interpretation *may have coexisted*.

3 THE ORIGIN OF GATHIC MONOTHEISM ILLUSTRATED.

Having concluded therefore to the entire propriety of an objective interpretation of the Gâthic pantheon, we must turn to the allied question, whether Zarathushtra created the subordinate divinities and placed them beneath an already existent supreme deity, or invented a supreme deity over an already existent pantheon, by a hierarchical method subsuming the *old* manifold under the *new* unity?

Comparative Religion has, again, an example how such changes *actually occur*. When, on the return from the Babylonish captivity the Hebrew high-priest Joshua established the full ritual law, its searching severities aroused deep and lasting, even if subdued resentment. This led to malicious reflections and criticisms of the scriptures attributed to the Giver thereof. The result was a realizing discovery of its many apparent moral crudities, and the conclusion of the *minim* or Jewish heretics was that the Law was bad, and that the scriptures were inspired by a God morally imperfect. The orthodox Jews answered by closing their eyes to the apparent facts (all that could be done in that uncritical age) and reiterating firmly that the deity of the Scriptures was good. The uncritical *minim* therefore had the choice of losing all faith in the Biblical deity, or all their faith in goodness and morality. What did they do? They elected a third course: they superimposed a *good supreme* deity above the misunderstood *prima-facie* crude Jewish Creator. This solution was very convenient inasmuch as it provided a classification for foreign divinities, which the Jews had, till then, fortunately or unfortunately, been able to ignore, but which the Romans now forced upon their consideration. Indeed, this solution would have carried the day but that Christianity arrived, and with sublime instinct refused to bate one jot of its faith in the divine, while introducing the intellectual discipline which solved whatever real problems there were, by relegating the responsibility for any apparent crudities to where they properly belonged — the imperfections of the divine Spirit's instruments.

This historical development shows us that if Zarathushtra attempted to cure the polytheism of his day by the superimposition of a Supreme, he did nothing unnatural, unexampled, incredible. How could it have happened that his followers were known as *Ashavans* (and not *Mazdeans*, as from the Supreme whom he proclaimed !) unless they had previously been known and recognised as partisans and worshippers of *Asha?* Zarathushtra's insistence that Mazdâh is the *father* of Asha (47.2) now appears in its true light as a *politic introduction of the supremacy of Mazdah to Ashaists.* Later than the Gâthas these thus subordinated divinities were regularly organized into a coherent group of seven *Bountiful Immortals* or *Ameshaspends,* which term may not unfittingly be rendered *archangels.* But it occurred only in the later times of the Haptanghāiti, Yasnas 35-42, and this idea should not be reflected back into the Gâthas, forming an anachronism.

4 Ethnology Fixes thl Period of Certain Gathic Ideas.

Let us take a glance at the Egyptian pyramids. It is not so very long since the Egyptian pyramids were looked at with awe as unexplained miracles testifying to some mystic knowledge and power of prehistoric races. When, later, pyramids were discovered in Yucatan, it was supposed that they were built by immigrants from Egypt. But gradually it was discovered that there were pyramids everywhere, and that many of the so-called pyramids were no more than the Stone Age's facing of hills, and hence seem to have been no more than mounds more permanent than those of the mound-builders; and the discovery in Egypt of remains of the earlier periods of the Stone Age support this.

Just like the pyramids of Egypt, the Gâthas can never receive their true interpretation until they are withdrawn from their splendid isolation, and are compared with the facts and customs of the period in which they originated. Zarathushtra's great solicitude for the Cow will not be interpreted as humanitarianism so much as the establishment of a settled pastoral community. The uncertain word maga which Bartholomæ (1109) renders as a *covenant* or *secret religious society*, will only remind us that Diogenes Laertes and Herodotus supposed the word *Magi* was the name of his tribe, which its gifted son turned into the appellation of priests and wonder-workers, enshrined in our modern words *magic* and *magician*. But whence did the tribe get its name? Perhaps from maga, *a hole*, if Zarathushtra, according to Y 50, led his fellow-tribesmen out of some dark ravine or cleft into open agricultural lands. This would further agree with the interpretation of Zarathushtra's social significance as that of the world-wide change from nomadic to agricultural or pastoral society; and in those early days (as it should also be more realized in our own days) social and religious problems were inseparable—the demagogue was *ipso facto* a prophet; social economy was discussed in religious terms. Social need furnished the steam, while the religious zeal acted as the guiding lever of progressive civilization.

IV. The Facts Themselves.

Thus having constructed a comparatively modern frame-work, let us now put therein what actual facts we do know of Zarathushtra's life, and notice if they do not fit those surroundings.

BARTHOLOMÆ (GdA 124) well speaks of the narrow conditions under which the Gâthas arose. We hear of a few enemies, Gerĕhma and Bĕñdva; of one supporter, Dĕjâmâspa Hvôgva. Zarathushtra thunders excommunications because (?) on a cold winter's night he, his companion and beast have not been hospitably sheltered, 51.12. Slaughtering of cattle seems to be the chief sin, 32.8,14. The prophet cries to the Divinity and appeals to Destiny about no more than the possession of some house in the neighborhood (?) 50.3. Against enemies, violence and even murder are meritorious, 53.8. A pair of cows in heaven is the promise made to believers, 33.3; 44.6; 50.2; 51.5; and for himself Zarathushtra urges the Divinity for ten mares with stallions, and a camel, 44.18. Thus does BARTHOLOMÆ conclude:

'The reformation which attaches to the name of Zarathushtra is not exclusively religious, but also agricultural, attempting to accustom the nomadic tribes of Eastern Iran to permanency of settlement, and consequent rational agriculture and cattle-raising. The local tradition derives Zarathushtra from Western Iran, and the local agricultural conditions support this. Western Iran stood then doubtless in a higher cultural position than the East. This would explain why Zarathushtra attempted to spread the blessings of orderly conditions which he had experienced in the West, to the East, the scene of his activities; and it is quite comprehensible that Vishtâspa, as an enlightened ruler, favored the Prophet primarily for his agricultural aims, and supported him therefor.'

U. Conclusion.

We might characterize Zarathushtra as combining the sociological and political activities of a Joshua with the theogony and agricultural teachings of a Hesiod. The books of Joshua and Judges represent very tellingly the Gâthic struggles with the demon-opponents and all their deeds of blood; while Hesiod's teaching of a supreme God, the dualism of the original *Eris* (love celestial and physical), the *Fire*, the *Guardian Spirits* (OeD 121-126), *agriculture,* and *morality* are strikingly duplicated in the message of Zarathushtra. Of course, Hesiod lived a century later, and represents sociologically a subsequent stage of development, that from pastoral to agricultural civilization; for though Zarathushtra may have taught this step, according to our interpretation of Yasna 50, there is no doubt that he *primarily* represents that earlier sociological step—the dawn of pastoral life among the nomads of Western Iran.

It should not be thought that this sociological interpretation or valuation of Zarathushtra's *religion* diminishes or degrades it. On the contrary, it exalts it. First, that religion is drawn down from the nebulous region of speculation into the clear, sane light of historical actuality. Secondly, Zarathushtra shines all the brighter by contrast with the greater obscurity. It only adds to his glory that he was willing and able successfully to implant his monotheism, his personal devotion, his passion for righteousness and his humanitarianism among those blood-stained nomads.

In conclusion, let us gather from him all the good we may without repeating that immortal error of *deifying his errors also.*

CHAPTER II

CRITICISM of the GATHIC PANTHEON.

1. Methods of the Criticism.

Why any criticism at all? Criticism is certainly out of place where all is consistent; but a chaos demands from intelligent beings, endowed with the desires of knowledge and progress of truth, a stand, an attitude, an explanation of some sort.

Nor does criticism usually come from enemies. Much knowledge and more interest are needed to induce human beings to spend their time in a profitless venture. It is a sign of interest and should be welcomed as such, apart from the enlightenment it may yield.

The subject-index shows that we have in the Gathic field full justification for critical consideration. We have a bewildering array of divinities, and these divinities seem to conflict in their claims, functions, and nature. In one place some appear as supreme, or first-rank divinities, in others only as agents. Again, the real (not the legendary) biography of Zarathushtra will remain unknown unless we succeed in puzzling it out from these hymns; and so compelling is this problem that Mills has already attempted to change the order of some of the hymns in order to secure a more consistent sequence.

Having therefore good grounds to apply critical methods to the Gathas, we may begin to do so by the preliminary stage of searching analysis; by recording

(1) Duplicates;

(2) Distinctions between the various members of such duplications, and other parties in general;

(3) These will lead us to examine what groups of thought, or associations exist between these various members; which, when contrasted will lead to some provisionary

(4) Reconstruction on a coherent scheme.

Duplications, in the Gathas, appear to be of two kinds, the general and the detailed.

2. General Duplication*.

The general duplications here pointed out appear in the tentative parallel arrangement of the two coherent Gathic groups Ahunavaiti, Yasnas 28-34; and Yasnas 43-51, 53 as duplicate biographies of Zarathusthra, whose details are worked out in the *Harmony of the Gathas* prefixed to the *Life of Zarathushtra*. The general reasons for this parallel arrangement, are as follows:

1. The two Hymns on Dualism, 30 and 45. Each begins with a declaration of intention to speak, and an exhortation to the hearer to hear, mark, learn, and inwardly digest; followed by the definite announcement of dualism, 30.3, 4; 45.2.

2. The coherence of the two groups, 28-34, and 43-51,53, divided by the differing *Haptanghaiti*, 35-42. The first group has 3 lines to a stanza; the latter has varying stanzas.

3. The explicit or formal salutatory beginning of 43, and the affecting ending of 34, praying that all mankind become progressive.

4. The duplicate choice of the cattle and appointment as Judge.

5. The duplicate mention of the names of the Zarathushtrian heroes, (Vishtaspa; and the other ones.)

6. Question about the origin of the heavens, 31.7; 44.3.

Guided by these definite duplications, the minor parallelisms fall into fair order, as the reader may judge by comparing the left-hand with the right-hand pages of the *Life of Zarathushtra*.

3. Detailed Duplications.

1. The contrast between Vohu Manah and Aka Manah, and Spenta Mainyu and Angro Mainyu. We may add to this Asha and the Druj. We have here three cults, the Asha-Druj or Moral cult; the Manah or Mental cult; the Mainyu or Spirit cult.

2. The path of Asha, 33.5, 6; 51.13; the path of Vohu Manah, 34.12; 51.16; the path of the cow, of free will, 31.9; the path of profit, 43.3; the path of good teaching, 46.4; the path of the daenas of the Saoshyant, 53.2, with the way of Vohu Manah and the daenas, 34.13; and the Milky Way, 44.3.

3. *Asha* and *Ashay* are evident duplications; and, indeed, we find *Ashay* almost exclusively connected with Vohu Manah.

4. There is the manifold designations of the abode beyond:

a. The house of the Clever.
b. The house of the Best or Worst Mind.

    c. The house of the Druj.

    d. In harm, in harmlessness, 46.17.

    e. Garodman.

All these may be synonyms, but certainly originated in different surroundings.

    5. There are many words for *knowledge* or *word,* each belonging to a different complex or group of ideas and thought.

    6. There is *Armaiti* and *Tushnamaiti.* The first is certainly grouped with *Asha,* the latter occurs 43.15, contrasted with Ashaists.

    7. We also have the duplication or contradiction of the Spirit wearing the heavens and their lights as a robe, 30.5; and *Zarathushtra's* question about it as if unknown to him, 31.7.

    8. *Ada* is a duplication of *Adana;* and so we find the latter in the Vohu Manist, 30.7; the former in the Spenta Mainyuist, 33.12; 33.11 and 48.1 are not definite.

    9. We have another duplication, *patha,* f, in the first document, 31.9; and *pathman,* n, in the second, 46.4.

    10. We have the duplications of *tare-maiti,* 33.4; and *pairi-maiti,* 32.3; the former opposed to Armaiti, the latter possibly to Tushna-maiti, as we shall see later.

4. Distinctions.

    1. Kavay Vishtaspa only *attains* to the Magian leadership, 46.14; 51.16; hence he did not possess it originally.

    2. The Daevas rushed over together to Aeshma, 30.6. Hence they were not with him originally, presumably belonging to another party.

    3. The Kavay *assist* the Druj, 32.14; hence they are distinct from them.

26. They 'who utter just words' had communion with Drujists, hence they need a warning not to do so, 49.9.

27. Jamaspa is invited to join with the Ashaists, 49.10. Hence he did not belong to them before.

28. The daena of the Druj (who has gone over to him) therefore destroys the 'just-straight' (path), 51.13; which must, therefore, differ from the Druj.

29. Zarathushtra is not yet a recipient of Asha in 51.17.

30. Zarathushtra mentions, 33.2, as meritorious, actions, either the killing of a Druj, or the instruction of a comrade. This implies that not all comrades were believers.

31. Zarathushtra opposes Daevas, Druj, and *Pairi-maiti* (the Proud), 32.3. Who were these latter? Were they the unbelieving Clever?

32. *Tare-maiti* (33.4, see 45.11) is to be removed from the nobility by magic practice. The word contrasts naturally with *Ar-maiti;* just as *Vohu Manah* contrasts with *Aka Manah;* and *Spenta Mainyu,* with *Angro Mainyu.*

33. The juxtaposition of Daevas and Men (or, Mortals, Doomed-to-Die.), shows that the designation *Men* was the appellation of a particular class, 29.4; 48.1. In 34.5, the division seems to be three-fold, Savages, Daevas, and Men (Doomed). Again, 45.11, the division is Daevas, Scorners, and the Lukewarm, as opposed to the faithful followers. So preponderating seems the influence of the Daevas, 32.4, that the term seems to apply to all renegades from Vohu Manah, Ahura Mazdah, or Asha.

34. Some know Vohu Manah, but turn difficulties of doctrines to their own advantage, 34.7. This implies a Vohumanist cult that is recognized publicly.

4. Friendly to the Magians are the Karapans, 51.14; and the Turas, 46.12. Hence they are not identical with them.

5. Aeshma is mentioned along with the Druj, 29.2; hence is not understood to be one of them.

6. *Grehma* is friendly enough with the Clever to be able to pervert them to becoming Drujists; but he is in open warfare with the Ashaists whom he slaughters, 32.10. Hence the Clever and the Ashaists differ from each other, for some of the Clever were in union (*sar*) with the Drujists, 49.9.

7. The clever are *worthy of* Vohu Manah's closer acquaintance; hence they are not already his followers.

8. Zarathushtra, promises to be a support for the Ashaists, 43.8. Hence he did not originate among them.

9. Bartholomae, 645, had already noted that *tash* (creating) is a word which occurs only in connection with *gav,* the kine.

10. Zarathushtra consults Vohu-Manah how he should adore Ahura Mazdah, 45.6. Hence Zarathushtra was not, originally, a worshipper of *Ahura Mazdah.*

11. Tushnamaiti, 43.15, is contrasted with both Ashaists and Drujists, and represents a party conciliatory of Drujists.

12. The Cattle was created for the herdsman and for the farmer, 29.6. Hence the two latter are not identical.

13. Zarathushtra was the only one who had heard the teachings of Asha *and* Vohu Manah before his appointment as Judge, 29.8. Hence, the teachings of Asha and Vohu Manah are not identical.

14. *Such as You,* 29.11, shows a multiplicity of cults, or of divine beings.

15. The free choice of the Cattle, 31.9, indicates a further change from pastoral to agricultural life.

16. Stanza 7 of 51 seems to distinguish
    (*a*) Cattle, Water and Plants;
    (*b*) Spenta Mainyu, Health and Immortality; and
    (*c*) Vohu Manah, *sengha*-teachings; *tevishi,* firmness, and *utayuiti,* endurance.

17. Asha is distinct from the Shaper of the Cattle, 29.2; for he converses with him.

18. The *daenas* are to be taught about Asha, 33.13; hence they are not yet acquainted with Asha.

19. How will *Armaiti* extend over those to whom the *daena* was announced? 44.11. Evidently *Armaiti* did not yet extend over them.

20. This was the purpose of Zarathushtra's *first* call, 44.11. Does this infer he had a later one too?

21. Vishtaspa, the Spitamians and Frashaoshtra (all Spenta Mainyians) are to Convert the *daenas* of Vohu Manah, 53.2. Hence they were not of the same cult with Vohu Manah.

22. The *daenas* are invited by instruction about Compensations, 33.13; 48.4; 49.5. Hence the *daenas* were not yet familiar with these compensations.

23. Zarathushtra's adherents were among the various cults, 45.11.

24. The Karapans and Kavays, though politically powerful, do not seem to be aware that their own souls and spirits will meet them at the Judgment-bridge (a Dathaist doctrine); hence, they are 'fools,' 46.11. Evidently they did not belong to the 'Clever' or Dathaist party.

25. 'May yet establish the Daevic gods through the *daenas* (converted to) of the Drujists,' 49.5. This seems to refer to some definite event which Zarathushtra anticipated.

5. Asha *and* Vohu Manah Contrasted.

Similarities of Asha and Vohu Manah.

1. A and VM are joined together, 8 times.
    49.7, 12; 50.1, 4, 7; 51.3, 15, 16.
2. Both are created by their father AM, A 4, VM 2.
    A 31.7, 8; 44.3; 47.2.
    VM 31.8; 44.4.
3. They are joined with AM, A 23, VM 10.
A 28.9; 30.9, 10; 31.21; 32.6, 9; 33.14; 34.3, 5, 6; 46.18; 48.9, 12;
    49.6, 7; 50.1, 4, 5, 8, 9, 10; 51.3.
    VM 28.2, 6, 9; 30.10; 31.21; 32.4; 34.5, 6; 49.7; 50.1.
4. They abide with AM in heaven, A 4, VM 8.
    A 30.7; 33.3, 5, 6.
    VM 30.7; 31.7; 32.15; 33.3; 43.6; 44.9; 46.14, 16.
5. They are like-willed with AM, A 5, VM 2.
    A 28.8; 29.7; 51.20; 49.6; 51.20.   VM 32.2; 51.20.
6. They are sung, prayed, sacrificed to, served and wor-
    shipped, A 17, VM 7.
A 28.1, 3, 9; 31.4; 33.8; 34.3; 49.12; 51.22; 50.4, 7, 8, 9, 10, 11;
    51.2; 51.10, 22.   VM 28.1, 9; 30.1; 33.8; 28.2, 3; 49.12.
7. They are to be part of the beatific vision, A 5, VM 1.
    A 28.5; 30.1; 32.13; 43.10; 48.9.   VM 28.5.
8. They make covenants, have allies, demand loyalty
    and support, A 27, VM 4.
A The 23 references to Ashavans, given above; 31.22; 33.9; 49.2, 9.
    VM 32.11; 49.3, 5; 51.11.
9. They are the counsellor of AM and of the faithful,
    A 5, VM 3.
A 31.3; 34.12; 46.9, 17; 51.11.   VM 44.13; 45.6; 47.3.
10. They teach, have words of life, A 7, VM 7.
A 34.15; 44.8; 46.2; 43.12; 48.13; 50.5; hints leading to Para-
    dise B 51.3.   VM 34.15; 44.8; 46.14; 46.9; 47.2; 48.3; 51.3.
11. They have straight paths, A 5, VM 3.
    A 33.5, 6; 34.13; 51.13, 16.   VM 34.12, 13; 51.16.
12. They make men worthy, A 2, VM 2.
    A 28.10, 11.   VM 28.10, 11.

13. They are to be realized in good action, A 6, VM 2.
> A 46.15; 48.7, 12; 51.1, 21; 53.5.
> VM 50.9; 53.5; to strive for the life of VM.

14. Are a prize to be attained and treasured, A 8, VM 5.
> A 28.4; 34.1; 43.1; 44.13; 46.3, 12; 51.4, 17.
> VM 32.9; 33.13; 43.1; 46.2; 53.4.

15. They protect the poor, A 1, VM 1.
> A 34.5.   VM ib

16. They grant and promote power, A 13, VM 5.
A   power, 29.10; 33.12; 31.16, body, 33.10; wealth, 33.11; con-
> gregation, 34.13, 43.14; 44.1; welfare, 44.10, 15; 47.6; plants,
> 48.6; cattle, 51.5.
VM   rule, 29.10; body, 33.10; wealth, 33.11; house and farm,
> 46.13; strength and subsistence, 51.7.

17. They grant awards, realms, happiness, A 16, VM 18.
A   28.2, 6, 7; 43.2; 44.18; H and Am, 45.10; 49.9, 12; 50.3; 48.7;
> 51.1, 2, 8, 15, 22; 53.1.
VM   30.8; 31.4, 6; 33.12; 34.7, 14; 43.2, 16; 44.6; H and Am,
> 45.10; 46.7, 10, 12, 18; 49.12; 51.2, 15, 21.

18. They watch over men, A 1, VM 1.
> A 44.2.   VM 28.4.

19. They are the responsible agents to appoint a judge,
> A 4, VM 6.
> A 29.2, 3; 49.9; 44.6.   VM 29.7; 43.7, 9, 11, 13, 15.

20. They are intimate friends, A 2, VM 1.
> A 49.8, 5.   VM 45.9.

21. They punish the wicked, A 4, VM 1.
> A 30.8; 31.1; 44.14; 51.13.   VM 49.1.

22. They are means, agents, mediators, A 25, VM 13.
> See above.
VM   32.6; 33.12; 34.3, 14; 46.9, 10, 18; 48.3; 50.6, 11; 51.27,
> 15, 21.

23. They take part in the judgment, A 5, VM 3.
> A 31.5; 32.6; 29.2, 3(?); 46.9(?).   .
> VM 33.12; 43.16; 44.6.

The reader is reminded much of this is illusory, and
no more than suggestion, depending on the translations.

2. DIFFERENCES BETWEEN Asha *and* Vohu Manah.

1. Rule, VM; A, power. A is the more active one. 29.10.
2. Through A, AM gives glories; 53.1 through VM, the realm. Both active. 51.21.
3. VM promotes realm of A 46.7. Asha and VM active.
4. Through VM, Z hears what AM and A consulted, 46.9. Both.
5. VM admits to realm those among whom A appears. 46.12. Both.
6. VM's glories given by A. 28 7. A active.
7. A dependents are loyal to VM. 32.11. A active.
8. Those who lack VM refuse Arm, and are avoided by A. 34.9. A.
9. VM's realm promoted by Arm and A. 34.11. A active.
10. AM grants VM's blessings through A. 43.2. A active.
11. VM takes men to A to be instructed. 43.12. A active.
12. Through A, men get acquainted with VM. 45.9. A active.
13. AM teaches through A what the possession of VM is. 46.2. A active.
14. A counsels with VM, and creates cattle. 47 3. A active.
15. Through A, the faithful wish to assure themselves of reward of VM. 48.7. A active.
16. Attachment of VM occurs through intimacy with A. 49.5. A active.
17. What AM has promised through VM he gives through A. 50.3. A active.

3. PECULIARITITES OF VM.

1. Helps to distinguish, understand. 31 5.
2. AM promotes VM, 31.10, and through VM what is consistent with his will. 50.11.
3. VM brings the spirit, 33.9, and praises it in words. 47.2.
4. AM promises rewards through VM. 50.3, 48.7.
5. Those who possess VM believe in the realm. 51.18.

4. PECULIARITIES OF A.

1. Destroys druj. 30.8; reciprocally 31.1, 44.14, 51.13.
2. Is fire 34.4, 43.4, 9 (46.7; 47.6; 51.13?)
3. Is connected with Armaiti 7 times, with VM 3 times.

34.9, 10, 11; 46.16; 48.11; 49.5; 51.2.
34.9, 10, 11.

4. Is a friend.
    32.2; 50.6(?); 43.14; 44.1; 45.6; 46.13; 49.5, 8; 50.6.
5. Is the means of knowing, is inter-relation between God'
    and man. 31.13 45.8 44.2 45.9.
6. Is the main principle.
    29.8; 31.6, 19; 33.13; 34.2, 7, 8; 49.3; 51.18.
7. Give bliss and good lot. 51.8; 51.10.
8. Is judge. 29.2. 3; 46.9; 31.5; 32.6.

Summary.

Summarizing the above data, it will be seen that Asha
and Vohumano are, on the whole, identical; but Vohumano is the weaker, less exteriorly active, and less individual of the two.

Of the common characteristics, Vohumano is more
frequently mentioned in three (Nos. 4, 17 and 19, the
latter being repetitions); the same in four (Nos. 10, 12,
15, 18, all minor ones); and by far less in the remaining
15 characteristics. Adding all the cases together, Asha
is mentioned 192 times and Vohumano only 110, or 57
per cent.

Of the characteristics in which Asha and Vohumano
are contrasted, Asha seems in 12 cases to be the more
active (Nos. 6-17); in Nos. 1 and 2 the distinction is not
very striking, while in Nos. 3, 4 and 5 the activity seems
equal. Apparently, then, Vohumano seems interior and
operative, while Asha is exteriorly active.

Of the 5 characteristics peculiar to Vohumano, none
is peculiarly striking—with only 8 references; of the 8
peculiarities of Asha, there are 41 references, an average
of 6. And these peculiarities are strong; partnership
with Armaiti, being the divine fore, being the divine
friend, and the main principle or doctrine.

It might then seem as if Vohumano were merely a
later replica of Asha, the name *Asha-dependents* given to
the faithful sufficiently suggesting and confirming this
conclusion.

CHAPTER III.

GROUPING *of the* ASSOCIATIONS.

We have now analyzed the Gathas and found a number of striking parallelisms and distinctions. We must now sort these out into groups or associations which shall, if possible, be internally coherent. We may do this under the following heads:

1. The Daevas.
2. The Armaitians.
3. The Ashaists.
4. The Vohu Manians.
5. The Spenta Mainyuists.
6. The 'Clever,' or Dathaists.
7. The Magians.

1. *The* Daevic Cult.

The Daevas were a political race, possibly descended from, or of the same race as the Vohu Manists, 32.3. Zarathushtra's attitude towards them seems to have changed from friendly to hostile, and, at the same time, he refers to them in such terms of general commonsense as were probably in common use at that day.

The Daevas became bad because they chose wrong; while choosing, they were deluded, 30.6. Again, in 32.1, it would seem that the Daevas attended Zarathushtra's reception, and were, without blame, included in the enumeration of the persons present; and possibly, among his converts.

b. Hostile.

Their deeds are long since known to the seventh (region of) the earth, 32.3. Hence they predominate so much that all other heretics are confused with them, 32.4. Their Kings had not ruled well, 44.20. Their prophet (Grehma) destroyed the second life, 32.5, through his utterances; Grehma, therefore, seems to have held doctrines at variance with Zarathushtra's eschatology.

It has long since been announced what may be awaited by daevas and men, 48.1. Whoever hates them is the friend of Zarathushtra, 45.11. Their evil destiny is 'the house of the Daevas,' 49.4. Were they the *proud* of 32.3?

c. Matters *of* Common Speech.

Mazdah is mindful of the plans executed formerly by Daevas and Men, 29.4. Zarathushtra separates himself from all Savages, Daevas, and Men, 34.5.

They are called refuse of intoxication, *mada,* 11.10; possibly with *haoma,* Y9.17, 11.10; or something fermented (?) which Kings or princes might indulge in, 48.10. Excrement, *muthra,* 11.89, suggests fermentation of decayed matter. They are strong, 34.8, and cruel, 29.3.

The Karapans had agriculture, but were unskilful or misinformed and hence unsuccessful, 51.14.

Grehma has a special name of opprobrium given him, *tkaesa,* 49.2.

They tried to please people, to seem generous, to *satisfy* (xsnav); as in the case of Yima distributing flesh, 32.8 (as gift?); which might seem necessary in case of leaders and politicians.

By irony of fate, it is from among these very Daevas (Kavays, one of whom had rejected Zarathushtra inhospitably, 51.12) that Kavay Vishtaspa, 28.7; 41.16; 51.16; 53.2 (meaning *possessing scary-horses?*) arose; who attained, 51.16, a position at the head of the Magian tribe, or cause; it seems implied that he added to this

(1) The Vohumanian followers (*padebis?*).

(2) The Ashaist followers (*manta cistim asha*).

d. Daevic Religion.

Of their religion little can be made out, except (*a*) that they opposed the eschatological message of Zarathushtra, 32.10 (see 46.11). This might explain Zarathushtra's violent opposition to them; together with his evident relations with them (Vishtaspa, and 51.12), which is quite possible as they were friendly in disposition, 32.8. (*b*) The demon Aeshma, 29.2; 30.6; 48.12; evidently represents the fury of the meat-eaters, 29.1; 48.7; 44.20; 49.4; such as Yima was. The Daevas therefore appeared to the Armaitians as 'furious,' merely because they were destructive of the fertile cow.

There seems to be also some purely daevic words, such as *hunav,* son, 51.10; *ham-dvar,* 30.6, to rush together, the verb *dvar* being chiefly used of Daevas (B). May it not refer to the use of horses among them (Jam-aspa, Haecat-aspa, Visht-aspa)?

2. *The* Armaitian Cow-Cult.

This Armaiti cow-cult may have represented the beginning (in Iran at least) of pastoral civilization. To Zarathushtra we must not attribute its origination, but only its championship. The 'path of free will,' 31.9, 10, offered to the cow does not contain even a hint of any help from Zarathushtra or any other leader; and rightly enough, for such developments of civilization operate blindly; and the famous names associated with them frequently were only their drift-wood; which, indeed, shows clearly enough which way the current is moving. Zarathushtra, according to 29.8, 9, only joined the movement, and championed it.

It is to this cult that we must attribute

(1) The 'Shaper of the Bull,' who is the Spirit of wisdom, who creates kine, waters, and plants, 31.9; 51.7; 29.2.

(2) The Soul of the Kine, *geus-urvan*, who appears as its advocate, 29.

(3) The personified, dramatized cow, 29.

(4) The actual cow.

(5) The paridisiacal cow (see references).

The chief adjectives of the cow are fortune-bringing, 44.6; 47.3; 50.2; and *pregnant* or *calving*, 29.5; 34.14; 46.19. Fertility is the chief idea; so we find Armaiti feminine, the mother-goddess, so to speak, whose devotion and humility bears a striking resemblance to the gentleness characteristic of cows. Her logical opponent was *Tare-matay* the Proud-mind, 33.4; 45.11. Hence we have as opponents of her followers the Proud, of 32.3, the Pairi-matayists. It will be noticed that (33.4) Zarathushtra would exorcise this *high-mindedness* from the gentlemen-by-birth, the nobility, *xvaetav*. These were, no doubt, then as now, opposed or separate from the *verezena*, or group of laborers.

Such a group of laborers, by their very *armatay* (gentleness) needed a leader. Had they been prouder, they might have asked for a king; but these simpleminded herdsmen asked for no more than a Judge, *ratav*.

So we find the kine demanding one, 29.2; insisting upon her inability to manage without one, 29.1; from divinities that seemed none too willing, 29.6. Indeed, her ideal of one seems to have been so high that she breaks out into tears at the appointment of a mere man such as Zarathushtra, 29.9.

As to the word *ratav* itself, the references, 29.2, 6; 33.1 seem connected with the kine, and with the judging of the two parties, and of the *mixed* (were these the Armaitians?). The 'two parties' are certainly Ashaist and Drujist, 31.2; 51.5; while in 44.16, the Judge is mentioned and distinguished from Vohu Manah and Sraosha.

Reverence of son for father betokens the same gentleness and dependence as of the cow, 29.10; 44.7.

Probably the difficulty of attaining peace made the Armaitians long for it, 47.3, 48.11; as associated with the growing of good pasture; which may explain, 33.3, the 'pastures of Asha and Vohu Manah' in heaven.

It would be quite logical if among the partisans of the pregnant, fertile cow arose the idea of Saviors, *saoshyant,* strictly, *profiters* (from *sav*), and Helpers, who were *'profiters,'* literally.

Understanding (xratav, 535) is a word predominantly Ashaist, 42 per cent., as against 25 per cent. Vohu Manist, and 32 per cent. uncertain; may be connected with the Creator of the Kine, the Spirit of Understanding; it was inevitable that a people who had chosen the pastoral life would have attributed some such compliment as *understanding* to the representant of that avocation.

We have in this cult also the peculiar word for wisdom *cyana,* 44.7, 29.6; in both cases connected with the Shaper, and Kine; and the word *tash* to create (discussed elsewhere).

3. *The* Ashaist Cult.

The Ashaist is the most picturesque of the Gathic cults, because of its vivid contrast between Ashaist and Drujist, so familiar both in itself, and in its religious consequences of dualism. We owe to it both the drama, 29, and the vaticination, 30; each of which represents one of its component elements. Both of these we shall have to study. The *denouement* of the drama pictures the political consolidation of Armaitians and Ashaists, while those Ashaists who did not accept Zarathushtra's leadership were driven into opposition, acquiring the undesirable appellation of *Drujists;* indeed, that vaticination (Y. 30) may have been uttered in order to make the split complete, and drive the Drujists out from among Zarathushtra's loyal adherents, 44.13; as they may have occupied neighboring houses, 50.3.

Zarathushtra's uncompromising attitude on partisanship we have seen elsewhere; but there is a danger of misunderstanding it, by looking at him from our own day when law-courts and police make partisanship almost unnecessary. It was otherwise with a beginning pastoral civilization which had to enforce the idea of settlements and limits on nomads by personal valor.

Nevertheless, Zarathushtra's violent end seems but a fitting reward for his frantic appeals to force: he that draweth the sword shall perish by it.

(1) The reason for this arising of dualistic animosity is simple enough when we consider the bitter feuds among farmers even at our late day. The pastoral settlers had the cow to fight about; hence a strict division between friends, and enemies.

(2) Hence also the need for champions or Saviors, among whom Zarathusthra appears as the first, to lead

the war against the Daevas or meat-eaters and slaughter-
ers; and this war was bitter enough to discourage even
Zarathushtra, 46.1, 50.1.

Marriage between divinities is not an unexampled
symbol of the union of two races; so when we read that
Armaiti was the *hitha* or Companion of Asha, we may
suppose (34.10) that this represents the formation of
this political bond (48.7) to which every bounteous man
will belong. No doubt the Cow's desire for a Judge represented her failure to assert herself against the flesh-
eating Druj, 29.1; and the expedient was to unite with
the Ashaists, under the judge-ship of Zarathushtra.
From now Tare-Matay retreats into the background,
until later (Yasna, 60.5) once more restored to his former prominence.

Is it possible that we have another indication of the
union of these two parties, the Armaitians and Ashaists?
We have, in 47.6 and 31.3, the peculiar association of the
Spirit (*spenta*) and fire at the distribution of the *good*,
47.6; and *satisfaction*, 31.3; (therefore not harm and
loss), to both *ranas* or parties. Does the *Spirit* here represent the 'Shaper of the Kine,' who was the 'spirit of
wisdom'? This application would seem very apt indeed.

The other occurrences of parties are, 51.9: the Ashaist
and Drujist. 31.19: the *ahumbis*, life-healing friend (?)
by red fire gives *good* to both parties.

The parties are called *asa* (dual), referring to Ashaist
and Drujist, and the Judge, 31.2.

As the prophet was called to come to Asha, he was
told to arise before Ashay and Sraosha arose to judgment, 43.12.

Did Asha, in these references, have especial connection
with the fire of the eschatological metal, 30.7; 51.9; 32.7?
(All which are Ashaist references.) The connection between Asha and fire, 43.4; 34.4; 31.3? is definite, so
that this is not impossible; and we have seen that the

eschatological metal might not impossibly be connected with the *Sword* of armed partisanship: and here we have 'asa' as their name. May we take this complex of ideas as the origin of the Ashaist cult?

But how did the fiery partisan Asha come to mean *right,* or *justice?* The root *sa,* which appears in profit (*sav, savah, saoshyant*) reappears in *sangha* or teaching (of the Saviors?); which is a distinctly Ashaist word, 32.6; 34.7; 43.6; 44.14; 46.3, 17; 45.2; and among Vohu Manists only once, 49.9, and then qualified by *guzra,* 'mysterious.'

This teaching seems promoted by Saviors rather than Teachers; the verb *kaeth* (428), the only other one meaning to teach not already appropriated by Vohu Manists is doubtful (Ashaist, 33.2, 47.5, 46.9; Vohu Manist, 44.6, 10; 46.18; 50.3; (?) 51.15); also *sah* (1574) (Vohu Manist, 34.12; 45.6; 50.6; Ashaist, 43.3; 48.3).

It must therefore have occurred, then as now, that one's own side appeared to be the *right* side and the opposite the *wrong;* to the right *truth,* is opposed the wrong *lie,* or *Druj.*

The Drujist, with his hell of the 'House of the Druj,' as opposed to the Ashaist, is well-known; but it would seem that another name of theirs was the *Doomed* (who had no second life), *martiya* or *mashya.* An identification seems to be made, in 48.1. When Asha overcomes the Druj, then the long prophecy of what is to happen to the Daevas and the Doomed will be realized. They are paired with the Daevas (as the Drujists would be), 45.11; 34.5. In 48.1 they are called *daeva darlings;* robbed of second life, 32.5; 46.11 (see 30.11; 32.8; 43.1; 48.5).

We must look among them for bitter animosity against the Druj—the 'harm or convert' spirit of 33.2, illustrates this abundantly; for the fiery partisan (*asayae, ashahya*)

Asha could see no middle ground. The partner of the divine Cow, *Armaiti,* would be the divine Bull, *Asha,* whose pastures we hear of in heaven, 33.3, 50.2? The Bull is connected with the Dawn, *ushas,* 46.3; and the good days, 50.10. Once more we have a connection between Armaitians and Ashaists when the Daeva states that the two worst things to see are the Cow and the Sun, 32.10; for the days imply light or fire, 43.4; 44.4; and the priest of Asha, 50.11; 33.6; will think of Asha as he brings an offering to the flames, 43.9.

No doubt we have here the germs of fire-worship, and without question this ever remained Zarathushtra's main interest.

4. *The* Vohu-Manist Cult.

Vohu Manah is practically identical with Asha in most respects; but if any difference is observed (see elsewhere) he is less individual; he lacks the *fire* of Asha. His name must have meant *'good nature.'*

This same characteristic is marked in Vohu Manah's followers. They are friendly to the Druj, 32.3, 5; 43.15; 49.9; and this is all the more marked as Zarathushtra finds fault with the *just-speaking man* (having the right saying, B.) for friendliness to the Drujist. This appears to Zarathushtra from his self-centred stand-point, as *hypocrisy,* 34.7.

'Are they faithful to thee, O Ahura Mazdah, who, *though they know of Vohu Manah,* turn the difficulties of doctrines to their own advantage by sophistries? As for me, I know none but *You, O Asha.'* This friendliness seems to have been returned, 47.5.

They were the literary men, and their submission to the Magian cause under Vishtaspa is described by the *padebis* (51.16) of Vohu Manah. More striking even than this, the word *daxsh,* to teach, 43.15, 33.13; and *fradaxshta,* teacher, (31.17, 51.3; occur nowhere except in immediately Vohu Manist passages (see the words). The rarer words *xsha,* 46.2, to teach, and *dah,* 43.11, to teach, also appear in Vohu Manist passages.

This *xsha* root, connected evidently with *xshathra* (like *da* and *dathra*), suggests that the latter word may, *at least among them,* have meant not *realm* or *power,* but something analogous to a *school* or *college.* Indisputable, however, it is that *xshathra,* 29.10; 32.4; 43.4; 44.6; 45.10; is associated with Vohu Manah.

The *sasna* are also distinctly Vohu Manist; in 29.8, and 48.3, undoubtedly so; in 31.18, nearest to Vohu Manah of 31.17 e, and mentioned as of the Druj, with whom we have seen the Vohu Manists sympathized. In 53.1, they are 'of the *good daena,*' both Vohu Manist terms. If we scrutinize the Vohu Manist duplicating divinities (Ashay, Tushnamaiti, College-xshathra) it would seem that they were an Euhemerist interpretation of the less moralized tribal deities of the Cow-cult (Asha Armaiti, Xshathra-xshay-power). This is just what we might expect from a non-partisan, student sect, who could not be prevented from reflecting on, or moralizing about, their divinities.

Ashay, for instance, is indubitably connected with Vohu Manah in 28.7, 33.13, 43.16, 46.10, 51.21, 43.1e; while in 34.12 the paths are *of* Vohu Manah, though taught (by Zarathushtra?) through Asha; in 43.5, we have the *akem,* and *vanguhim* ear-marks; in 48.8 the *good* spirit and *good* Xshathra; in 49.12 Vohu Manah is nearest to Ashay, as also in 50.9, where we have works of Vohu Manah; in 51, we have the *best* deeds, which must refer to the *good* Manah; the *good* Xshathra, also.

It is among them (43.15) we find *Tushn-amaiti,* no doubt a racial variant for the Ashaist *Armaiti.* Vohu Manah grants *tevishi* and *utayuiti,* 51.7. These are not

to be superficially attributed to Haurvatat and Ameretat, because in the passages where these *vitality* and
enduring are approached to Haurvatat and Ameretat,
they are separated off from them very evidently, 51.7;
43.1; 48.8a; as if it were an eclectic comparative identification of things known to be of different origin.

The psychological 'tang' to Bartholomae's translation of *daena,* i. e., *Ego,* or *individuality* seems too artificial for so early a period; yet we cannot well go further
away from psychology than to translate it *Spirit.* Even
so, it remains a word testifying to *reflection* and *study*
on the part of the users thereof; and, as it happens, its
chief connection is with the Vohu Manist cult, 33.13;
44.9; 53.4; 34.13; 49.5; of whom we otherwise have
gathered that they were unpartisan students.

Their hell was the ' Home of' their 'Bad Mind,' or
'Worst Mind.'

Were the Vohu Manists the *proud,* 32.3, *pair-
imatoisca?* In this 32.3 the *proud* are those who 'will
dare to reverence the *Daevas,*' and who 'will be considered as belonging to the *Druj.*' Hence, the proud were
originally neither *Daevas* nor *Druj*—what else could
they be but Vohu-Manists, seeing that *Aka-Manah* is
mentioned in line 172? Secondly, the intellectual Vohu-
Manists, might well have been so termed by the Armaitians, who were no more than humble cow-herders, to
whom the gentlemen, *xvaetav* might well appear *proud.*
Thirdly, there seems to be a contrast or opposition between the humble Armaitians of verse 2, and the *proud*
of verse 3. Now, we have no record of any opposition
within the ranks of the simple-minded *verezena,* or
group of laboring cow-herders.

It would seem as if *chisti,* sophia—wisdom, was associated with the Vohu Manist cult, 46.9; 48.11; 47.2;
51.16, 18.

Likewise the Magian cause is distinctly, 51.11, 16,

grouped with Vohu Manah alone, and among others, in 33.7; 46.14; also with Vohu Manah and Xshathra in 29.11, in the cow-drama.

Does the meaning of *Tushna* (matay, 658, *silent* devotion) have any connection with the *guzra* (secret) teachings? This would seem the fitting cult, in order of importance. In 28.5, the *mathras* of the Knower were not unknown among the Vohu Manists; who were rather, the chief association thereof.

Who were the Savages, *æshafstras?* The only indications we have are:

(*a*) 34.5; Zarathushtra preached to Daevas, Doomed (druj), and Savages. This would imply they belonged to a sect other than Daevic or Ashaist—the only other definitely well-known sect of whom it could be said Zarathushtra had preached to them was the Vohu Manist.

(*b*) The non-Vohu Manists are shunned by Asha, as much as Savages are shunned by us, 34.9. Does this suggest that Zarathushtra, like his divinity Asha, separated himself from the non-Vohu Manist Savages?

Why should they be called "small beasts of prey," *æshafstras?* Possibly like the treason which Zarathushtra attributes to certain Vohu Manists who, though they know the truth, use it for their own purposes, 34.7; they held a variant of Armaiti, as "stealing" it. However, in 49.9, the *Sasna* is taught by Asha (or the Ashaist prophet?) while Vohu Manah has the *guzra-sangha,* the Secret teachings.

We must accept Yasna, 30, as the Vohu Manist school of Dualism; and from it we must gather the following ideas: the Spirit being clothed with the Stone-heavens as a garment, 5; and the lights, 1; *Adana,* as duplicate of Spenta—Mainyuist *Ada,* 7; *maetha* and *vicitha* for *crisis;* that *Better* and the *Bad* spirits, showing it Vohu Manist.

The only association that does not seem to fit is Aeshma, 30.7, who, as *sickness,* should logically belong to the cult of Health, Haurvatat. Still, sickness is only a minor result of rapine and violence, which without question is Daevic, for it was to Aeshma that the wrong choosing Daevas rushed.

5. *The* Spenta-Mainyuist Cult.

It is only with the greatest reluctance that the writer even considers the recognition of another cult; for the following reasons seem decisive:

(1) The parallelism between the dualism of 30 and 45 demands a group other than the Vohu Manists, who were philosophical enough to be appealed to by a Dualism; and this could be neither the Daevas, bent on rapine, nor the Ashaists-Armaitians, bent on cow-herding and fire-worship and fanatic opposition to the Druj.

(2) We have *Spenta* and *Angro Mainyu,* as another group of divinities. True, *spenta* recalls Armaiti the bounteously fertile, and *Mainyu* recalls the Armaitian 'Shaper,' the Spirit of Wisdom. But the Armaitians were perhaps the most ancient and simple, cow-cult, whereas Yasna 45 contains a group of late ideas, we shall see later. Sraosha, the Cinvat-bridge, Garodman, and Haurvatat and Ameretat, ignored in 30.6. Again, there would be among the Armaitians no room for *Angro-Mainyu,* as no opponent is mentioned to the Shaper-of-the-Cow, the Spirit of Wisdom; the opponent there was *Tare-maiti,* corresponding to *Ar-maiti.*

(3) We have, as compensation, *ada* (directly associated with *Spenta Mainyu,* 33.12, though not in 33.11; 48.1) and *adana,* 30.7; a duplication, showing that we must hold apart the Vohu Manist *adana* from the Spenta Mainyuist *ada* group, whichever it be.

(4) The Savages, as we have already seen, were Vohu Manist; the foreigners, *voaxema,* 34.5, must have been different from them, and would suggest later comers, such as would hold the more advanced Spenta Mainyuist doctrines, which we will next see.   Neither Daevas nor Druj would be addressed as 'foreigners.'

(5) The chief reason for the recognition of a different and later group is that in 30.6, 7 we have *tevishi* and *utayuiti* given to a sick man, without mention of *Haurvatat,* if not of *Ameretat;* whereas in 45.7, these qualities of *tevishi* and *utayuiti,* are as always later, properly connected with *Haurvatat* and *Ameretat,* 45.7, 10.   These divinities must then have been either unknown to, or ignored by, 30.7; this later alternative would be unlikely, because no reason could well be advanced for purposive ignoring of them.

Again, in 32.5, Ameretat appears not with her later twin companion Haurvatat, but with *Hujyatay,* showing the formative stage of the later twin-doctrine of *Haurvatat* and *Ameretat.*

(6) We have a special eschatology, Sraosha as Judge, and *Garodman,* 45.5, 8, which would conflict with 'House of the Best Mind' or 'House of Druj' and of *Asha.   Garodman* is a later idea, taken up by the later Mazdeans.   While the Vohu Manist's psychological cast of thought held to the crisis, *vicitha* and *maetha,* 30.2, 9, we have in 45.7 the *Preparer,* who was later to stand with Sroasha at the (bridge) of judgment, 46.17.

(7) The *cinvat-bridge,* 46.10, 11; 51.13; shows a developed (and later Mazdean) view.   The prophet will go over it first, 46.10, certainly developed from the simple *ratav* of the herdsmen.   In 46.11, while connected with the house of Druj, the fact that their daena will meet the Karpan and Kavays there is mentioned as something they do not seem to have known yet.   So,

in 51.13, there is a manifestation (of new doctrinal description?) for those who have left the way of Asha, with the *daenas* as destroyers of the good reward. While *daenas,* as we have seen, were frequently connected with Vohu Manah, nevertheless the whole picturesque picture, employing both Vohu Manist and Ashaist conceptions, is a strikingly new *ensemble.*

(8) We find also in Yasna 45 a more advanced psychological scheme of eight elements; *manah, sengha, xratav, varana, shyaothana, daena,* and *urvan,* (mind, doctrine, understanding, thought, teaching, deeds, spirit, soul) in 45.8; while in 30.2 we have only the traditional threefold division of *manah, vacah,* and *shyaothana,* mind, word, and deed.

(9) All the other names for men being appropriated (*vir* to Armaitians, as used with *pasav; mashyia* to the Druj-doomed), we may be impressed by the appearance of *maretan* (reminding of the latter *gayomart*) in the classic passage, 45.5. In 46.13 *sasta* precedes it, and the 'hearing' is connected with *Sraosha.* In 29.7 the cow asks who would intercede for her with men (probably the *daevas?*); yet the cow's Creator was the Spirit of Wisdom. Again, in 30.6, the connection is with Aeshma, and hence daevic, unless we consider his role as sickness-producer as being Spenta Mainyuist, as opposed to *Haurvatat* and *Ameretat.* (The references are, 29.7; 45.5; 46.13—30.6; 32.12.)

(10) In considering the special doctrines of the Spenta Mainyuist group, *Haurvatat* might appear as an innovation. We have seen two stages of growth towards this; first, when Haurvatat was ignored, and secondly, when she appeared as *Hujyatay.* The idea of health and sickness therefore may have been characteristic of this group. Did the *ahumbis,* 31.19; 44.2; have anything to do with this? In 31.19 applied to Zarathushtra, and in 44.2 to Ahura Mazdah, it may have

shown another stage in the development of the healing idea, with *Aeshma* imported from *daevas,* as opponent, 30.6. At any rate *urvatha* as friend appears in 45.11.

(11) There is the following complex of associations, all connecting with the Spenta Mainyuists:

    a. The *Clever* are sifted by Sraosha, 46.17.

    b. The *Preparer* (Zarathushtra himself) will stand for them with Sraosha, 46.17.

    c. The Preparers wish for profits of *Ameretat,* 45.7.

Are the *Clever* Spenta Mainyuists? On the whole, they seem to have relations mainly with Zarathushtra himself, and as *Grehma* does not believe in the second coming or life, 32.10; 46.11; does it mean that the Clever did believe in it before Grehma perverts them to being Drujists?

Sraosha, obedience, would of itself, mean obedience to Zarathushtra himself. He is associated with the Preparer and Judgment in 46.17; 44.16; 43.12; and in 45.5 with Ameretat (Spenta Mainyuist); with Haurvatat and Ameretat, in 45.5.

6. The Clever, or Mazdists.

The *Gnostic* cult includes *Mazdah,* from the verb *mazda* (B 1163) to mind, or remember. In connection therewith we have the *Knower vidvae,* 31.6; the Knowing, 45.3; the Clever, datha, 732; 46.17; with their special heaven, the house of the Clever, 32.10; with their opposite the Fools, or Non-clever, 46.17.

7. The Magians.

The Magians were apparently a well established tribe, with a special name, *magavan,* 33.7, 51.15.

They were perhaps *Daevas,* for Vishtaspa the Kava-yite attains their leadership, 46.14; 51.16; 53.2. They may, however (as many kindred tribes and persons have been to their relatives), have been bitterly hostile to them, or they may have drifted apart in some manner, so as to allow for Zarathushtra's opposition to their kindred the Daevas. Meat-eating, 32.8; and intoxication (by haoma?), 48.10; may have been elements in this disunion. In the Magian sections of the Gathas, 46.9-13; 51.11-22; 53; the cow-drama, 29; we have a prevalence of Mazdah Ahura together (except in 33, which has a slight preponderance of Mazdah only). The word *Mazdah* may therefore have been already prevalent, and known to Zarathushtra. The word *maga* meant a *hole.* Now if we suppose that the men who lived in the deep valley, which was not fitted for agriculture, wished to support themselves, pasturing cattle would be the only possibility. The dwellers on the high table-land were successful, powerful daevas; and at last, when driven to despair, Zarathushtra advises the Magians to settle 'cleverly' these open sunny lands, and engage in agriculture also, 50.1-4. This would account for all the facts, and allow a *role* for Zarathushtra as champion of the herdsmen, and his later alliances with the Daeva Frashaoshtra and Jamaspa.

Again, the Magians may have been troglodites, such as lived in the Hauran. Fire would be very necessary to them; hence perhaps their preserving or being favorable to that element of nature-worship. However, such introspective lives as troglodites must necessarily live would favor the preservation or development of memory and mindfulness, the *Mazdah* concept.

Indeed, the verb 'mazda,' to remember, is found in one of the Magian sections, 53.5; the other occurrence is in the Spenta Mainyuist, 45-45.1, which cult Zarathushtra was seeking. We may therefore conclude it was in general use. But the famous Yasna 30 (dualism) also begins with the expression that the prophet will now utter things *memorable, mazdatha*. These no doubt were the secrets of the Mazdean theologians, common among all of the various cult-tribes.

Did *Mazdah* alone of all the other divinities, have no opponent? Seeing that the name *Mazdah* is after all kindred to *Manah, Mainyu,* and *Maiti,* all these words meaning *thought* in some shape, such an isolation would seem improbable. But what opponent have we for him? The later *Ormuzd* and *Ahriman* betrays it. *Ahura* was an opponent of *Mazdah.* Hence Zarathushtra's long effort to ,recognize *Mazdah* as the Supreme *Ahura;* hence we have *Ahuras of Mazdah,* and *Ahuras Mazdah,* 31.4; 30.9; before the final crystallization occurs. Hence also we have the conjuring of disobedience (*Asrushtay*) from *Mazdah Ahura,* 33.4, so as to leave *Ahura* as holy and universal a name as it has since become.

The secular use of Ahura, 29.2; 31.8, 10; 46.9; 53.9; as judge is *attributed* to Mazdah in 31.8; 46.9; to a man in 29.2; 31.10; 53.9; and in the latter case it refers to a conqueror who would murder and imprison. So we have both

      a. Ahura as sufficiently different from Mazdah as to be attributed to him;

      b. As containing the idea of bloodshed and violence, which makes the point of the '*spentem*' and '*ashavanem*' added to it in 46.9.

While originally then the idea may have been that of an opposing divinity (still reflected in Zarathushtra's code of ethics against his enemies, 43.8; 28.9; 46.4, 18; 31.18) he insisted that Ahura and Mazdah were the same, 31.8; 46.9; Ahura becoming 'bounteous' and 'just.'

We have this *asrushtay* in 33.4; 44.13; 43.12; really the opponent of Sraosha.

Outline of Pre-Zoroastrian Cults.

I. DAEVAS.

Meat-eaters, butchers of cows; refuse, intoxication (with haōma?) Friendly; agricultural, but employing methods different from Zarathushtra's. Grêhma their *tkaēsa* (prophet) teaches an eschatology different from Zarathushtra's, 32.10. They are politically prominent, and have a wide reputation, and ally themselves with Aēshma. They use hunav for *son*.

II. ARMAITIAN BOVINE FERTILITY WORSHIP.

Armaiti the productive, cow-like, gentle, is pasture. *Fashioner* (tash) of the Bovine; gêus urvan, *Soul of the Bovine.* Bull-god with pasture. They demand a *Judge* who shall dispense *profit* and *loss*. They honor *understanding, reverence,* and *peace.* Vira for *man.* Opponent to Armaiti is Tare-*maiti.* They combine with

III. ASHAIST PARTISANS, Yasnas 28, 43, 44, 48.

Asha is opposed to the Druj*ists*, who are called *the doomed*, or *mortals.* 'Injure or convert them!' cry the *champions* or *saviors.* Their law is the sêñgha: their Judgment occurs by red fire and molten metal (the burning of sword-wounds[3]) *Home of Druj*, hell

IV. VOHU-MANISTS, Yasnas 30, 34.

Friendly to all, hence also to Drujists, hence they appear to Zarathushtra hypocritical, 34.7, and *proud*, 32.3, pairi-matōiscā, as opposed to their Tushnā-maiti; Ashay is their version of Asha To their *Vohu* is opposed *Aka* Manah, in the *Home of the Worst Mind*, whither go the *Savages*, by retribution, ādāna. They are the intellectuals, interpreting doctrines; having verses; teaching, daxsh, xshā, sāsnā, cistay-*sophia, secret teachings,* of which the legend of the stone-heaven may have formed part for the *daēnas.*

V. SPENTA-MAINYUISTS, Yasnas 45, 47, 49.

Dualism of *Speñta* versus *Añgro Mainyav; Sraosha* versus *Asrushtay.* From among all *men* (maretan) and *foreigners* (vaōxemā) Sraosha sifts out the *clever* who, following the *Preparer* over the *cinvat* bridge, in the *Garodman* attain *Haurvatat* and *Ameretat.* They had an eightfold psychological division. Retribution is ādā

VI. MAGIANS, Yasnas 29, 33, 46.9-13, 51.11-22, 53.

A tribe living in a deep valley, by despair driven out into open lands, 50.1-6, submitting to the Daēva ruler Vishtāspa. Their divinity Mazdāh is united to his erst-while opponent Ahura from whom Zarathushtra as *knower* of the *mysteries* conjures away all evil, then superimposing him above all other gods as the *supreme*

DEVEL

Amidst th
think of as i
of some mou
tra must have

In studying
sage we must
(1) As in
youth, are as
(2) We m
arose he was
Hence, in
we should go
his relations a
whom he is r
outside of or
surval had be
therefore ima
In this sec
legendary ma
the picturesqu
scaffed. For
the enquiry a
has taught th
are not alway

CHAPTER IV.

DEVELOPMENT *of* ZARATHUSHTRA

Amidst these groups or tribes (which we must not think of as large nations, but perhaps as fellow-settlers of some mountain—group or table—land), Zarathushtra must have grown up and worked.

1. *The* Magian Youth.

In studying the origin of Zarathushtra and his message we must keep certain things in mind.

(1) As in other religions, the accounts of his early youth, are among the least reliable documents.

(2) We must change perspective: when Zarathushtra arose he was unnoticed, and the world around him great.

Hence, in asking ourselves to what tribe he belonged we should go to the later years of his life, and see what his relations are . Here we find the Magian tribe, among whom he is not satisfied to teach; he wants to preach outside of or 'before' it, 33.7. This would not have occurred had he not belonged to it by birth. We must therefore imagine him a youth of the Magian tribe.

In this account of the life of Zarathushtra all the legendary material which would have added much to the picturesqueness of the scenes has been purposely omitted. For the purpose of this work has been to limit the enquiry strictly to the *Gathas*. Biblical criticism has taught that popular—and even orthodox traditions are not always the safest guides.

CHAPTER IV.

DEVELOPMENT *of* ZARATHUSHTRA

Amidst these groups or tribes (which we must not think of as large nations, but perhaps as fellow-settlers of some mountain—group or table—land), Zarathushtra must have grown up and worked.

1. *The* Magian Youth.

In studying the origin of Zarathushtra and his message we must keep certain things in mind.

(1) As in other religions, the accounts of his early youth, are among the least reliable documents.

(2) We must change perspective: when Zarathushtra arose he was unnoticed, and the world around him great.

Hence, in asking ourselves to what tribe he belonged we should go to the later years of his life, and see what his relations are. Here we find the Magian tribe, among whom he is not satisfied to teach; he wants to preach outside of or 'before' it, 33.7. This would not have occurred had he not belonged to it by birth. We must therefore imagine him a youth of the Magian tribe.

In this account of the life of Zarathushtra all the legendary material which would have added much to the picturesqueness of the scenes has been purposely omitted. For the purpose of this work has been to limit the enquiry strictly to the *Gathas*. Biblical criticism has taught that popular—and even orthodox traditions are not always the safest guides.

The location of Zarathushtra's birth in the neighborhood of lake Urumyah finds absolutely no support in the Gathas whose ignoring of sea and lake (mentioning water but in 44.4; 51.7) is particularly striking. If his visions occurred by a river or lake, the hymns do not mention it.

2. As Student with the Vohu Manists.

What may we suppose that the possibly shy, homesick, distressed Magian youth may have learnt with the Vohu Manist teachers? Elsewhere we have seen all the special doctrines they may have introduced to him; but the most certain of all is that they taught him to address Vohu Manah as a present help in trouble, for never, as long as he lived, was the impressionable Magian to fail to raise his prayers and adorations to the Good Mind who dwelt above the heavens.

"We would not vex the best Mind because of the expected benefactions, 28.9. He would always teach hymns worthy of the life of Vohu Manah, 30.1. He watched over the issues of human life with Vohu Manah, 28.4. He would always advance his interests through Vohu Manah, 33.8. Would Vohu Manah have the power to protect his poor? 34.5. The lot of Vohu Manah was composed of the incomparable things of the coming kingdom, 33.13. It was the power of Vohu Manah that should be the portion of him who withstood the divine fire, 43.4; for Vohu Manah appoints the proper punishments, and will come, and utter judgments, 43.5, 6."

And so our young prophet was instructed in verses or oracular utterances, 43.11, which no doubt never entirely faded from his mind.

But Vohu Manah, the good natured, full of good sense, could not be bigoted; and when the time came the young Magian was ready to progress further, it was that Divinity itself which told him, 'Thou shouldst go to some Ashaist fane, to be instructed,' 43.12. And no doubt with tears he bade farewell to his friends of the cheerful, debonair disposition. These, however, seem to have left upon the youth the indelible eschatological interest which pursued him all through life—for we have seen, 33.12, 13, that Vohu Manah was the divinity associated most closely with the distribution of compensations.

3. As Student with the Ashaists.

However delightful the gracious young Magian's stay may have been among the Vohu Manians, and however serious the eschatological interest may have been that he brought with him, his joy of being a priest, 33.6, 14; 43.9; among the Ashaists never forsook him. Years later when celebrating the heroes of the Devaist struggles he would sing to Asha 'as never before,' 28.3, his mind going backwards to when he had done so first.

'When will I behold thee, as a Knower, O Asha?' he should cry, 28.5.
me the realm, O Vohu Manah! 31.4.

If Asha is at all willing to be invoked, so attain for 'What help hast thou for me, O Asha? 49.12.

'I would remain your eulogist, O Mazdah and Asha, as long as I live!' 50.11.

Such were the reminiscent sentiments which he carried with him all his life; of this early sojourn among the Ashaists, whose details the reader may find elsewhere; however, it may be well to note down the chief points thereof:

First, a theophany of Asha in person, 34.7, 8; 43.9, 10.

Second, a Vision of the uncertainties of life ended by a decision to support the Ashaists against their enemies the druj—a 'naturalization' so to speak, among them, 31.12, 13; 43.7, 8.

Third, a touching prayer for sufficient divine grace, to carry out Asha's decrees on his enemies, 30.8-11; 43.15, 16.

Fourth, no doubt, admission to the Bond-society of Ashaists, *hithav,* 48.7; which association remained with him to the end of his daevic struggles; for in his vision Armaiti the divine *hitha,* 34.10, of Asha (his wife?), appears and aligns the parties.

This was the sunny, 32.2, portion of Zarathushtra's life—for Asha had his strength through fire, 34.4; and no doubt our young Magian began at this time those ritualistic, reverential fire-worshipping rites, 43.9; through which he may have more than once beheld the divinities themselves. Indeed, he referred to himself even later as the friend of Asha, 50.6.

But neither did this satisfy Zarathushtra's soul: the fire may have led him to seek the Spirit's wisdom, 33.6, which for the present was to be withheld from him, 30.6, 7; 33.6; 44.18. So in disappointment he went by himself—and called on the nameless lord Ahura—from whom, as we shall see, he was to attain treasures that passed his understanding.

When Zarathushtra left the Ashaists he wrote, 33.6:

'I who, as (Ashaist) priest, coming through Asha from the Best (Mind), desire (to walk) the just (paths of the Holy) Ghost

From us (the Ashaist priests) (going) towards the pastures which advisory-managers ought to work through the (Vohu) Manah (disposition);

For these two objects I wish, O Ahura Mazdah, to consult together visibly (the Best Spirit and thee).'

4. *The* Ahurian Experience*s*—Reflexion.

We must now study the mental experiences of our young prophet while studying with the Ahuraians, to whose name *Mazdah* he was to give so much prominence; our sources will accordingly be on the one hand, 34.12-15; 31.3-5, 7, 8, 11, 14-17; and on the other, 44, except 17 and 18.

In 31.6, 7 Zarathushtra asks a number of questions. What is the answer? From whom does it come? (8)

'Whereupon, when Zarathushtra with his (own) eye (by looking at nature) and through (his) mind (by puzzling out its significance) comprehended.'   He thought it over himself; he 'minded' it; the first step towards being reminded of it.

So in 44.8, he asks Ahura Mazdah what his purposes are that he may be mindful of them, and the utterances about which he had asked through Vohu Manah's aid. Evidently it was his purpose to remember them; he had just gone through so many cults it was highly important that he should systematize and fix them in his own mind.

In 50.8; 51.16; we have him stepping before Ahura Mazdah with the *verses* (the feet) 'which are as famous as those of zeal with stretched-out arms encompass you O Mazdah.' They are the verses of Vohu Manah, 51.16. It was at a time such as the one where we are now that he was producing them.

If he was familiar with the verb *mazda,* as we have suggested, this would fit this memorizing effort exactly; and the God who would help him to it would indeed be the 'mindful lord.'

5. *The* Ahurian Experience*s*—Teaching*s*.

This was the very psychological moment, and introspective mood for him to draw from the crucible his
mind full of the Vohu Manist and Ashaist teachings he
had just received any combination, deduction, or addition. Let us now put together the results of his intro-
spection:

31.8. Ahura Mazdah is first and youngest of creation; is the father of Vohu Manah; *thy* Vohu Manah,
32.6. The genuine creator of Asha; the owner of Armaiti and of the Shaper-of-the-Bovine creation, who
was the understanding of the Spirit.

11. Creator of *gaetha* and *daena,* establisher of body
and life, etc.

Let us go to 44:

(1) Friend.
(2) *Ahumbis.*
(3) Who was the first father of Asha?
(4) Who is creator of Vohu Manah?

For whom didst thou create the cattle? (A prelude
to the drama of 29.)

(7) 'Sons reverent to their fathers' (meant Asha
and Vohu Manah were made subject to Ahura Mazdah).

(7) Who created Armaiti? (45.4, is daughter.)

(9) He wants to help the *daenas.* He wants to learn
the dwelling of Vohu Manah and Ahura Mazdah.

(10) *Cista,* wisdom, mysteries.

(11) How to spread the religion for which he was
chosen—all other (divinities) he regards with suspicion.

(18) He wants the mystic *mathra* of Haurvatat and
Ameretat; and the ten mares and camel to enable him
to start in his work.

Evidently he had combined the former cults of **Asha** and **Vohu Manah**, and had superimposed above them a supreme father and Creator, which new revelation should unite the warring cults under one banner.

The name was already at his hand—the lord who was mindful of all this; himself was henceforth an Expert-Knower (*vidvae*), one of the clever (*dathra*); and he now had a secret (*guzra sangha*) which united him to all cults and enabled him to seek converts among them all.

CHAPTER V.

CRITICAL RESULTS.

It is now time to cast a very tentative general bird's eye view on the ground we have traversed, in order to approach to its significance.

1. Chronological Significance of 'Mazdah.'

Should we suppose that the occurrence of the name *Mazdah* was in some one hymn shown to be predominant, would it imply that that hymn was early or late? The decision would be, that it was late, because:

(1) The later Zoroastrian religion is distinctly Mazdean, the name Ahura dropping out to some extent, or coalescing with Mazda into Auharmazd, Ormuzd.

(2) There was a time, as we have seen, 43; when Zarathushtra learnt the supremacy of Mazdah.

(3) The use of *Ahuras* in the plural, the *Ahuras Mazdas,* the plural pronoun, all point to an earlier polytheism.

Gathic Occurrence of Divine Names.

Yasna 28: Ahura, 8; Ahura Mazdāh, 2,3,4,5,6,9,10,11. Mazdāh, 1,7.

29 A, 5; AM, 4,6,7,10,11; M, 5,8; None, 1,2,3,9.

30 A, 1; AM, 5,8,9; M, 10,11; None, 2,3,4,6,7.

31 A, 8,15; AM, 2,4,5,7,9,14,16,17,19,21,22; M, 1,3,6,8,10,11,13; —12,18,20.

32 A, 0. AM, 1,2,4,6,7,16; M, 8,9,11,12,13; —3,5,10,14,15.

33 A, 3,13; AM, 2,5,6,11,12; M, 4,7,8,9,10,14. —1.

34 A, 0; AM, 1,3,4,10,13,14,15; AM, 2,5,6,7,8,9,11,12.

---

43 A, 0; AM, 1,3,5,7,9,11,13,15,16; M, 2,4,6,8,14; —10,12.

44 A, 1-19; M, 1,2,3,4,7,8,9,10,11,14,15,16,18,20.

45 A, 11; AM, 3-11; —1,2.

46 A, 6,9,15; AM, 1,2,3,5,7,10,12,13,14,16,17; M, 4,8,18,19. —11.

47 AM, 1,5,6; M, 2,3,4.

48 A, 1,7; AM, 2,3,6,8; M, 4,9,10,11,12; —5.

49 AM, 5,6,7,8,12; M, 1,2,3,10; —4,9,11.

50 AM, 1,3,5,10; M, 2,4,6,7,8,9,11.

51 AM, 2,3,6,15,16,17,18,21,22; M, 1,4,7,8,9,10,11,19,20; —5,12,13,14.

53 AM, 1,2,4,9; M. 3; —5,6,7,8.

2. Inference*s of* Occurrence*s of* divine Name*s,*

If any conclusion can be drawn from the occurrences of divine names in the Gathas it would be as follows:

a. Comparing 30 and 45, we find in the latter later writing a far greater number of divine names.

b. In the early series of Yasnas *Ahura Mazda* predominates; in the later, *Mazdah* alone.

c. Yasna 44 has the most uses of *Ahura* alone on the first lines of each stanza, and therefore may be earliest; showing genuineness of Zarathushtra's desire for truth.

d. Yasna 43 has *Mazdah* alone predominating over Ahura alone; hence it is a late writing up of Zarathushtra's early experiences, which is also somewhat the case with 34.

e. If we accept 45 as a Spenta Mainyuist writing, we have an immense predominance of *Mazdah Ahura* together. But 47 (Spirit Song) is as neutral as 30.

f. The Daeva struggle Yasnas 33 (32 less so); 48-51; have strong predominance of *Mazdah* alone, hence late, under stress. See 44.20, where Daeva struggle is mentioned, and has Mazdah alone.

g. 46, with Magian cause, is early, showing predominance of Ahura Mazdah. The latter verses of 51. 15-18, 21, 22; which also mention the Magian cause, have a strong predominance of Ahura Mazdah also.

Development of the Gathas according to the Divine Names

Earliest—*Ahura* Predominates, Used Independently of *Mazdah*

44 Heart-searchings.

Early—*Ahura Mazdah* Used Together; *Ahura* Preponderates

45 Dualism, Spenta-Mainyuist.

Late—*Ahura Mazdah* Used Together, *Mazdah* Preponderates

28 The Heroes and their Mission.
29 Drama of Cow.
30 Dualism, Vohu-Manist.
31 Great Communion with Divinity.
33 High-priestly Prayer.
46 Preparations for Struggle, Magian.
48 Appeal for Champions.

Latest—*Ahura alone* Absent; *Mazdah alone* Frequent

32 Vituperation of Grehma and Opponents.
34 Early Experiences, Shorter Document.
43 Early Experiences, Longer Document.
47 Battle-hymn of the Spirit.
49 Appeal for Defenders from Bendva.
50 Exodus of the Magians.
51 Proclamation of the Kingdom.
53 Securing a Champion by Marriage.

Results.

1 The struggle antiquated *Ahura* and established *Mazdah*.
2 The priestly influence worked in the same direction.
3 The Second, Longer, Personal Document was earliest, both as to Personal Experiences and Dualism.
4 Account of Early Experiences is later than Heart-searchings.
5 The Cow-drama is too artificial to be early, *in its present form*.

The Magian sections of the Gathas are then 46.9-13; 51.11-22; 53; 29; 33.

The Spenta Mainyuist, 45; 47; 49 (Ada).

The Ashaist sections: 28; 43; 44; 48.

The Vohu Manist section: 30; 34.

The parallelisms of 30-45; 34-43, 44; suggest that the earlier part of the life was paralleled by Vohu Manist and Ashaist influences; the latter by Magian and Spenta Mainyuist, though the latter two both had bonds together, and belonged to the later document.

3, Authorship of the Gathas.

What bearing would the above critical suggestions have on the authorship of the Gathas? If we have two parallel accounts, it is not likely Zarathushtra wrote both. If we have to choose, it would be the simpler, the shorter, and probably earlier. But even here we have the advanced notions of a priest, 33.6, 14; of penances, 31.13; implying an established organization, of fire-sacrifices, 31.7; with rubbing-sticks, 31.19, Mills. On the other hand, 43 and 44 seem in parts so sincere, as to be original. Again, it is doubtful whether a work so rude as turning civilization from nomadic to pastoral, 29; and from pastoral to agricultural, 50; would justify finished metrical, parallel accounts of Zarathushtra's life.

On the whole it may be said to be certain that genuine sources underlie both versions, with preference for the second, longer, and more personal account.

4. Amplification *of the* Authorship Question.

How far may we attribute the authorship of the *Gathas* to Zarathushtra? We must first choose between he Shorter and Longer Documents (28-34; 43-51, 53), is it is not likely that both were written by the same nan; why should one man write both?

Analogy from Biblical Criticism would lead us to :hoose the Shorter Document as the earliest; but, on the :ontrary, we seem to be led to decide for the Longer Document, as more personal; and less advanced in the ise of *Mazdah alone*—the Chapters on Dualism 45 and 30, and the Personal experiences, 44 and 34 showing this the Shorter Document (28-34) is the Priestly one: we have a decided unity of metre; a mention of Zarathushtra as *priest* (33.6; 14?); of *penances* (31.13), which imply an organized and effective ecclesiastical authority; *fire-sacrifices* (the *lights* of 31.7, and *rubbing-sticks* of Mills; 31.19); the Cow-drama, 29, while no doubt representing one of the earliest incidents, uses *Mazdah* preponderatingly, and is already Magian in writing, 29.11. On the whole, therefore, if Zarathushtra wrote one of the two documents, it is more likely it was the Longer and more Personal Section 43-51, 53.

In any event, we may with certainty assert Zarathushtra was the author of the materials which are written up in the *Gathas*.

5. Uncertainty of Conclusions.

In conclusion, the writer would state once more the utmost diffidence with which he advances these his suggestions. Even if they were well-grounded, he knows, by the history of other literary controversies, how much ridicule and contempt they may attract to him. The great majority of mankind have a mind quite able and willing to accept contradictories; it is only the few who can feel the impossibility of a chaos, and who would feel compelled to seek some sort of explanation. It is to them only that these critical suggestions are offered. The reader may be sure that it was only in spite of himself the writer gave so much time and space to reflections which would do himself no good; but anything is preferable to confusion and chaos, just as Basilides said: "I will affirm anything rather than that God is unjust."

CHAPTER VI.

ZARATHUSHTRA'S Personal SIGNIFICANCE.

1. Summary *of the* Message.

What significance does Zarathushtra himself bear? This may perhaps be best discussed negatively, to clear the ground; and then it will be seen what remains.

Negatively: 1. Not originator of pastoral life, but its judge or champion.

2. Not Magian leader.

Positively: 1. Eclecticism.

2. Personality as judge-protector of Bovines.

3. Partisanship or Dualism.

4. Both Lives.

5. The teaching.

6. Mazdeanism.

2. Negative Significance.

(1) We have already seen that the description, 31.9, 10, of the original choice of the Bovine creation, which must be looked on as the poetic description of the establishment of pastoral life mentions no leader; it is only later that she finds she needs a judge, 29.1, 2, 9, 11; or guardian; which Zarathushtra, 10, undertakes to be.

(2) The *Magian* name arises as a tribe apparently, Zarathushtra, 33.7; wishing to preach outside of it; the cattle are adopted into it, 29.9; and who will by good actions regard it, 51.11; until Vishtaspa is Ahura Mazdah's friend for it, 46.14; 51.16; and the Jamaspa couple, 53.7; are established in it, and threatened if they leave it.

During that earlier period it seems to have been leaderless; Zarathushtra even wishes to leave it.

3. Eclecticism.

The dogmatic chaos of the Gathas has, in this work, been analyzed; but the question remains, was this chaos possibly purposive? And what we can gather of Zarathushtra's life would suggest that it was so; his life purpose seems to have been to get converts among all the cults, and to unite them all. So we find Vohu Manah telling him to go to Asha, 43.12, at a time 'when he first learned Your teachings', 43.11. And then the use of the plural pronoun would be most naturally explained by the result of just such an eclectic education. The uniting all of them by superimposing over them as father Mazdah would leave the existing pantheon intact.

4. Personality as Judge-Protector of Bovines.

The dramatic Yasna 29 describes the call of Zarathushtra for the purpose of protecting the Bovine creation from the nomadic meat-eaters, 29.1a, b, 5b; and establishment of agriculture, 29.1c, 5c.

The Bovine-Soul expects, 9.c, future energetic help.

Zarathushtra prays for peace, 10; for the creation, and for reception among men that he may teach them the Magian cause, 11b; on account of which obedience is yielded to him, 11c.

This judge-ship Zarathushtra was not ashamed of, and he considered that it was divinely acknowledged, or caused 'noted,' 31.2; and the assembled multitude are to seek their salvation only in the measure in which he announces it, 32.1; and some of the audience at least accepts his terms, 32.2.

The question before us now is, how far was he successful? His policy of partisanship we have seen elsewhere; and however close the friendships it may have given rise to, it must have raised very much bad blood in every party involved.

Bendva for a long time opposed him, 49.12; and was so powerful as to make Zarathushtra feel his material poverty, 46.2. Perhaps that was the reason he wanted the ten mares and the camel, 44.18.

The nobility, the peers, the laboring-guild, the Druj and the Daevas all seemed to work against him, 46.1; whither shall he fly?

Bendva, 31.15; 32.5; 46.4, 7; 50.3; and Grehma, 31.18; 32.14; 44.12; seem to trip him up at every turn.

On the whole, the acknowledgment of the Daevic Vishtaspa as Magian chief amounts to a confession of failure, just as among the ancient Hebrews the day of the 'judge' faded before that of the 'king,' whose permanence of authority, and whose unquestioned or unquestionable authority alone could deal with the inner and outer dangers and difficulties.

Finally, in despair, Zarathushtra advises his adherents to settle open lands among the Druj, like the *Clever* ones do—hence diplomatically, 50.1-6.

5. Partisanship Founded on Dualism.

Dualism is taught in 30.3, 4 and 45.2. In both cases the teaching is preceded by

a. An announcement of the prophet's intention to teach an important doctrine, 30.2; 45.1; and

b. An exhortation to those who are *willing* to hear, 30.1; to open their ears and eyes, 30.2; and remember, 45.1b; and

c. A statement that it is important in respect to the

personal responsibility, 30.2b; for a great crisis—interpreted both eschatologically (B) and politically (M); but distinctly referred to Grehma the false prophet and the second life, 45.1b, c; again interpreted eschatologically (B) and politically (M).

This threefold preliminary, in duplicate, should emphasize the importance of the dualistic revelation.

Zarathushtra's effort seems to have been to create divisions, to 'draw the line,' to establish a party. So he accuses the Vohu Manists of treachery for friendliness to the Druj, 34.7; his revelations from Armaiti are to sunder himself from daevas, savages, and the doomed-men, 43.15; 49.9; 34.9; 43.7, 8; 34.5. He is angry because Grehma is on sufficiently good terms with the 'Clever' to pervert them to Drujdom, 32.10; and these fierce Daevas seem to have been anxious to *please* (*xsnav*) people, and generously give them food as Yima, 32.8. The druj seem to have lived among the Ashaists, and Zarathushtra was the one to eject them, 44.13. On the whole the various opposing parties seem to have been anxious to get along as peaceably as possible together, while Zarathushtra's main purpose seems to have been:

(1) To create an impassable barrier between Ashaist and Drujist ('injure or convert,' 33.2; who injures him pleases God, 31.18; 45.11; 46.4).

(2) To disunite Daevas, Clever, Vohu Manist, and Savages (see references above);

(3) To separate himself from all of them, 49.3; 34.5; and

(4) To make personal service to himself the test of orthodoxy; whoever opposes him is an enemy to humanity, 46.13; 51.12, 10; 46.18, 19.

While this unconciliatory attitude may not seem lovely, it may be doubted whether any great positive work could ever be begun or carried on, on any less positive a basis.

6. Both Lives.

Both lives.   There is no doubt Zarathushtra taught *two lives,* a present and a second life, an *acpi zatha,* or *second birth* or *regeneration,* 48.5.   He called his enemies the Druj, the 'doomed,' as such meaning will alone explain the enumeration of *daevas, savages,* and *men-mortals* or *doomed,* 45.11; 34.5; 48.1.   Grehma with his doctrines destroys the plans of life, 32.9 (which however may refer only to present-day regulations).   His threats and picturesque representations of the House of the Druj assure he taught a good life.   All uses of the word *nar* are in connection with promises of blessings or eternity.   Besides, Zarathushtra took himself very seriously.   He was the preparer and Savior *par excellence,* and was to stand next to Sraosha at the Last Judgment, 46.17; and he recommended his utterances on the ground he was able to justify them at the Last Day, 31.19.   No wonder that his enemies were *the Doomed!*

7. The Teaching of Mazdeanism.

The *cistay* or teaching (secular and religious) appears in

> 48.5 as the *good* cistay, composed of
> > (*a*) the second birth;
> > (*b*) agriculture for pastoral society.
> 44.10 as the *maya* or mystic cistay, where we have
> > (*a*) undefined goods of Ahura Mazdah;
> > (*b*) words and deeds of Armaiti, the purpose of 44.9, 10 being, how will the believers succeed in *holding together* or combining the practical and theoretical side of my teaching.

CHAPTER VII

ETHNOLOGICAL SIGNIFICANCE OF ZARATHUSHTRA

1. Dialects *of* Thought-Religion.

The personal significance of Zarathushtra was an eclectic union, under the predominance of the *Mazdah Ahura*, of a number of pre-existent cults,—we might say, a realignment of parties for and against himself personally. This Zoroastrian pantheon has been shown to be no ready made hierarchy of archangels (impossible because of the evolving, and not devolving trend of humanity), but a number of different cults.

But not until we have discovered how these cults originated can we understand them, and in consequence, Zarathushtra. For we have seen that his personal significance was not that of an originator, but a monotheistic organizer of a pre-existing polytheism. But what was this polytheism? The most sublime and abstract polytheism the world ever saw. For we have, in four different dialects (and it was because of the differences of dialect that we were able to do our critical work), one and the same Mind or Thought-religion —(1) *Armaiti-Tushnamaiti* versus *Tare-Maiti* and *Pairi-maiti;* (2) *Vohu Manah* versus *Aka Manah;* (3) *Spenta Mainyu* versus *Angro Mainyu;* (4) *Mazdah* versus *Ahura* (Ahriman); (5) *Sraosha* versus *Asrushtay.* Zarathushtra's personal influence on the world around him depended not on the amount he changed that world's pre-existing religions, but on the faithfulness with which he represented them, after having inrited them into a pantheon which has since survived as archangels and arch-demons. This was indeed rather of a misfortune, but perhaps the only possible way to reunite the sundered Thought religion. Granting therefore that the four pre-Zoroastrian cults were only four dialects of the same Thought-religion, the burning question of our whole enquiry is, Whence may this have arisen? And in order to find this origin, we must again scour the Gathas for any touch with the then surrounding world. Here, again, we are surprised at the comparatively faint reflection of surrounding conditions; we hardly have a name or a fact to point out the ethnological relation.

2. Elements of Gathic Religion.

1° There is, however, in the Gathas an element of magic and fetichistic fire worship.

2° There is the Cow-group (Aryan?).

3° There is the Horse-group—the names Jamaspa, Haecat-aspas, Vishtaspa (Arabian?).

4° There is the Camel-cult, the names Zarathushtra, Frashaoshtra (Tartar?).

5° There ar the Daevas, who are possibly connected with the Hindu devas-worshippers.

Zarathushtra may have united the camel-tribes (Tartars), horse-tribes (Arabs) and cow-tribes (Aryans) into a single religion enunciated by himself, while remaining, in fire worship and sacrifices, the last remainders of the magic nature worship, including the fetichistic 'second life' reanimations, denied by the more cultured Daevas.

3. Ethnological Origin *of* Gathic Element*s*.

But the grouping of these ethnological elements does not yet explain the singularly pure Thought-religion. Looking over to the deva-worshiping Hindu Aryans, we find very much the same phenomena, however; so that we may look on it as a racial inheritance, from before the time of the revolt of certain of the Thought-religionists against the more materialistic, anthropomorphic, of the deva-worshippers. The cow-forces here were not, as with the Hindus, in the majority; and hence were forced to fuse with the other cults, instead of having them fuse with it, as in India. This, of itself, may have brought on a split with the Daevas, who remained as an opposition when Zarathushtra lured from them Vishtaspa, and put him at the head of the now predominating Magian tribe. The purity of the thought religion is an Aryan trait, hence its simultaneous appearance in the varying dialects of the Thought-religion. Zarathushtra then united with it the remainder of the nature-worship of the troglodytic Magian tribe, and thus produced his eclectic whole from

(1) Troglodytic, nature (fire) worshipping Magians.

(2) Four dialect-versions of the Thought-religion;

(3) Merging of the Cow-forces into the Camel-forces;

(4) Splitting the Daeva Horse-forces so as that the remainder was sufficiently small to be later turned into demons, and to disappear from the actual scene of conflict.

4. *The* Aryan Race'*s* Thought-Innovation.

We must therefore hark back to the origin of the Aryan race as the first self-conscious development of man as thinker, and consciousness, or conscience. The inheritance is therefore racial, and Zarathushtra's merit would lie in having fixed the Thought-religion into a dogmatic system early enough so as to become a survival, striking and suggestive, among more materialistically developed Hindu pantheons.

While, apparently, we are finding a purer religion the earlier we go up the stream of time, this need not conflict with the evolutional progress of the race. There are times of birth and of growth; of progress and temporary regression. The beginning of the Aryan race was such a time of progress, followed by compensating regression; then, a further progress manifested among some other race, and then receded there. The result of this alternate, cyclic progress, occurring simultaneously in various races, does at times give rise to the impression that the old was the best; but it is not really so, on the whole. It may remain the best *for that race,* but other races will lift up new and higher ideals, or will turn back to old symbols, interpreting them more purely. And so it has come to pass that even Zarathushtra's eclectic fusion of the various dialects of the Aryan Thought-religion has been left behind in some senses, though it will, to all eternity, retain a racy flavor of the soil of far-off Iran, and remain an inspiration; and a memorial of what that wonderful Aryan race in its infancy was.

FAMILIAR ZOROASTRIAN PHRASES.

WHO does not believe that "God at sundry times and in divers manners spake in time past unto the fathers by the prophets"? Vital interest can therefore not be lacking in such prophetic utterances as the Gāthās or Hymns of Zarathushtra, which have the first right to be considered his, if any portion of the Avesta can make that claim. These Gāthās contain incidental touches which sound so very familiar to us, that they may well command our attention in a leisure hour.

Certainly the greater number of these incidental touches cannot be considered in the light of direct influences of either the Old or New Testament, because they are so remote in time and place, and because many of them form no more than commonplaces of religious sentiment. Yet may they wake an echo in our hearts, cheering us by the thought that God has not left Himself without at least indirect witnesses to the utmost ends of the earth. Such at least was the faith of Justin Martyr when he wrote: "And those who lived according to reason are Christians, even though accounted atheists, such as among the Greeks, Sokrates and Herakleitos, and those who resemble them."

I. ESCHATOLOGICAL ECHOES.

The Judgment.

In this connection it may not be without point to refer to Herakleitus's 25th fragment, which shows that in 500 B.C., at Ephesus, the Gāthic judgment by fire (*Yasna* 31.3,19; 34.4; 43.4; 47.6; 51.9) was not unknown:

"For the fire coming upon [the earth] will judge and seize all things."

This judgment, the great crisis 'maētha,' 'vicitha,' 'māh,' whether interpreted as referring to the earthly 'sacred wars,' or to the 'end of the age,' is an undeniable element in the teaching of the Gāthās. It is variously represented as occurring by spirit and fire with molten metal, or as a bridge of sifting, with Sraosha as Sifter, while the Preparer, Zarathushtra himself, will stand with Sraosha (46.17) to vindicate his words (31.19) and lead the faithful into Heaven (46.10).

Regeneration.

Connected with the judgment by fire is regeneration (cp. *John* 3.3). In 48.5 we find the word 'aipizath' meaning literally 'again-birth.' It has been frequently attempted to minimise the force of this expression, but without much success, if the plain meaning of the words is not openly denied. The context however demands it, for in the next verse we hear of the birth of the 'first life':

"Armaiti, with good deeds, perfects for mortal men an 'again-birth,' good dwelling, enduringness and vitality; and for cattle she produced plants at the birth of the first life."

Whatever doctrinal distinctions we may please to associate therewith, 'regeneration' is the quite literal rendering of 'aipizath.'

The Second Life.

Zarathushtra taught a second life. For what else can we conclude from his doctrine of regeneration, or from his opposition to Grehma because, by his teaching, he destroys the second life (45.1)? So also the Karapans (46.11) destroy the (second) life of men through evil deeds; for if this does not mean 'second' life it would mean wholesale murder, which is absurd.

"I entreat thee, O Ahura, to grant me both lives, both that of the body and of the mind;   .   .   .   with the felicity with which Mazdāh, through Asha, supports [those to whom] Mazdāh, gives the two lives for their comfort" (28.2).

The Resurrection.

The notion of a resurrection also was very probably current in the Zoroastrian religion. Söderblom (p. 244) has brought together the external evidence such as that of Æneas of Gaza. Diogenes Laërtius (*Int.* 2) asserts that the Magi kept up a regular succession from the time of Zoroaster, which he puts at 6000 years before Xerxes, under the names of Ostanes, and Astrampsychos, and Gobryas and Pazatas, until the destruction of the Persian empire by Alexander. Plutarch (*De Is. et Os.* 46, 47) quotes Theopompus, the historian of Philip of Macedon, as to dualism, and the final struggle, when, after alternate periods of 3000 years, Hades shall fail, and men shall be happy, neither requiring food, nor constructing shelter. Herodotus (3.62) mentions (about 400 B.C.) that Prexaspeo, the executor of Smerdis, said: "If the dead rise up again, expect that Astyages the Mede will rise up against you; but if it is now as formerly, nothing new can spring up for you from him."

A number of passages from the Pahlavi Huzvaresh glosses and versions have been claimed to refer to the resurrection (28.5; 30.2,7,10; 31.4; 33.10; 34.6,14; 48.9). Perhaps the most striking is (30.7): "And Armatay conferred on the bodies persistence and firmness so that he by thy retributions through the metal may become the first of them." Most of the other passages, however, contain no literal reference to the resurrection on properly objective translation.

The Gospel.

The word 'hu-meretay' (in 31.10) has by all later tradition been interpreted as 'good news' or 'evangel.' But Jackson thinks it should be translated 'good marks' or record at the judgment.

The Unpardonable Sin.

When 'hu-meretay' was taken to mean 'gospel,' it appeared that the following quotation signified that the nomad should not be admitted to its blessings, even should he desire them. But Professor Jackson points out that this would conflict with the strong proselytising tendency of the Zarathustrian religion. It seems therefore safer to interpret the passage (31.10) as follows:

"Then [the cow] chose for herself among the two [possible lords, the herdsman or nomad] the herdsman who would fatten her;

"[Namely] the Ashaist who feels that it is in his mission to see to it that all things that belong to Vohu Manah prosper and who-in-return-is-prospered-by him;

"[Whereas] the nomad shall not get a share of Vohu Manah's favourable report [at the judgment, as in verse 14, not 'gospel'] even though he should urge for it [so long as he will not herd cattle]."

The Second Coming.

We are also struck by a 'second coming,' not however of the second person of the divinity, but of the first, as in 43.5,6:

"A bad compensation for the bad, and a good compensation for the good,

"[which is to occur], with thy skill, at the last crisis of creation;

"At which crisis come thou, O Mazdāh, with Spenta Mainyu, Xshathra, and Vohu Manah."

The Preparer.

We also hear of a Preparer. 'Rād' means to prepare, to get ready; hence 'rāda' means the 'preparing one,' corresponding somewhat to the Taxōn of *The Assumption of Moses,* and reminding us of John's message to "Prepare the paths of the Lord" (*Mt.* 3.3).

Yasna 46.17 is uncertain, but has all the appearance of admonishing the faithful to sing praises to the Preparer who will stand with Sraosha at the judgment. However this may be, Zarathushtra prays: "Grant, thou greatest ruler, a hearing to the Preparer with the Word" (28.7). The kine lament that so impotent a Preparer is appointed for them (29.9). "Let the 'Preparers' wish for the compensations" (45.7). Whoever prepares the world for Zarathushtra (46.13) shall receive great rewards.

The Saviour.

The Gāthās moreover have the idea of a Helper or Saviour. The word 'saoshyant' is the present participle of the verb 'sao,' to 'profit,' 'gain'; hence it means literally the 'profiting one.' It is applied in the singular to Zarathushtra (45.11; 48.9; 53.2), and in the plural to his helpers (34.13; 46.3; 48.12).

There is also the word 'saregan' (29.3), of uncertain derivation, used by Asha, in conversation with the

shaper of the kine, in reference to there being no
'helper' for the cow. Whoever will take sides with
Zarathushtra will be the Saviour's friend, brother, or
father (45.11).

"The daevas [spirits of the Saviours] are walking
along Asha's path to their rewards" (34.13).

II. Gnostic Echoes.

The Æon or Age.

In close connection with the 'second coming' is the
idea of the 'age,' in Greek 'aiōn,' and Semitic 'ōlam,'
which may well start a short series of extremely curious
Gnostic echoes. The Gāthic divinity, Ahura or the
Lord Mazdāh (and we also have the plural Ahuras, reminding us of Elohīm), was the 'mindful' or 'memorable,' hence knowing one. The Gnostics also founded
their systems on the idea of knowledge.

We have for 'age' or 'eternity' the word 'yav,' and
its dative 'yavōi,' which is used adverbially in the sense
of 'ever.' It may frequently be translated for 'all
eternity' (49.8; 46.11; [41.2; 40.2;] 53.4), or may mean
'always' (49.1; 43.13). So we read in 49.8: "While
both of us wish to be thy messengers for ever in the
age." Or in 53.4: "May Ahura Mazdāh grant thee
[the fruit of Vohu Manah] for all eternity." Or again,
in 28.8: "And for whomsoever thou wouldest grant
Asha (Justice) for all the age of Vohu Manah (Good
Disposition)."

The Plērōma or Fulness.

For Fulness or Plērōma, the corresponding Avestan
word is 'būr' as in 31.21: "From the resources of his
innate glory Ahura Mazdāh shall grant sustained communion and fulness of Health and Immortality."

The Mysteries.

There is also a 'guzra-sangha' or secret teaching, reminding us of the Mysteries of the Kingdom, as in *Yasna* 48.3:

"[The Knower knows] bounteous secrets, which are expressed [in] the doctrine."

The right path is not always the most obvious (31.2). Possibly also the word 'maya' may mean 'mysteries.' Thus (43.2, Mills):

"O Ahura Mazdāh, reveal all those mysteries which thou givest through Asha."

The Word and the Prophet.

'Mathra,' the 'word,' forms 'mathran,' the 'worder,' or prophet (from Gk. 'phēmi,' to say) utterer.

(*a*) Such 'mathras' are directly connected with the gnostic or spiritual Knower (45.3; 51.8; 31.6; 28.5; 43.14; (*b*) 'mathra' appears as a divine word of (magic) efficiency (31.18; 43.14; 44.14; 45.3; 31.6; 29.7); (*c*) as a word of promise (44.17; 28.5); (*d*) as the word of a prophet (50.6).

Its result is choice of the cause of Ahura Mazdāh (28.5) and communion with Ahura Mazdāh (44.17). It provides food for the cattle (29.7); it reveals [a mystery] about Haurvatat and Ameretat and about Vohu Manah (31.6). It is to be 'worked' or practised as Ahura Mazdāh considers and declares it should be (45.3). It has the power to smite down the Druj (44.14), and arouses those who scorn Ahura Mazdāh's teachings (43.14). In short, it is a magic utterance of the 'mathran' (41.5; 50.5,6; 32.13; 28.7; 51.8), or prophet, who seeks a hearing (28.7); it is his word which will be sought by the evil in hell (32.13); it is the utterance of the prophet (51.8) who rejoices at the gift of the spirit to the missionaries.

The Gnostic.

The Gnostic is the 'vidvāo' (past participle of 'vaēd,' to know), the 'knower,' and the expression is applied even to the divinity (48.3): "The Knower, who is one like Thee." So we read (28.5): "When shall I behold Thee, as a knower?" Or (34.9): "Those who drive away Armaiti, prized by the Knower." Or (48.3): "Tell me, O Ahura, for Thou indeed art the Knower." Or again (51.8): "Tell me, O Mazdāh, for the knower should be told." In another place it is said: "Let the Knower (Mazdāh) speak to me the knower." (Cp. also 45.8 and 48.2.)

The Antichrist.

In the Gāthās we find several opponents to divinities. For instance, Angra Mainyu to Spenta Mainyu; Aka Manah to Vohu Manah; to Ar-matay (Docile, Devoted Thought) we have Tare-matay (33.4), who in *Yasna* 60.5 became her direct opponent, meaning 'Thought going beyond'; again, to Tushna-matay (Silent Thought) we have opposed the Paira-matay-ists (32.3) whose name means thinking-up or forward.

The Lie.

In 2 *Thess.* 11.9-12, the great apostasy consists in trusting in the Lie. In the Gāthās the Lie is the Druj (32.3), enumerated along with the proud opponents, 'Paira-matay.'

III. Picturesque Chance Echoes.

Since human nature is the same all the world over, and in all ages, we should be more surprised if we did not find coincidences of emotional expression, than when we do. With considerable interest we may trace in the Gāthās picturesque images with which we have grown very familiar.

Family-Extension.

When we remember: "Whosoever shall do the will of my Father which is in heaven, the same is my brother and sister and mother" (*Mt.* 12.46-50), we cannot fail to be struck by:

"Whoever therefore in the future scorns the daēvas and the men who scorn him [Zarathushtra], and all others except whoever is devoted to him, shall be considered by the bounteous individuality of Zarathushtra, who is saviour and master of the house, as his friend, brother or father, O Ahura Mazdāh."

Dives and Lazarus.

Nor can we avoid thinking of the Parable of Dives and Lazarus when we read (32.13):

"Through which Xshathra-power [of the above Asha, Justice] Grehma will be degraded to hell, the dwelling of the Worst Mind, [wherein dwell] the destroyers of this life; and [then], O Mazdāh, he will complain, being moved by a desire for the message of thy Prophet, who then however will keep him from beholding Asha (Justice)." Or again (53.8): "[On the contrary let the malefactors through whom are effected] murder and bloody deed, let them all be abandoned, and cry upwards in vain."

The Reward of Apostles.

Another picturesque coincidence is that of the Galilean Apostles' very human and comprehensible cry: "Behold, we have forsaken all and followed thee; what shall we have therefor?" (*Mt.* 19.27-29). If the Apostles of the Lord did not hesitate to ask this question, can we find fault with Zarathushtra for not being

insensible to personal reward? "The saviour would like
to know how his compensation should be [given] to him"
(48.9); he would know also, of lesser things, when he
shall receive the reward promised him, of ten mares and
stallions and one camel, together with Haurvatat and
Ameretat (44.18).

The Loss of One's Own Soul.

"Thou fool! This night shall thy soul be required
of thee; then whose shall those things be which thou hast
provided?" (*Lk.* 12.20). Not very unlike the thought
in these inspired words are those of the Gāthist:

"The Karapans, through their political power join
the Kavays,

"To destroy the [second] life of men through evil
deeds;

"[Fools! Whereas] their own souls and spirits will
terrify them,

"When they shall come to the Sifter's bridge of
judgment;

"As companions they will be admitted to the Home
of the Druj for ever" (46.11).

Ears to Hear.

"He that hath ears to hear, let him hear," cried the
Utterer of the Parables of the Kingdom (*Mt.* 11.15);
the strong Singer of the Gāthās cries:

"Listen with your ears to the best [information];
behold with [your] sight, and with [your] mind" (30.2).

Was, Is, and Shall Be.

The expression of eternity, 'was, is, and shall be,'
common in all lands, is found also in the Gāthās, as
for instance (29.4): "The Lord knows all the plans
achieved in the past, and [to be] in the future, and it
is he who decides about the present ones; it is whatever

he wills that happens to us."   (Cp. also 33.10; 57.22.)

The First and Last.

We are reminded of the Alpha and Omega (*Rev.* 22.13), when we read in 31.8: "Then Zarathushtra understood that Mazdāh was both the first and youngest of creation."

The Poor.

Zarathushtra seems to have been poor himself; he prays for ten mares and a camel (44.18), and he ascribes his failure to his poverty in flocks (46.2). No doubt this caused his sympathy with the poor, for whom he prays (53.9):

"What Lord will destroy the Drujist and establish the Kingdom by which, O Mazdāh, Thou wilt give to the justly living poor that better [part]?"

And again (34.5): "Have You the power to protect your poor?"

Whosoever Will.

"Whosoever will," cries the Revelator (22.17). Compare this with *Yasna* 43, which opens with the salutatory: "Success to me, to you, and to whosoever will"; while *Yasna* 30 begins in a style somewhat reminding us of the Sermon on the Mount:

"But thus, O [souls] desirous [of hearing], I will utter (1) those things worthy of being remembered by the expert-knower; (2) the praises for Ahura, and (3) hymns [worthy] of Vohu Manah, and (4) things well remembered by the aid of Asha. Listen with your ears to the best [information]; behold with [your] sight, and with [your] mind;

"Man by man, each for his own person, distinguishing between both confessions, before the great crisis. Consider again!"

Come Quickly!

In the last verse but one of the Gāthās, Zarathushtra invokes peace on the believers' villages, peace which is to be produced by the slaughter of the enemy, adding "and may it come soon!" Compare this with the great cry for the coming of the Prince of Peace: "Even so, Lord Jesus, come quickly!" (*Rev.* 22.17,20).

Pity on the Misled Crowds.

As Jesus felt compassion for the misled crowds (*Mt.* 9.36) which the Jews hindered Him from calling to Himself, so Zarathushtra opens one of his immortal hymns with a poignant expression of his grief:

"Ever has Bendva hindered me [and proved himself the] greater [of us two], when I, O Mazdāh, was trying-to-satisfy the misled [crowds] through Asha (Justice)."

IV. Minor Echoes.

Angel or Apostle.

The word 'dūta' (168) which comes from 'dav,' to send off, should strictly represent 'apostle' (Gk. 'apostellō'). But 'dūtya' (204) means 'message,' which would represent the Greek 'aggelía,' while 'aggelos,' the Greek for 'messenger,' is the English 'angel.' So both shades of meaning fall together.

'Fraēshta' is derived from 'fra' and 'aēsh,' or 'off' and to 'get-into-hasty-motion'; it would thus be more closely rendered 'emissary' or 'apostle,' not 'angel'; while 'vat,' to 'announce,' which would exactly represent 'aggelos,' is only used in the passive about an event, and not of the function of a person. Perhaps then it would be wiser to render these words into English by the less familiar 'messenger.'

"May we be thy messengers, to hold off those who hostilely deceive thee" (32.1 [168]).

"The message of thy prophet, who will keep them from beholding Asha" (32.13 [204]).

"As we [Frashaoshtra and Zarathushtra] wish to be thy messengers for-ever-in-the-age" (49.8 [738]).

The Token.

Again we may notice 'daxshta,' meaning a 'token,' 'pledge,' or 'earnest,' and compare it with 2 *Cor.* 1.22; 5.9; *Eph.* 1.14. Thus:

"And do thou, O Mazdāh, within [the nature of] both contending parties set satisfaction as a token [of the accuracy of my prophecy of the judgment by]

"The metal, molten through thy red fire [which as a sifter] shall

"Harm the Drujist, but profit the Ashaist" (51.9).

The Spiritual Israel.

It was suggested by Herodotus that the Magi were a tribe. No doubt they were at first; but the threat of Zarathushtra to the newly married couple (53.7) that if they ever abandoned the Magian cause they would cry 'Woe!' at the end of life, suggests that it had become already a religious organisation which could be left at will.

The Robe of Heaven.

The Most Bounteous Spirit wears the adamantine heavens as a robe (30.5). "As a vesture shalt thou fold them up," sings the writer of *The Epistle to the Hebrews* (1.12).

The Mediation.

It is well known that in the Gāthās Ahura Mazdāh never does anything directly, but only through some one of the other Ahuras, as agent. So for instance in 33.12,

Zarathushtra prays that Ahura Mazdāh may grant him through Armaiti, vitality; through Spenta Mainyu, strength; through Ada, retribution; through Asha, might; and through Vohu Manah, compensation.

The Divine Inheritance.

The Gāthās, as well as the New Testament (*Eph.* 1.14, ff), promise man a divine inheritance ('raēxenah') and epoch of judgment, of rewards or punishments (30.11). So also, of Haurvatat and Ameretat (33.10). "Can they be faithful who through their teachings turn into sorrow sure inheritances for Vohu Manah?" (34.7) asks the sorrowing prophet, reminding us of Elijah, who thought himself left the only faithful soul (1 *Kings* 19.10).

The Giving of the Spirit.

Zarathushtra would have the new settlers act as missionaries (50.3). Nor is he jealous of them, any more than Elijah was jealous of Elisha's double portion of the spirit, or Moses of the elders of the congregation when Jahvè spoke unto them also. "The prophet rejoices through the word which is told the expert knower" (51.8).

Foolish and Wise Virgins.

"I will tell you how to sift the clever from the foolish" (46.15).

"By uttering praises of the Preparer who will stand for them together with obedience,

"Who will sift the clever from the foolish" (46.17).

This sundering of the wise from the foolish reminds us in a distant way of the Parable of the Wise and Foolish Virgins.

The Faithful.

The word 'aredrā' means 'trustworthy' or 'faithful'

(48.8; 50.4,8) ; it is applied both to men and God.

"Are they faithful to Thee, O Ahura Mazdāh, who, though they know of Vohu Manah, turn the difficulties of traditionally inherited doctrine to their own advantage?" (34.7).

"[Zarathushtra] who is faithful like Thee, O Mazdāh" (43.3).

"Who is the faithful one, who first taught" (46.9) ?

"O Frashaoshtra, go thou with the faithful to where we both desire to be with the Beloved" (46.16).

"Will thy realm please the faithful [believers]" (48.8) ?

"Zarathushtra hears the faithful entering their new homes singing with joy" (50.4).

"Zarathushtra will encompass Asha with the reverence of the faithful" (50.8).

"God is faithful" (1 Cor. 1.9), Paul does not hesitate to say, nor does the Gāthist.

Faith and Works.

Not less in Zarathushtra's day than in the days of Paul and James, were human hearts torn with the ever recurring question of faith and works. The Gāthist, no doubt in some moment of despair, cried:

"Is the message I am about to proclaim genuine? Does Armaiti (Loving Devotion) support Asha (Justice) through deeds" (44.6) ?

The End Known to God.

The "end of the Lord" (Jas. 5.11) is the end of human actions, known to, and brought about by, the Lord.

"The knower is not to commit any of these deeds of violence, whose [fatal] end, thou, O Ahura Mazdāh, best knowest" (32.7).

The Better Part.

The word ('vahyō') 'better' is in the Gāthās frequently used absolutely in a way which it is difficult to translate in any way other than the 'better part.' For instance:

"O Maidyaimangha! Zarathushtra, who has given his daughter Chisti, to this Yamaspa, and who as having known through his spirit the [first] life, is again wishing [the second], says that thou [hast] the better [part] of life, having [practised] the decrees of Mazdāh through thy deeds" (51.19).

The Beloved, 'David.'

There is very little love, apparently, in the Gāthās, but we have the word 'ushtā,' meaning 'at will' (from 'var'), used as an exclamation: Success to you! hail! (33.10: 43.1; 41.4; 51.16; 51.8; 30.11), which in 46.16 appears as follows to mean the 'desired,' the 'beloved':

"O Frashaoshtra Hvogva, go thou with the faithful to where we both desire to be, with those who are beloved (or desired)."

Jeshurun.

There is in the Gāthās a strange similarity between the name and office of Geūsh Urvan, the Soul of the Kine, the representative of the whole bovine creation, and the representative of Israel, Jeshurun (*Dt.* 32.15; 33.5,26; *Is.* 44.2) who "waxed fat and kicked"—inevitably suggesting a bovine creature. The resemblance goes further. Jeshurun is said to belong to the Lord, and in *Yasna* 29 the kine come to the divinities with a complaint demanding protection, and ending with a profession of devotion. As Jeshurun is the chosen of the Lord, so Geūsh Urvan represents in the midst of human violence the chosen, accepted nature of pious

devotion. The lateness of the books in which Jeshurun
appears, suggests that not impossibly the name might
have become familiar to the Jews when the Persian
Cyrus freed them from captivity; and the Jews' friendliness to his religion might easily be inferred from their
calling Cyrus the Anointed or Messiah of the Lord.
This occurs in *Is.* 45.1, very near the Jeshurun reference,
Is. 44.2.

No other reasonable derivation has ever been attempted; Cheyne's arbitrary and mechanical juggling
of words is the counsel of despair, and purely individual
and fanciful. Arbitrary interpretations, such as the
'Straight' by Aquila, Symmachus, and Theodotion, do
not give the least explanation of why the 'Just' or
'Straight' one should wax fat or kick. The above suggestion therefore deserves at least thoughtful consideration.

We may close this hasty review of echoes that happen to be familiar to us, with a literary similarity that
is all the more striking from the fact, that from its very
nature it can be no more than a coincident expression
of human nature guided by instincts more or less divine.
For we must not fail to note that, though the Gathic
hymn to which we refer is beautiful, it cannot hope to
pose as a rival to the sublimity of the mystic utterance
into connection with which we bring it.

Yasna 33 (except the first three verses, which
complete the subject of *Yasna* 32), contains a high-
priestly prayer which reminds us not only as a whole,
but even in its structure, of the parting prayer of Jesus
in *John* 17. We are forced, however, to make one trans-
position, before we can get an entirely similar outline
of prayer:

First, for self-glorification (*Y*. 33.4-7; *J*. 17.1-8).

Second, for protection of his followers (*Y*. 33.11-14; *J*. 17.9-19).

Third, for universal conversion (*Y*. 33.8-10; *J*. 17.20-26).

The Gāthic prayer then closes with a touching eucharistic oblation of the Gāthist's own being:

"As oblation, Zarathushtra would bring the life of his own body, the first fruits of his good thoughts, deeds and utterances, his obedience, and whatever power be his, [to offer them] to the mindful Mazdāh and to the justice [of] Asha!"

PART IV.

Dictionary *and* Grammar.

Abbreviations.

Numbers followed by S *or* P indicate that person of Singular or Plural.

Numbers following Pr indicate a particular one of the many collateral forms of the Present.

A, with verbs, active voice.
A, Acc, with nouns, accusative
Abl, ablative case.
Adj, adjective, part of speech.
Aor, aorist tense, past action.
Aug, formed with an augment
B, Bartholomae.
Comp, comparative degree.
Conj, conjunction.
D, Dat, dative case.
D, Du, dual gender.
Des., desiderative mood.
F, feminine gender.
G, genitive case.
I, Inf, infinitive of a verb.
Im, Imp, imperfect tense.
Imp, Imp-at, imperative.
Ind, indicative mood.
Inj, injunctive.
In Comp, in composition.
In, Ins, Is, instrumental case
K, conjunctive voice or mood.
L, locative case.
M, *m*, masculine gender.

M, Mills.
M, *with verbs*, middle voice.
N, *n*, neuter gender.
N, nominative case.
O, optative mood.
P, Pl, plural number.
P, Pr, present tense form.
  When followed by a number, this shows which of the many collateral present-forms it is.
Pass, passive voice.
Pf, perfect tense.
Part, participle, which appears in the following forms, which are also declined, taking case, number, and gender:
PP, PrPa, present participle.
PfP, perfect *or* past participle.
Pron, pronoun.
S, Sg, singular number.
Su, subjunctive mood.
Sup. superlative degree.
s-Aor, an Aorist with an s-stem.
V, vocative.

NOTE. The necessarily hurried choice of the designation *Dictionary* was since much regretted, as too pompous. It was hit on to indicate the following attempt at complete references.

A

a-, *in composition,* not, without.

ā, also, towards, at, in (48.7), on, upon, off, until, near, on account of [*References incomplete*].

ā-baxshō.hvā, 33.10, to distritute, —baxsh.

a-bi.frā, 33.13, unique, without equal (-a)

ā-būshtīs, 43.8, developing, (-ay)—bav.

ābyā, 32.15, *pron.* by the two.

ab.yastā, 53.5, zealous seeking for (-ay)—yat.

acishta, worst, *sup. of* aka, bad. 30.4,5,6; 32.10,13; 33.4.

a.cistā, he is considerate, 51.11,—3S, kaēt.

adā, then. 29.2, 30.10.

ādā, *f,* retribution. 33.11,12, 49.1; adāis, 48.1.

ā-dam, house, 48.7, 49.10.—dam.

ādāna, retribution, 30.7,—ādā.

ā-darê, 43.15, 3PPrA; a-das, 46.5; ā-dāt, 31.18. 51.14;—dā.

a-dāthascā, 46.15; -emcā, 46.17; those who are not clever, the stupid—dātha.

adê, 44.4, under, beneath.

ā-debaomā, *m,* 30.6, delusion.

ā-demānē, 32.15, from, or to the dwelling—deman.

ā-dishtis, *f,* 44.8, purpose [-ay].

ā-dīvyeiñtī, 44.13, they strive, —dyav.

ā-drêñg, 29.3, AccPl of ādra, dependent.

a-drujyañt-ō, 31.15, deceptive.

a-dvaēsha, 29.3, not harming, innocuous.

advān, *m,* way. 34.13, 44.3; 31.2, advāe, NS.

aēibyō, *pron.,* to, *or* from these, 28.10, 29.10, 30.8, 31.1, 32.2,12, 34.8,9 43.6, 44.20, 45.3, 46.12.

aēm, *pron.,* 29.8, this one, NS.

aēnah, *n,* violence, 30.8, 31.15, 32.6,7,8; 34.4.

aēnah, *adj.,* maleficent, 30.8, 31.13,15, 34.4.

aēnanhē, *I,* to commit violence, 32.16, 46.7,8.

āenhāmā, we may be, OPfA of ah, to be; 32.1, 49.8.

āenhan, *m*, mouth, 31.3.

āenharê, they may be, *or* were, OPfA of ah, to be, 33.10; 44.20; 45.7, 51.22

aēs, to be master over; isē, 3SPM, 50.1; isāi, 28.4, 43.9, 50.11; isōyā, 1SPM, 43.8.

āescā, *pron.*, one of these two, 30.3.

aēsh, to seek, desire; aēshasā, seeking, 53.9. P ishasā, *which see: also* pait-ishā*t*.

aēsha, potent, able, 28.4; 43.10; 44.17; 45.7.

aēsham, *pron.*, of these *or* those, 30.7,8; 32.7,8; 34.1.

aēshema, *m*, fury, rapine, 29.1, 44.20, 48.7, 49.4; *personified as* demon thereof, 29.2, 30.6, 48.12.

aēurus, shimmering, shining; 50.10; *from* aērav?

aēvā, aēvō, single, only, 29.6,8. (-a)

ā-frashta, counselled with; 51.11—fras.

ā-fseratus, compensations, 51.4. AccPl (-tav)—feseratū.

afshmān-ī, harm, trouble, 46.17, *n*, AccPl.

a-fshuyant-ō, non-fatteners (of cattle), nomads, 49.4—fshav.

ā-gema*t*, 44.8, 3SPrM *of* gam.

a-gushta, unheard, unbearable, 31.1—gaosh.

a-*g*zao.nvamnem not decreasing, 28.3, AccS.

āh, *or* êeāh, *n*, mouth, 28.11; 31.3, 47.2?

ah, to be, *irregular; see under each form.*

ahav, that.

ā-hêmusta, repulsive, 46.4.

ahī, thou art, 32.7, 43.7, 47.3, 51.3—ah. 34.11

ā-hishāyā, they oppress, 29.1—hā(y).

ahmāi, to me, *or* this, 29.3, 30.2,7; 31.6, 43.1 44.16,19; 45.5,10; 46.8,13,18t 47.1,3; 49.2,3; 50.2,3, 51.6,19.

ahmāibyācā, to *or* with us, 28.6.

ahmākêñg, our, 32.8, 45.9.

ahmā*t*, *or* ahma*t*, by *or* from this, *or* us, AblS, 34.9, 44.13, 45.11, 47.4, 51.10. Henceforward, 33.6.

ahmī, I am, 32.8, 46.2, (ah).—To this, (a), *or* me, 43.6.—51.12?

ā-hōithōi, *I*, to subject, oppress, 32.14—hā(y).

ahū, a*n*hū, *m*, a*n*ūhi, *f*, master, mistress, 29.6, 32.11.

ahūm, life, 30.6, 31.20, 34.15, 45.1, 46.11,13, 51.19, 53.5,6;
—AccS of aꞑhav, *m*.

ahūm.bis, life-healing [B], 31.19, 44.2,16.

ahura, *m*, master, 29.2,10, 53.9. Divine lord, *see* Table of Occurrence of Divine Names. *Polytheistic plural*, 30.9, 31.4, 33.11

ā-hu.shitay, dwelling in a good place, 30.10,—shay.

ahvā, we both were, *or* might be, 29.5,—1DPrA, ah.

ahyā, of this, 28.1 29.10 31.12 32.1,13,14 34.6,9,10 43.3,9 44.15,19 45.3,4,6 46.8 47.1,3,5
48.4,10 49.1,2 53.7.

aḥyāi, ahyāi, to this, 31.9,10 46.19 48.6.

ahvā *or* aꞑhvā, *f*, life. *AP* ahvāe, 28.2; *LP* ahvāhū, 51.9.

ā-ḥvaithya, *adj*, personally, 33.7.

aibī, upon, towards, to, unto, 31.13 32.15 43.7 51.9,19

aibī-bairishtem, most bearable, 51.1, (AccS of -a)—bar.

aibī-dereshta, visible, 50.5 *adj*.

aibī-dereshtā, clear sight, 31.2 *f*, (-tay).

aibī-gemen, they come to, *or* arrive at, 46.11,—gam.

aibī-jamyat, he may come to, *or* arrive at, 43.3;—gam.

aibī-mōist, he may send along, 46.12,—maēth.

āidūm, come! 33.7,—*Imperative*, ay.

ainīm, reciprocal, 53.5,—GP1 anya.

aipī, likewise, also, 30.11 32.3,8 48.5.

aipī-cithīt, in the future, 29.4.

aipī-débāvayat, he may again delude, *or* deceive, 31.17—dab.

aipī-zath, 'again-birth', re-generation, 48.5, *m*.

airyaman, noble, peer, *m*, 32.1 33.3,4 46.1 49.7.

āis, *adv*, consequently, 28.11 31.2 44.11.

āis, *pron*, with these, 53.8.

ā-itē, to go to, 31.9,—*Inf* of ay.

ā-itī, that which is now going, the present, 31.14.—3SKA of ay.

aithīs-cīt 32.16, *or* āithis, 48.9, destruction,—NS āthay, *f*.

a-jēn, they may drive, 48.10,—3SPrA, gan.

ā-jimat, he may come, 43.12,—gam.

a-jyāitim.cā, non-life, non-existence, 30.4,—AccS, -tay, *f*.

a-gzaonvamnem, not decreasing, 28.3,—AS, -na, *adj*.

aka, bad; *comp*, ashyah; *sup*, acishta. 30.3 32.5,10 33.2,4 43.5 45.1 46.17
47.5 49.11 51.6.

ikā, manifest, open, cleared, 48.8 50.4 51.13.

ikā-stēñg, 50.2, 'open-standing', cleared land, farms (?). *Bartholomae* makes of it the eschatological revealing of secrets.

i-keretis, message, news, 48.2,—NS, -tay, *f.*

ıkōyā, threat, 51.8, *f.*

i-manaṇhā, purpose, 49.6, —*n*, NPl. -ha.

ımeretāt, immortality, *f.* 32.5 33.8 34.1,11 44.17,18 45.5,7,10 47.1 48.1 51.7.

i-mōyastrā baranā, company-bearing, associates, 30.9,—NPl.

ınā, with this, 28.5.

ın-aēsha, impotent, 29.9 46.2.

ın-afshmanam, harm-lessness,*B*; immaterial, 46.17,—GPl, *n.*

ınāis (ā), thereby, 28.9 32.15 53.6,8.

ı-nasat, 53.7; a.nāshē, 44.14,—nas, to perish, disappear.

ıñgra, hostile, inimical, 43.15 44.12 45.2 48.10.

ınhācā, I may be, 50.11,—1SPrSu, ah.

ınhaitī, he, she, it (is, was, shall) may be, 30.11 31.5,22 56.3 53.7 —ah.

ınhat, he, she, it might be, 3SOPf of ah; 29.4,9 30.4,7,9 31.5,6,9,16 32.2 33.3 44.12,19 45.3 47.4 48.4,9 49.7 53.5,7.

ınhen, they might be, 31.1,4,14 48.12 49.11.

ınhēus, *GS of* aṇhav, *m,* life.　31.8 32.13 33.1 34.6 43.3,5 44.2,8 45.2,3,4 46.3,10 48.2,6 50.11 51.6.

ınhus, same as above, 28.11 30.4.

ınhvascā, of a master, 32.11.

ınman, firmness, eternity, 30.7 44.20 45.10,—*n.*

ıñtare, 33.7; añtarē, 49.3; among.

ıñtare-caraitī, he between-makes, procures, 51.1,—3SKA, **kar**

ıñtare-mruyē, to 'swear-off', renounce, 49.3,—*I*, mrav.

ınus-haxs, successive, 31.12.

ınya, other, 29.1 34.7 44.3,11 45.11 46.7 50.1 53.5.

ınyāthā, otherwise, 51.10.

ıoderescā, of cold, 51.12,—GS, aodar, *n.*

ıog, to preach, aojāi, 50.11, *I*; aojī, 43.8, 1SPr; aogedā, 32.10, 3SPr; pairy.aogzā, 43.12, 2SPr.

ıogō, with strength, 29.10, *Is. of* aogah, *n.*

ıojaṇhā, 50.3; aojaṇhō, 43,4, physical strength,—aojah, *n.*

ıojyāe, stronger, 34.8, *adj, comp. of* aojah, Sup. aojishtō, 29.3.

aojōi, to commit, *I*, 32.7.

aojōṅghvat, being strong, 28.6 31.4 43.8,16 ; aojōnhvañtem, 34.4—aojahvañt.

aojy.aēshū, worthy of renown, 46.12, *LP*. 34.8, -āe, comp. -jah

aorāca, downwards, 53.7.

aoshō, the destructions, 49.1—AccP, -ah, *n.*

apā, off, 33.4.

ā-paithī, on the path, 50.4—pathī, *f.*

āpanāis, with attainments, 28.10—*n*, -a, IsPl. ap.

apānō, may reach, 33.5—ap.

a-paourvīm, not as at first, as never before, 28.3.—parav.

apara, later, hinder, 31.20, 45.11—*comp. of* apā.

apascā, waters; 51.7,—AccPl, āp, *f.*

apa.yañt-ā, holding off, 32.9,—Ins.S, PrP, yam.

apa.yeitī, to take away, 32.11—*I*, yam.

apēma, last, hindermost, 30.4 43.5 44.19 45.3 48.4 51.6,14 53.7—*sup.,* apā.

api.vaitī, it was announced, *or* promised, 44.18—3SPr, vat.

apō, off, 32.9—*same as* apā.

apō, of water, 44.4—GS āp, *f.*

ar, to arouse, *I*, arōi, 33.9, 50.5; ārem, 1SPr, 43.10; uz.āresh-vā, 33.12, īratū, 53.8. *Imp-at.*

ā-radāe, preparing, 28.7,—NS, -ah, *adj, from* rad.

a.rapā, come hither! 49.1, —*imp-at. of* ā-rap.

āredat, prospers, 50.11—3SPrKo, ared.

aredra, faithful, 34.7 43.3 46.9,16 48.8 50.4,8.

arejat, is worthy, of value, 50.10—3SPr, areg.

arêm, properly, 44.8 45.11 51.14.

ārem, have I come, 43.10, —*contraction for* ā-erem, *from* ar.

arêm-pithwā, mid-day, noon, 44.5, *f.*

aretha, duty, affair, 33.8 43.13 44.5—*n.*

ārezvā, the just deeds, 33.1—NPn, ā-erezvan.

ārmaitī, an Ahura, 'adaptable thought,' love; *Mills:* alert and ready mind to act. —*From* arêm-maitī, proper thought ?

ā-rōi, to grant, 33.9 34.3 50.5—*I*, ar.

ārōis, sorrow, grief, 51.4, GS; 14, AccPl— āray, *f.*

arshnavaitīs, be-stallioned, 44.18—Acc.Pl.f. of -vañt, PresPart.

as, he was, 31.9, 34.8; ascīt, there would be, 46.18—*impf,* ah.

asashutā, he arrives at, 48.1,—3SPrM *of as.*

asayāe, the two parties, 31.2—only in Dual; G of *asa, m.*

ā-sêñdā, they effect, 51.14—Pr, sand.

asênō, the stone (-quarried) heavens, 30.5,—AccPl, asan, *m.*

asha, *n,* justice, right; *or,* an Ahura. *References incomplete.—*
   ashahyā, G; ashāi, D; ashem, Acc; ashā*t,* Abl.

ā-shaêitī, dwells with, 43.3,—Pr, shay.

ashao.xshayañtāe, the Ashaist discipline, *or,* life, 33.9, —gen.du.
   of -añ*t, from* ashāvan *and* xshāy.

ashāvan, a follower *or* devotee of Asha, an Ashaist. ashaunō,
   gen.sing.; -ē, -aēcā, 43.4, dat.; -*a*m, 49.10, gen.pl. 30.4,11
   31.14,17,20; 32.10,11; 33.1,3,9; 43. 4,8,15; 44.12; 45.7; 46.5,
   6,9,14; 47.4,5; 48.2; 49.10; 51.9; 53.4,9.

ashibyā, to, *or* with both eyes, 32.10, —dat.dual *of* ash, *n.*

ashis, (nom.sg.) compensation; an Ahura, 28.4,7 31.4 33.13 34.12 43.4,5,
   12,16 46.10 48.8,9 50.3,9 51.5,10,21.—ashay, *f.* ashōis, gen.sg.. ashīm,
   acc.sg. ashī, ashicā, inst.sg., ashīs, acc.pl. ashivāe, 51.5, consonantal dual, acc.

ashōis, *see above.*

ashtō, to find shelter, 51.12;—*I,* as.

ash*y*ah, worse, *comp. of* aka, bad. -ō, 51.6, acc.pl; -ascā,
   48.4, gen.sg. *or* nom., acc. pl.

ā-sh*y*as, dwelling with, 47.5,—nom.sg.pres.part. shay.

a-sīshtay, promise, *f,* -ā, loc.sg.. 30.10; -īs, acc.pl., 44.9.—sāh

a-sīshtīm, 34.4, acc.sg. *either* of above (B); *or* of superlative of
   āsav, swift, (M). *See* āsū.

ā-sketīm, attachment, 44.17, acc.sg. āskitay, from hak.

asnam, of days, 46.3. 50.10—gen.pl. azan, *n.*

asnā*t,* from near, 45.1,—adverbial ablative of a*s*na, near.

aspāe, mares, 44.18,—acc.pl. of aspa, *f.*

a-spêñcā, 45.9; -cī*t,* 34.7, misfortunes,—acc.pl. aspā, *n.*

asperezatā, he strives for, 31.16,—Pr, spare*z.*

a-srushtay, disobedience; -īm, acc.sg. 33.4; -tā, loc.sg. 43.12;
   -tōis, gen.sg. 44.13.—srav.

a-srūdūm, badly heard, evil reputed, 32.3.—srav, passive.

a-srvātem, they both heard, *or,* became conscious, 30.3,—3 dual, augmented, srav.

asta, hate,— -tā, ins.sg., 34.8; -ascā, acc.pl. 44.14; -āi, dat. 46.18.

astāi, to make enemies of, 46.18—inf. of ans ? *or* dative above?

astay, companion,— -is, nom.sg. 31.22; -īm, acc.sg; 33.2; -ayō, nom. or acc. pl. 46.11, 49.11.

ā-stīs, places, worlds, 43.3,—acc.pl. stay, *f.*

astvat, corporeal, 28.2 31.11 34.14 43.3,16— -vañt, ast, bone.

āsū, swift, 44.4,—ac.pl. āsav. *adj.*

a-sūnā, effective, compelling, 28.10,—nom.pl. -na.

a-sūrahyā, im-potent, weak, 29.9,—gen.sg. sūra.

at, āat, but, thereupon, *frequent.*

athā, so, thus, therefore, 29.1,4 31.18 32.6 34.6,7 44.6 51.16 53.3,5.

athrā, there, 31.12 46.16.

āthrā, through fire, 31.3,19 47.6 51.9,—ins.sg. ātar, *m.*

āthrē, to fire, 43.9,—dat.sg. ātar.

āthris, misfortune, 46.8,—nom.sg. āthray, *f.*

āthrō, of fire, 43.4,—gen.sg. ātar, *m.*

ātrêm, fire, 34.4,—acc.sg. ātar.

aurunā, ? wild, swift, (aurva) red (M) 34.9.

aurvatō, of ardent, *or* speedy, 50.7—gen.sg. -vañt.

avā, down, 33.6, 44.13; avō, 30.10.

avā, with that, 44.17, ins. sg.

avāe, those, 43.4, acc.pl.

a-vaēnā, behold! investigate! 46.2; a-vaēnatā, 30.2—imp.vaēna

avaēsham, of those, 29.3, gen.pl. 'of those not one understands.' i

avaētās, curses, crying of woe, 31.20—acc.pl. -tāt; from avōi.

avāis, with those, 32.15, 44.15,—ins.pl.

avam, of those, 44.19,—gen.pl.

avāmī, I strive, 44.7,—av.

avanhā, with help, 51.5,—ins.sg. avah, *n.*

ava-nhānē, in the consummation, 33.5,—loc.sg. -na.*n.*

avanhē, to help, 50.7 dat.sg. avah, *n.*

avanhem, help, 34.4,—acc.sg. *above, as adj. m.*

avanhō, of help, 49.12, 50.1,—gen.sg. *above.*

ava-pastōis, to fall down, 44.4,—inf. pat.

avarĕ, help, 29.11,—acc. avar, *n, same as* avah.

avarenāe, of both confessions, *or* beliefs, 30.2—GDDu -na, *m.*

a-vāstryō, the non-pasturer, nomad; 31.10,—NS of -a, *adj.*

avat, so much, 28.4; *correlate to* yavat.

avat, that, 29.10 31.6,15,16 49.12.

ava-zazat, they are driven off, 34.9,—zā(y).

avĕm, to be guardian, 49.10; inf. av.

ā-veretō, in the conviction, 45.1,—loc.sg. -ay, *f.*

āvis, manifestly, 33.7.

āvīshyā, manifest, 31.13, 50.5,—ins.sg, -a, *adj.*

āvō, help, 29.9 30.10 32.14,—nom, acc.pl, avah, *n.*

avōi, woe! 45.3, 53.6,7,—*interjection.*

ā-xsō, I ask instruction, 46.2,—xsā.

axshtat, they procure, find, 51.4,—stā.

ay, to go, inf. itē, 43.13, āitē, 31.9; pres.part. acc.sg. ayañtem,
46.5; imperat. āidūm, 33.7, idī, 46.16; āyōi, (ā-iyōi) I come
to, 31.2; āitī, it goes, present things, KA, 31.14; āyat, 31.20,
āyāt, 46.6, he goes to; ayenī, 46.1, 50.9; ayēnī 34.6, I go.

ayāe, of both these, 30.5,6 31.2,10 33.9 44.15.—gen.dual.

ayamaitē, inflicts. holds, 31.13,—yam.

ayanhā, with metal, 30.7, 32.7 51.9,—ins.sg. ayah, *n.*

ayaptā, with felicity, 28.2, ins.sg; felicities, acc.pl. 28.7, 53.1.

ayārĕ, the days, 43.2,7, acc.pl. ayar, *n.*

ayĕm, this, 44.12,—nom.sg. *like* āēm.

i.yesē, they desire, 53.6, yās.

ayū, lasting, 31.20,—acc.sg. ayav, *adj, n.*

azāthā, you may drive, *or* go. 50.7,—zā.

azdā, knowingly, certainly, 50.1, *adv.*

azdyāi, to reach to, 51.17,—inf. *as.*

azem, I, 44.7,11,—nom.sg.

azĕm, 43.14, *should read* (B) a-zĕ, to go, arouse, inf. zā.

azī, both calving, pregnant, bearing, 46.19,—nom.du., azī, *adj.f.*

azīm, calving, 44.6,—acc.sg. *same.*

azī, 31.18, *is* ā-zī, *particles.*

azus, zeal, 53.7,—NS, āzav, *m,*

ā-zūtay, *f,* fat. solid food; -itiscā, NS,49.5. -tōis, gen.sg. 29.7

azyāe, of calving, pregnant, bearing, 29.5, 34.14, gen.sg.

B

baga, piece, lot, *n*; -ā, acc.pl. **bāgem,** 51.1, acc.sg.

bairyāeñtē, may they both be borne, 32.15,—bar.

banayen, they will afflict with disease, 30.6,—ban.

baodañtō, to consider, 30.2,—*inf. as imperative.*

baraitī, 31.12, 50.6, they raise; **baretū,** 33.9, let me bring up; **baranā,** 30.9, bearing,—bar.

barātā, brother, 45.11,—nom.sg. *m, for* brātar.

bavat, 28.11, 30.9, it becomes; **bavaitī,** 30.10, it may become; **bavaiñtī,** 33.10, the are becoming,—bav. (bvañticā, būzdyāi)

baxshtā, he shares, 31.10; **baxshaitī,** he shall share, 47.5,50.3, 3SKA.—baxsh. (ā-baxsh).

bêedus, 53.4, ?

Bêñdva, a daēvic oppcnent of Zarathushtra, 49.1, NS; 49.2, GS.

berexdam, prized, valued, AS, 32.9, 34.9, 44.7, 51.17; VS, 48.5, -ē.

būjem, penance, 'loosing,— AS, **būg,** *f, from* baog. 31.13.

būmyāe, of the earth, 32.3,—GS, **būmī,** *f.*

būnōi, to the ground, 53.7,—DS, **būna,** *m.*

būrōis, of fulness, 31.21; GS, **būray,** *f.*

būzdyāi, to develop, 44.17,—bav, *inf. of* s-*aorist.*

bvañticā, those who are becoming, 45.7,—bav.

byeñtē, they are intimidating, 34.8,—3PIP, bay.

C

-cā, and,—is added to other words.

cagedō, offering, affording, 51.20.— AP, cag*ed*, *adj.*

cagvā*e*, offering, granting, 46.2,—NS, cagvah, *adj.*

caraitī, he makes, 51.1, 3SKA; carānī, I shall practise; 44.17—kar, to make, *or* do.

carā*t*, he is going on, 46.4; caratascā, both driven along, 51.12, 3DPrA,—kar, to move along.

car*ekerethrā*, thoughts, 29.8,—APl. *n*, -a.

*c*ashmainī, in his eye, 31.8, 45.8, LS; cashm*ēñg*, eyes, 31.13, cashm*am*, eyes, 50.10, APl,—cashman, *n.*

*c*āxnar*ê*, they desire, 44.13,—kan, 2 Pf.

*c*axrayō, transforming into. 34.7,—NPl, caxray, *f.*

*c*ayascā, who, 45.5,—NPl, kā.

*c*azdōñ*n*hvad*e*byō, being enlightened, 31.3, DAblPl; cazdēñgh-vañt*êm*, enlightened, 44.5, AS.—?

*c*īcā, and why, 47.5. *See* cya*n*ha*t.*

*c*īcīthwā, through thoughtful, caring, 43.2—IsS, cīcītav; ka*ê*t.

*c*ikōiter*es*, they have consulted, 32.11,—ka*ê*t, 1Pf.

*c*ina*s*, thou hast destined, 44.6,—kaēsh, 3SPrA.

*c*invatō, of sifting, 46.10,11; 51.13,—GS, PrPart. kay. -vañ*t.*

*c*is? who? 31.18, 43.7.

*c*istā, seeks, prays, promises, 51.5; kaēsh, 3SPrM.

*c*istis, wisdom, 30.9, 48.11, NS; cistōis, 44.10, 46.4, 48.5, GS; -tī, 47.2, 51.21, IsS; -tīm, AS,—-tay, *f.*

cī*t*, some one, *frequent.*

*c*ithenā, untranslatable sign of a question.

*c*ithrā, clearly, 31.22, 34.4, 44.16, *adv.*

*c*ithrā*e*, clear, 33.7, NAPl; -r*ê*, 45.1, NS, *adj.* -a.

*c*ithr*em*, a race of people, 32.3,—AS, -a, *n.*

*c*ivīshī, I teach, taught, 51.15, IsPrM; civishtā, thou hast assigned, 34.13,—kav.

*c*ixshnushā, I was satisfying, 49.1; -ō, *inf.* 32.8, 43.15, 45.9,—xshnav, Pr16, *desiderative.*

cīzdī, designate! decide! 44.16,—kaēsh, imperat. (cinas).

cōis, 31.3, 47.5. 2SPrA; cōisht. 45.10, 50.3, 51.15; cōishem, 46.18;—kaēsh, to decide, teach, designate.

cōithaṯ, 46.9, 3SPrA. cōithaitē, 33.2;—kaēth, to teach, promise.

cōreṯ, he made, rendered, 44.7, 45.9,—kar. See Bartholomae's Handbuch, 298.3b.

cyanhaṯ, *is* cī-anhaṯ, how is it? 44.12.

D

dā, to give, set, utter, decree, create. It appears as
ā-darê, 43.15, 3PPrA.
a-d*as*, 46.5, Pres. Part. N.
ā-dā*t*, 31.18, 51.14.
dadāe, 31.9, 16 44.15.
dadāitī, 33.14. 3PPA. dadaitī, 46.1.
dada*t*, 29.9 3SKA *or* 3PPrA, 32.14.
dadā*t*, 30.7,11 31.21 32.10 46.7,13 51.21 53.2,4.
dadātū, 53.8, 3S.
dad*en*, 30.8 K.
dadeñtē, 31.14. 3PKM.
daduyē, 46.15, 3PPM.
dā*e*, 28.6,7 31.3 34.15 43.1,2,4,5 46.6 47.6 49.8 thou mayest give, etc.
dā*enh*ā, 34.1 44.18 thou shalt give.
dāeñtē, 48.11. will give.
dā*est*ū, 28.7 grant thou.
dāhī, 53.9 thou shalt give. 2SKA.
dāidī, 28.6,7 40.2 51.2,7,18, give thou.
daidī*t*, 28.2 43.14,16 46.2
daidītā, 43.2 46.18. 3SOM.
daidyāi, 51.20 *inf.*
daidya*t*, 44.10.
daiñtī, 32.15 3PlPrA.
dāitē, 44.19.
dāitī, 44.19.
d*am*, 44.16.
dāmā, 34.3, we shall give.
d*an*, 45.5 47.1 3PKA.
dañtō, 32.4.
das*t*ē, 34.1
das*v*ā, 33.12, to present,
dā*t*, gives, 29.10 44.3,5 45.4 48.4,6 49.7 53.1,3 (31.18 51.14.
dātā, 29.2,10 31.5 33.1 34.2,6,14. 43.1,13 48.12; 44.20, 2PPrM.

dā—*continued*. For meanings, see text-references.

  dātū, 51.17. *imperative.*

  dāvōi, *inf,* 28.2 44.14 51.9.

  dāyā*t,* 43.1 46.10 50.5, K.

  dāyetē, 31.11.

  dazdē, 46.8 51.6,19. 3SPM, and 3 DPfM 30.4.

  dyā, 43.8 1SOM.

  dyāi, 29.8.

  dy*a*m, 44.14 1SOA.

  dyā*t,* 43.10 45.9.

  ni-dāmā, 45.8.

  nī-dā*t*em, 49.3.

  vī-d*a*m, 32.6, 3SIM.

  vī-dāyā*t,* 43.12.

  vī-dīshemnāis, 51.1 ?

da*b*, to deceive, to defraud,—dābayeitī, he deceives, 43.6; da*b*en, they deceived, 53.1; daibishentī, they deceive, 32.1; de*b*ena-otā, you will defraud, 32.5, 2PPrA; *see* daibishyañ*t.*

dadē, 29.4 *see* mand.

dā*d*rē, he maintained, 51.8,—1Pf, dar.

daduyē, 46.15, *see* dā.

dā*e,* (as) a gift, 28.6,—NS da*h, n. See* dā.

daē-doisht, (*literally,* given and shown), promised, 51.17.

daēna, *f,* spirit, *covering both* religion *and* individuality.   31.11,20; 33.13 34.13 44.9,10,11 45.2,11 46.6,7,11 48.4 49.4,5,6,9 51.13,17,19,21 53.1,2,4,5.

dā*e*nhā, 34.1 44.18,—dā. As noun, *f,* NS, giving.

dā*e*nhō, of the given (path), 53.2,—GS dā, *adj.*

daēs, to show,—

  daēdōisht, the valued, promised, 51.17.

  dāis, do thou show me, 43.10 2S s-AorA.

  dīshā, thou wilt appoint, 43.7 2S s-AorM.

  dōishā, show, assure me, 51.2, 2S s-AorM.

  dōisht, shown, 51.17, s-AorMPfPart.

daēva, *m,* an opponent of the Daēva tribe?—   29.4 30.6 32.1,3,5 34.5 44.20 45.11 48.1 49.4; daēvā-ci-nā, 30.6.

daēvō-zushtā, a beloved, darling of the Daēvas, 32.4.

dafshnyā, deluded, 53.8,—dab.
dāhī, thou shalt give, 53.9,—dā.
dahmahyā, (that part) of teaching, 32.16,—dahna, *adj.*
dāhvā, 50.2, ?—LPl dam, house?
dahyêus, of a province, 31.16 46.1,4,—GS, dahyav,- *f.*
dahyūm, 31.18,—AS, *same.*
dahyūnam, 48.10,—GP, *same.*
daibishyañt, deceiving, PrPart dab— -atō, GS, 28.6; -ē, DS, 34.4
daibisheñtī, they deceive, 32.1,—dab.
daibitā(nā), long since, 32.3 48.1 49.2.
daibitīm, the second, 45.1,—AS, daibitya, *adj.*
daidītā, *see* dā.
daidyāt, they observe, 44.10,—3PPrA. dāy.
daiñtī, 32.15, *see* dā.
dāis, do thou show me, 43.10,—2S s-AorA, daēs.
dam, to set, 44.16, *inf,* dā.
dam, *m,* house, —dāhvā, 50.2, LP; dêñg, AP, 45.11; ā-dam,
    49.10 48.7 LS.
dāman, *n,* house, 48.7, NP; 46.6, AP. *see* demāna.
dāmay, creating, creator, *adj,* -is, NS 31.7 44.4 45.7; -īm, AS, 31.8 34.10
dāmay, creation, *n,* -ōis, GS, 43.5 51.10.
dam, 47.1, 3PKA, dā.
dam, 45.10. 49.4, *same as* dam *from* dam.
dānē, 44.9, *completes* yaos *as from* yaozdā, to sanctify, 1SF.
dañgra, clever, 46.17.
dar, to maintain, hold, *forms*
    dādrē, 51.8, he maintains.
    dārayat, 31.7, he will maintain.
    dāresht, 43.13, maintained.
    deretā, 44.4. he was sustaining.
    dīdāreshatā, 46.7, he wishes to hold, prepares, *Desiderative* M
    dōresht, 49.2, to have maintained, K s-Aor.
    drītā, 46.5, he might maintain, O.
    dārayō, to hold off, 32.1,—inf. dar.
dar(e)ga, long,—30.11, 31.20 AS; 43.13 GS -ahyā; 33.5 -ō, *in comp.*
daregāyū, long-lasting, 28.6,—IsS, -yav, *f.*
daregōjyātōis, long-lived, 43.2, GS; -īm, AS, 33.5.— -tay, *f.*

dare*s*, to behold,—darshtōis, *inf,* 33.6; daresā*t, abl. of* -sa, *as inf.* 32.13 ; daresānī, I shall behold, 28.5 ; daresem, 43.5 ; daresōi, 43.16; vyā-daresem, 45.8; daresatā, 3SKM, 30.1.

dareshat*c*ā, visibly, 33.7.

darethrāi, to attain, 46.3,—inf. dar.

dasā, ten, 44.18.

dasemē, decade (M), gift, offering (B), 28.9,—*m.* -a, LS.

dastē, to give, 34.1,—inf. dā.

dastv*a*m, of teachings, 46.7,—GP -vā, *f.*

da*s*.vā, give! 33.12,—imp. dā.

dāta, law, *n*; -ā, 33.1, (yathā.āis) IsS. P?; -āis, IsP, 46.15, 49.7; dātōibyas*c*ā, 51.14. dātā, 51.19, AP.

dātar, giver, creator, *m*;—dātārem, AS 44.7; dātā, NS, 50.6,11.

dātha, clever,—*m*, -em, AS. 46.17, 50.2; -ē*ñ*g, AP, 28.10 32.10 46.15. dāthaēibyō, DAblP 51.5.

dāthran*a*m, of compensations, 31.14,—GP dāthra, *n.*

dathrem, assignment, 34.13,—AS -ra, *n.*

dav*a*s.ci.nā, though he should press, 31.10,—dav (dvaidī).

dāvōi, to give, 28.2 44.14 51.9,—inf. dā.

daxsha*t*, she taught, 43.15; fra-daxshayā, teach! 33.13;—daxsh.

daxshārā, with a token, 43.7,— IsS -āra, *m.*

daxshtem, token, 34.6 51.9; AS -ta, *n, from* PfP daxsh.

dāyā*t*, it might care for, 29.7; vī-d*a*s, NSPrP 33.3;—dāy, care for

dazdyāi, dazdē, *see* dā.

dēbāvaya*t*, he may delude, 31.17,— 3SPr30, debav.

debenaotā, you will defraud, 32.5,—2PPrA dab.

deb*a*zaitī, does she support, 44.6,—K, debaz.

deb*a*za*n*hā, with the support, 47.6,—IsS -zah, *n.*

Dejām-āspā, Jamaspa, the bridegroom, 46.17, 51.18.

dejī*t*-aretaēibyō, from the law-scorning, 53.6; -tā, IsS 53.9;— -ta.

demāna, *same as* dām*a*n, house, dwelling, *n,*— -nē, LS, 32.13,15 45.8 49.11 50.4 51.14,15; -nahyā, GS 31.16; -nāi, DS 46.11; -nem, AS 31.18.

dē*ñ*g, houses, 45.11,—AP dam.

deredyāi, to maintain hold, 43.1,—inf. dar.

derescā, attack of violence, 29.1,—deres, *f.*

dereshtā, visible, 34.4,—IsS -ta, PfP , dares.

dereṭā, he was supporting, 44.4,—PfP stem, dar.

derezā, with a bond, chain, 53.8,—IsS derez, *f.*

dīdainghē, I was taught, 43.11,—1SPrM *da*h.

dīdareshaṭā, he prepares, 46.7,—*desid.*IM dar.

dīd*as*, observing, 49.9,— NSPrPart dā(y) (daidyā*t*).

dīderezō, thou wish to hold fast to, 44.15,—*desid.*2S darez.

dīdra*g*zō.duyē, you wish to assure yourselves, 48.7,—*desid.*M *of* dra*n*g, to strengthen.

dīshā, thou wilt appoint, 43.7,—2S s-AorM daēs, *see.*

divamn*em*, holding afar, 31.20,—AS -na, *adj,* [diva].

diwzaidyāi, to deceive, 45.4,—inf. dab.

dōishā, show me! 51.2,—2S s-AorM, daēs.

dōishī, to show, 33.13,—inf. daēs.

dōresht, held, 49.2,—dar; *see* Bartholomae, Handbuch, 298.6b.

draonō, possessions, 33.8,—AP -nah, *n.*

dregvañṭ, lying, *applied to* certain opponents,—PrPart dreg.

     dregvāe, NS, 30.5 31.17 44.12 46.4,6,7 47.5 49.2 50.3.

     dregvāitē, DS *f,* 31.15 33.2 43.4,8 46.6 51.8.

     dregvañṭem, AS, 32.5,14 46.5 48.2 51.9.

     dregvañṭō, N,AP, 31.20 46.1 47.4.

     dregvasū, LP, 29.5 44.14.

     dregvataēcā, DS *m,* 33.1.

     dregvat*am*, GP 30.4.

     dregvatō, GS 31.18 32.10,16 43.15 45.7 49.4,11 51.13 53.7.

     dregvōdebīs, IsP, 29.2 48.11.

     dregvōdebyō, DAbIP, 30.11 31.14 53.6.

drigāovē, to the poor man, 53.9,—DS drigav.

drigūm, the poor man, 34.5,—AS *same.*

drīṭā, he might withhold, 46.5,—O, dar.

drug, druj, *f.* lie, deceit. *Appears as*

     drūjascā, GS *n,* 32.3.

     drujem, AS, 30.8 31.4 32.12 33.4 44.13 48.1. druj*êm* 44.14.

     drūjō, GS, *or* N,Apl, 30.10 31.1 46.6,11 49.11 51.10,14 53.6.

     druxs, NS, 49.3.

dugedā, daughter, 45.4; -dra*m*, AS, 53.3;— -dar, *f.*

dūirē, in the distance, 34.8.

dūrā*t*, from far, 45.1.

dūr.aosh*e*m, holding-afar, death-repelling, 32.14,—AS, -a, *adj.*

dus-*e*rethrīs, mis-led, 49.1,—AP *m*, -thrī, *adj.*

dus*e*-xshathrā, badly ruled, 48.5,10, NP; -êñg, 49.11, AP.

dushitācā, misfortune, bad dwelling, 31.18,—LS, -tay, *f.*

dus-*h*varethêm, bad food, 31.20, 53.6;—AS -tha, *f.*

dus-mana*n*hō, of bad mind, 49.11,—GS -nah, *m.*

dus-sastis, evil-teaching, 32.9, 45.1,—NS, -tay, *adj.*

dus-*sh*yaothana, evil-doing, *adj.*— -āi, DS 31.15; -ā, 34.9, NP; -êñg, 49.11, AP.

dus-xrathwā, evil-willed, 49.4,—NP -a, *f.*

dūtā*e*nhō, messengers, 32.1,—NP, dūta, *m.*

dūtīm, message, 32.13,—AS, dūtya, *f.*

du*z*-dā*e*nhō, evil-spirited, malicious, 30.3, GS; -dā*e*, NS, 51.10;— -dā(y), -dah, *adj.*

du*z*-azōbā*e*, being notorious, 46.4,—NS, -ā, -ah, *m.*

du*z*-daēnêñg, evil-minded, 49.11,—AP, -ā, *adj.*

du*z*-jyātōis, evil living, 46.8,—GS, -ay, *f.*

du*z*-vaca*n*hō, evil speaking. 49.11,—AP -ah, *adj.*

du*z*-varenāis, evil behaving, 53.9,—IsP -a, *m.*

du*z*-varshtā, evil-doing, 49.4,—AP -a.

du*z*-vareshna*n*hō, evil doing, 53.8,—NP -nah, *adj.*

dvaēshā*e*, hostile, NS 43.8; AP 28.6; -sha*n*hā, IsS, 44.11, 46.8;— -ah, *n.*

dvaēthā, threat, 32.16,—NS, *f.*

dvafshêñg, pains, torments, 44.14,—AP, -a, *m.*

dvafshō, pain, torment, 53.8,—NS, -āh, *n.*

dvaidī, we both shall urge, 29.5,—1DPrM, dav.

dvar, to rush, of Daēvas only; hêñ-dvāreñtā, 30.6, they rushed.

dva*n*maibyascā, to the clouds, 44.4,—DP, -man, *n.*

dyā, limited, 43.8,—GS, *n*, dyah, *adj.*

dyāta*m*, is limited, 48.7,—3SImM, *passive meaning*, nī-dyā.

dyāi, to give, 29.8,—inf. dā.

E

êeãenhã, with the mouth, 28.11,—IsS êeãh *or* ãh, ãenhō, GS, 31.3.
êeãnū, in the mouths of, 32.16 47.2,—LPl, êeãh; according to, B.
êeãvã, us both, 29.7,—ADu, *pron.*
êmavañt, powerful.—   -va*t*, AP 33.12;   -vañtem, AS*m*, 34.4;
    -vaitĭm, AS*f,* 44.14; -vat*a*m, GP 43.10.
ênãxshtã, he has succeeded, 32.6,—*augm.*3S s-AorM, na*s.*
êneitĭ, torment, pain, 30.11,—NS, intay *or* ênitay.
erejwō, worthy, 46.13,—NS, -a; *same as* erethwã.
ere*s,* justly, 30.3,6 32.11 44.1-19 48.9 49.6,9 51.5.
ere*s-*vacãe, just worded, 31.12, 49.9,—NS -cah, *adj.*
ereshi*s,* envy, 31.5,—NS -shay, *f.*
ereshvãi*s,* just-acting, 28.6, IsP; -vãenhō, 29.3, NP; -vã, 44.9, AP;
    -vō, NS, 51.5,11; -va, *adj.*
ere*t*hwêñg, just, worthy, 28.10; AP -wa, *adj.*
ereze-jĭs, right-living, 50.2, AS; -jyōi, 29.5, 53.9, DS; -jĭ, *adj.*
erezūc*a*m, in right speaking, 48.9,—GP *used adverbially,* -vacah
erezū*s,* straight, 33.5,6 43.3 53.2, AP; -zãus, 51.13, GS; -zav.
erez-uxd*a*i, to the right-worded, 31.19, DS; -d*a*, 44.19, IsS; -*d*a.
evistĭ, not to be sharer of, 34.9; NP*n, adverbial,* -tay, *adj.*
evĭdvãe, non-expert, 31.12,17,—NS -vah, *adj.*

F

ˈedrōi, to a father, 53.4,—DS pitar.

ˈerasābyō, with questions, 29.5, AblP; -sayāi, DS, 43.7; -sem, 43.9, AS; frasayā, 44.13, AP; -sā, *f.* frasā, 31-13, AP, -sa, *m.*

ˈerashêm, progressive, 30.9, 34.15,—AS -sha, *adj.*

ˈerasha.oshtra, Zarathushtra's father-in-law, DS 49.8; NS 51.17; VS 46.16.

ˈerashō-temem, suitable, 46.19 50.11,—AS -ma, *adj.*

ˈerash.vā, take counsel! 53.3,—*imp.* fras.

ˈera-srūidyāi, to hear from, 46.13,14,—inf, frā, srav.

ˈeseratūm, compensation, 33.12,—AS -ū, *f.* (51.4).

ˈrā, *in composition,* towards, away.

ˈra.cinas, he regulates, 32.5,—3SPrA, kaēsh.

ˈrād, to promote, prosper, frāda*t*, 46.13; frādeñtē, 43.6; frādōi*t*, 44.10; frādainghē, *inf.* 44.20.

ˈrāda*t*-gaēthem, prospering estates *or* world, 33.11,—AS -ā, *f.*

ˈra-dathāi; to fructify, 31.16 45.9.—inf. dā.

ˈra-daxshayā, thou mayest instruct, 33.13,—daxsh.

ˈra-daxshtā, teacher, 31.17, 51.3,—NS, -tar, *m.*

ˈrādō, of promotive, 34.14, 46.12,—GS frād, *adj.*

ˈraēshtāenhō, messengers, 49.8,—NP -ta, *m.*

ˈraēshyā, I urge, 49.6.—aēsh.

ˈrafrā, I precede, 46.10,—1SK, par.

ˈrāidīm, promotion, help, 53.6, AS*f.* frāday. *f.*

ˈraidivā, since long, 32.14.

ˈra-jyāitis, destruction, 29.5,—NS -tay, *f.*

ˈra-mīmathā, you have prepared, 32.4,—mā(y).

ˈraore*t*, cheerfully, 30.5, 53.2.

ˈra-oxtā, he arrives at, 48.1,—vak.

ˈrāreñtē, they rise, arrive, arouse, 46.3,—3PKM frā, ar.

ˈrasā, questions, 31.13,—AP, -sa, *m.*

ˈra-sastīm, observance, 49.7,—AS -tay, *f,* sāh. frasayā *see* fer-

ˈrasayā, questions,, 44.13,—AP *from* ferasā, *f.*

ˈrashī, I consulted, 44.8, 45.6,—Aor fras, to ask, *which appears*

as ferashvā 53.3, peresā 44.1-19, *and*

frashtā, he consulted, 49.2,— 3S s-AorM; *also* frashtā, 43.14;
   ā-frashtā, 51.11; hême-frashtā, 47.3.

fra-srūtā, famous, 50.8,—NSnPfP srav.

frā-vaocā, do thou reveal, 34.12,—vak.

fra-vaxshyā, I will speak out, 44.6 45.1,2,3,4,5,6,16.

fra-varetā, she chose out, 31.10,—var.

fra-vōividē, I was selected, 44.11,—vaēd.

fra-vōizdūm, to be selected, 33.8,—s-Aor vaēd.

frā-xshnenem, providing for, 43.14,—NSn(B); AS,

frā-xshnenē, to be instructed, 29.11, 43.12,—inf. xshnā.

fra-xshnī, to learn to know, 44.7,—inf. xshnā.

frīnāi, I placate, I sue for friendship, 49.12,—frāy.

frīnemnā, placate, 29.5,—NDm, frāy.

frō, forth, from, 28.11 33.8,12 45.6 46.3,4,5 49.6.

frō-gāe, progressing, 46.4,—NS -gay *or* -gah, *adj.*

frōretōis, to prosper, 46.4,—inf. frā, ar.

frō-syāt, he may intend to oppose, 46.8,—sā, Pr27?

fryāi, to a friend, 43.14 44.1 46.2, DS; fryā, 44.1, IsS; fryō, 46.2,6 NS;
   —frya, friendly.

Fryāna, friendly, 46.12,—a name?

fshêñghīm, prospered, 31.10, AS; fshêñghyō, 49.9, NS,— -a, *n.*

fshuyañt, fattening, PrPart. fshav; *appears as*
   fshuyeñtē, 29.5; fshuyantaēcā, 29.6, DS.
   fshuyañtem, 31.10, AS.
   fshuyasū, 49.4, LP.

fshuyō, should fatten 48.5,—fshav.

G

gāe, of both head-of-cattle, 46.4,—GD gav, *m.*

gaēmcā, life, 30.4, 43.1,—AS gaya, *m.*

gaēthā, substance, estate, world, *f,*— -tham, 50.3, AS; -thē, LS, 34.2; -thāhū, 43.7, LP; -thāe, AP, 31.1,11 34.3 43.6 44.10 46.8,12,13.

gaidī, come! 28.6 49.1,—imp. gam.

gairē, to watch, 28.4,—inf. gar.

gam, to come, *forms the following stems:* jam- jem-; Aor jêngh-

gam, the cattle, AS, 32.10 44.6,20 47.3 50.2 51.5,7.

gaodāyō, cattle-keepers, 29.2,—AP -yah, *m.*

garemā, hot, glowing, 43.4,—IsS -a.

garō, of praise, 45.8 50.4 51.15 GS; -ōbīs, IsP, 34.2.

gat-tē, 51.10; gat-tōi, 43.1, go,—inf. gam.

gāt, he steps on, is banished to, 46.6, —gā(y).

gāthā, hymn, *f.*

gātūm, place, throne, 28.5,—AS gātav, *m.*

gāus, of the Cattle, 32.8,14,— *same as* gêus, GS gav, *m.*

gāvā, both head-of-cattle, 46.,19—NDu gav, *m.*

gāvōi, to the Cattle, 29.3,7 33.3 48.5 51.14,—DS *same.*

gayehyā, of life, 51.19,—GS gaya, *m.*

gemen, they shall come, 46.11,—gam.

genā, woman, 46.10,—NS *f.*

gerebam, to hold fast to, 34.10,—inf. grab.

Gerêhma, a rival to Zarathushtra, 32.12,13,14.

gerezdā, he complained, 29.1,—3SPr garez.

gerezdā, through being recipient of, 50.9, IsS; -dīm, 51.17, AS; -day, *f.* gared.

gerezē, 32.9; gerezōi, 46.2;—I appeal, I complain, 1SPrM garez

gêus, gês, of Cattle, 28.1 29.1,3,7,9 31.9 32.12 33.4 34.14 46.9,—GS gav *m.*

gêus tashan, Creator 29.2 31.9 46.9 51.7; -ūrvan, Soul of Kine, 28.1 29.1,5,9

gêushā, ears, 51.3, NP; gêushāis, IsP, 30.2;— -sha, *m.*

gūsh(a)tā, heard, 29.8 31.18,19, PfP; gūshahvā-tū, 49.7 ; gūshōdūm, s-Aor, 45.1; *both imperatives of* gaosh.

gūzrā, secret, 48.3,—AP, gūzra.

H

ha-(demōi), the same, 44.9,—*pron.*

hā, that, sing, *f,* 47.6, 48.2,6.

haca, hacā, with, in consequence of, forthwith, forth, out, 28.2,11 29.6 31.2,14 32.2 43.14,17 45.4 46.19 47.1 51.5,22 53.1,6.

hacaitē, it may follow, 34.2, 48.4; hacaiñtē, 45.2, 46.16; hacāeñtē, 48.12;—hak.

hacêmnā, those following, 44.10,—hak, PfPM. In 44.13, Bartholomae reads hacênā, LS *of* hacênay, *f,* companionship.

hacimnō, following together, 43.10,12,—hak.

haciñtē, they are accompanying, 33.9,—hak.

hadā, together, 29.2, 46.17 50.4.

ha-demōi, in the same dwelling, 44.9, 46.14,—LS dam.

hādrōyā, through a desire, 32.7,—IsS, -yā, *f.*

Haēca*t*-aspā, friends to Zarathushtra, 46.15.

hafshī, I acknowledge, hold, 43.4,— hap.

hahmī, I may be, 34.5. B *reads* haxmī, I follow,—hak.

haithīm, genuinely, truly, 31.6,8 34.6 46.19 51.13—adv.acc. -thyā.

hāitīm, possession, 32.9,—AS hātā, piece, chapter, *used in all the hymn-headings.*—hā(y), to connect, *or* han, to earn.

haithya, veritable, genuine, 30.5 31.8 34.15 43.3,8 44.6 46.6 49.11 53.6. in 46.6, *read* haēthahyā, companions, AP*n,* -ya, *adj.*

haithyā-var*e*sht*a*m, genuine, realizable, 50.11,—AS -ta, *adj.*

hak, to follow, urge, *forms* hish-hak, haxshā, scañtū, PfP haxta, inf. haxtōi*t,* haxmī.

hākurenā, support, 44.1, AP; -em, AS 33.9; -a, *n.*

ham, hêm, together, 30.4 31.8 44.15 46.12 47.3 53.3.

hāmō, the same, 31.7, NS; hamêm, 32.16 AS.

hamāestārō, defeaters, conquerors, 48.12,— NP -tar, *m.*

han, to earn, hāneñtē, 44.19, 46.19; hanānī, 44.18.

hanar*e*, without, 31.15 47.5, *with abl.*

ha*n*hus, fruit, 53.4,—NS -hav, *n.*

haozathwā*t,* by proficiency, 45.9,—AblS -wa, *n.*

haptaithē, to the seventh, 32.3,—LS -tha, *n.*

hapti, he holds, 31.22—hap.

hārō, watching over, 31.13 44.2,—NS -a, *adj.*

has, being, 46.4,5 47.4 51.5, NS hañt. PsP *of* ah, *to be.*

hātam, of beings, 29.3 44.10, GP hañt *or of* hātā *m.* PfP han.

hātā-marānē, remembering merit, 32.6,—VS -nay, *f.*

hathrā, with, along with, 28.4 30.9.

haurvatāt, *f,* cheerful life, 'wholeness' health; an ahura. 31.6,21 33.8 34.1,11 44.17,18 45.5,10 51.7. Called hu-jyātay, 32.5. Chiefly used in dual with ameretāt.

haxmêñg, companions, 49.3 AP -man, *m.*

haxshāi, I will urge, 46.10,—hak.

haxtayāe, corporeally, *literally* of both thighs, 53.7.— haxt, *n.*

hazascā, power, might, 29.1,—NP -ah, *n. from* haz.

hazaoshāenhō, same pleasure, like-willed, 51.20 NP; hazaoshem, 28.8, AS.

hazê, might, power, 43.4,—AS, ê *for* -ah, *n. from* haz.

hazō, 33.12, AP *same.*

hêcā, 46.1 ?

hêm, *same as* ham, *prefix.*

hêm(e)-frashtā, counselled together, 47.3 53.3,—fras.

heme-myāsaitē, he combines, 33.1,—myas.

hêmithyāt, he would dismiss, 53.9,—maêth.

hêm-parshtōis, to counsel with, 33.6,—*inf.* fras.

hêm-tashat, shaped together, 47.3,—tash.

hêm-yañtū, they shall go together, 51.3,—ay.

hêñ-dvāreñtā, they rushed over, 30.6.—dvar.

hêñ-graben, he understood, 31.8,—grab.

hêñ-keretā, the compensations, 31.14,— AP -tay, *f.*

hêñtī, they are, 33.10 44.16 45.6 51.10,22.

hêñtū, let them be, 33.7 53.8.

hī, both of them, 30.3 31.10 44.18, hīcā, 32.14.

hīm, of them, 29.2 44.14,20 50.2.

hīs, with them, 33.10.

hīshasat, he will attain to, 32.13,—hant.

hitham, companion, fellow, 34.10,—AS -a, *adj.*

hithāus, of the company, 48.7,—GS -thav, *m.*

hizvā, tongue, IsS, 28.5 31.3 47.2; -vāe, LS 45.1 51.3; -vascā, GS 51.13; -vō, IsS 31.19 50.6; -zubīs, IsP 49.4;—hizū, *f.*

hōi, to him, 29.2,8,9 31.6 45.8,10,11 46.13 47.3 48.7,9 50.3 51.6,12,17 53.1,2,5.

hōis, with them, 53.6.

hu-cistīm, good teaching, 34.14 AS; -tōis, 46.4, GS; -tay, *f.*

hudāe, beneficent, 48.3 45.6; hudāenhō, 30.3 34.3, GS *or* NP; -hē, 31.22 DS; ābyō, 34.13, DAblP;—hudā(y), *n.* or *adj.*

hu-dānus, well-disposed, 31.16; -nāus, 44.9 50.9; hudān(vareshvā), 53.3,—NS hudānav, *adj.*

hudemêm, sweetness, loveliness, 29.8; AS, -ma, *m.*

hu-jyātōis, of good life, 32.5 46.8; hujītayō, NP, 33.10.

hu-karetā, well-formed, 34.13; IsS -a, *adj.*

hu-mazdrā, well-remembering, 30.1,—AP -dar, *m.*

hu-meretōis, of good marking, 31.10,—GS -tay, *f.*

hunāitī, he incites, 31.15,—hav.

hunarā, with skill, art, 43.5—IsS -ra, *m.*

hunaretātā, with ability, 50.8,—IsS -tāt, *f.*

hunus, a (daēvic) son, 51.10,—NS -av, *m.*

hus-haxā, with well-befriended, 32.2; -xāim, 46.13;—AS -xay, *adj*

hu-sheitīs, good dwelling, 29.10, IsP; -tōis, 30.10, GS; -tis, NS 48.11— -shitay, *f.*

hus-hênem, well-earning, 53.5,—AS -na, *adj.*

hu-shōithemā, good abodes, 48.6,—AP -man, *n.*

hu-shyaothanā, doing good deeds, 45.4,—NS -a, *adj,f.*

hu-xratus, understanding well, 34.10 51.5,—NS -tav, *adj.*

hu-xshathrā, ruling well, 44.20 48.5, NP; -rāis, 53.8, IsP;— -a.

hu-zêñtus(e), well-informed, 43.3 46.5 49.5,—NS, -tav, *adj.* (*n*).

*hv*aēcā, selves, 46.11.

*hv*aēnā, glowing, 32.7,—IsS -na, *adj.*

*hv*aētus, a gentleman, a noble by birth, 32.1 49.7, NS; -tū, 33.3 IsS; -têus, 33.4 46.1 GS; -tavē, 46.5; -taovē, 53.4, DS; -tav.

*hv*afenā, *pronoun*, each other, 30.3,—AP.

*hv*afnemcā, sleep, 44.5,—AS -na, *m.*

*hv*a*hy*āe, of himself, 33.14.

*hv*a*hy*āi, for himself, 30.2.

*hv*āis, with themselves, 31.20 46.4 49.4 51.13,22.

hva*n*hevīm, blissful life, 53.1,—AS -haoya.

hvāpā*e*, well-made, 44.5: NS *in line* 403, AP *in* 404,— -pah.

*hv*apaithyā*t*, self-glory, 31.21,—AblS -a, *n*.

*hv*araithyā, effective, 28.10—NP -a, *adj*.

hvarecā, the sun, 32.10; hvar*ê*, 50.2,—AS hvar, *n*.

*hv*āremnō, to be devoured, 32.8,—AP PfP *hv*ar.

*hv*arenā*e*, sunny, glorious, 51.18,—NS -ah, *adj*.

*hv*arethāi, for food, 34.11 48.5, DS; -thāis, IsP, 49.11,— -a, *n*.

hvarshtāis, well-done, good works, 49.4, IsP -a.

*hv*āthrā, complete life, glory, AP 31.7 33.9; -ē, 28.2 50.5, DS; -em, AS 43.9 53.6,— -a, *n*.

*hv*athrōyā, with his desire, 43.2,—IsS -ā, *f*.

*hv*ê, themselves, 46.11.

*hv*êñg, suns, 43.16 44.3,—AP *hv*ar, *n*.

*hv*ênva*t*, sunny, 53.4, NS*n*PrPart; -vātā, 32.2 IsS.

*hv*īticā, well-being, 30.11,—NS -tay, *f*.

hvō, that one, he, self, *frequent*,—NS hva, adverbially.

Hvō-gvā, a friendly tribe, 46.16,17 51.17,18.

*h*yāmā, we might be, 30.9,—O, ah.

*h*yā*t*, it might be, 43.15 16 44.17,—O, ah.

hya*t*, which, that, because, so that, *frequent*,—conj. *and* pron.

*h*yātā, you might be, 50.7,—O, ah.

*h*yêm, I might be, 43.8 50.9,—O, ah.

*h*yên, they might be, 51.4,—O, ah.

I

ī, *unrenderable*, 31.22 53.6,—conjunction.
ī, they, 34.2 44.2 49.6 53.5—NADuP?.
idā, here, 29.8.
idī, come! 46.16,—*imp.* ay.
īm, (this?), 30.9 44.19 45.1,3,4,11 46.5,8 51.12.
īrā, with zeal, 49.10,—IsS -a, *n.*
īratū, attack! 53.8,—imp. ar.
irixtem, an end, 32.7 44.2,—AS -a, *n.*
īs, *pronoun*, these? 30.6 31.18 32.13 44.14 46.12 51.14 53.8,9.
isāi(cā), I am able, 28.4 43.9 50.11; isē, 50.1 3SPM—aēs.
isemnō, he shall be able, shall stand up for, 46.6,—*adj.* PfPM.
īsh, desire, *f.* -ā, IsS 29.9; -em, AS 28.7; -ō, NP 50.4, AP 28.9.
īshā xshathrīm, 29.9,—AS -rya, *adj. f.*
ishāeñtī, let them seek, desire, 45.7—aēsh.
īshanam, desiring, imitating, 32.12 GP īshan, *adj.*
ishasā, I shall seek, 31.4,—aēsh.
ishasas, seeking, desiring, 51.19,—NS PrP aēsh.
ishasōit, he might seek, 50.2,—O, aēsh.
ishathā, you have come to seek, 45.1,—aēsh.
ishayas, deserving, caring, 50.9,—NSPrP Pr24 ishaya.
isheñtī, they are seeking, 46.9,—aēsh.
isheñtō, desirous, 30.1 47.6,—NPPrP aēsh.
īshtā, wealth, ability,   AP 46.16 49.12; īshtīm, AS 32.9 46.2;
    īshtis, NS 48.8 53.1; īshtīs, AP 34.5 44.10; ishtōis, GS 46,18
    51.2,18,—īshtay, *f.*
ishyā, prized, desired, 48.8 NP? -yam, AS 51.17 -yēñg, AP 32.16
ishudō, compensations, 31.14, NP; -dem, AS 34.15,—ishud, *f.*
isōyā, I would wish to be, 43.8,—1SPM, aēs.
isvā, disposing of, 47.4; ability, 43.14,—IsS isvan, *adj.*
īt, indeed, no doubt, *intensive*, 28.8 43.10 44.20.
īt, pronoun, this? 44.19 46.2
ithā, so, thus, therefore, 33.1 45.3 47.4 53.6.

ithyejō, dangers, 34.8,—NP -jah, *n.*
ivī-zayathā, you dismiss, 53.7,—2PPr zā(y).
Izācā, zeal, 49.5,10 51.1, NS; izayā*e,* 50.8, GS—*f.*
izyāi, I desire, 49.3,—āz.

J

jaidyāi, to kill, 32.14,—gan.
jamaētē, they shall both meet, 44.15, 3DKM,—gam, *which forms*
  jamaitī, it shall come, 30.8.
  jañtū, may come, 44.16.
  jasaētem, they both came, 30.4.
  jasāi, I will come, 51.22.
  jasat, he came, 30.6,7 (43.1-15); *in* 51.15 came *or* shall come.
  jasatā, do you come! 28.3.
  jasō, come thou! 43.6.
  jasōit, might come, 46.8,—O.
javarō, inciter, M, weighing, B. 48.8,—NS -a, *m.*
jayāis, with urgers, 50.7,—IsP jiya, *m.*
jênayō, women, 53.6,—NP genā, *f.*
jêneram, murder, killing, 53.8,—AS -ā, *f.*
jêñghaticā, they are coming, are future, 31.14,—Aor gam.
jīgerezat, he will complain, 32.13,—garez.
jimā, I come, 29.3,—gam, *which forms also*
  jimaitī, they will come, 48.2.
  jimat, it may come, 43.4 44.1 46.3 48.11.
  jimen, they shall come, 45.5.
jōyā, gain, desire, 32.7,—gay; IsS -ā, *f.*
jvā, they who were living, the past, 45.7;—gay, *which forms*
  jvāmahī, we may live, 31.2,—1PKA.
  jvañtō, all living, 31.3,—AP, PrP.
  jvas, living, 46.5,—NS, PrP.
jyāitīm, life, 33.5,—AS jyātay, *f, which forms*
  jyātêus, of life, 32.9,15 46,4 53.9,—GS. *m.* jyātav.
  jyōtūm, life, 31.15 32.11,12,—AS. *m.*

K

kā how? what? 34.5 44.8,19 48.8 51.11; kā-cīt, 46.8.
kadā, whether, when, 29.9 46.3 48.9; kadārêm, 31.17.
kaēibyō, to *or* from which? 44.6 46.3.
kaēnā, punishments, 30.8,—NP -nā, *f.*
kahmāi(cīt), to which? 29.1 43.1 44.16.
kahyā(cīt), of which? 43.7; kahyāicīt, to which? 33.11.
kainibyō, to maidens, 53.5,—DP -nyā, *f.*
kam, for the sake of, 44.20,—*preposition, with dative.*
kāmem, desire, 28.10, AS; -ē, 32.13, LS; -ahyā, 43.13, GS.—*m.*
kamna.fshvā, having few flocks, 46.2,— NP -a, *n.*
kamnā.nā, having few followers, 46.2,—NP kamnā-nar, *m.*
Karapā, a tribe, 44.20 *and* -anō, 46.11 48.10 NP; -pā, 32.12 *and* -pōtāescā
     32.15 AP.
kascīt, whoever, 49.5, NS.
kasêus(cīt), of little, few, 31.13 47.4,—GS kasav, *adj.*
kasnā, who? 44.3,4.
kastē, which, 29.7 46.14.
kat, what? 48.2 49.12 50.1.
kā-tā, how, which, 33.8.
katārêm, which of the two, 44.12.
kathā, with what, how, 29.2 43.7 44.2,9,11,13,14,17,18 46.1 50.2.
kāthê, the retributions, 44.2,—NP -tha, *n.*
kāthē, to show favors to, to entertain, 47.4,—kan.
Kavā, a tribe, 44.20 NP -yascīt, 32.14 46.11 AP; 46.14 51.16 53.2 NS.
kayā, may desire, 33.6,—kā.
kê, who, what? 29.1 44.3,4,5,7,12,16 46.9 49.7 50.1 51.11.
kehrpêm, body, 30.7 51.17,—AS kehrp, *n.*
kêm, whom? 29.2 46.7,—AS.
kêñg, whom? 48.11,—AP.
keredushā, protection, 29.3,—IsS -dush, *n.*
kerenāun, they make, 30.9,—kar.

keretā, he made, 44.4,—kar.

Kevīnō, of the Kavay tribe, 51.12, NS; -ītāescā, 32.15, AP.

kōi, who, 48.11,—NP.

kū, where? 53.9; ku-dā, 29.11.

kuthrā, whither, 34.7 44.15 46.1 51.4·

M

mā, not.

mā, me, 29.1 31.17,18 32.9 45.6 46.1,7,9 48.2,5 49.1,2 50.2 51.10.

mā, my, 46.2,—NP*n*.

madahyā, of this intoxication. 48.10,—GS mada, *m*,

mā*e*, the moon, 44.3, NS māh, *m*.

maēthā, unclear, undecided, separate, 30.9.—NP -a, *adj.*

maēthā, crisis, change, uncertainty, 31.12 33.9 34.6, -ā, *f.*

magahyā, 48.10, B *reads* madahyā.

Maga, Magian tribe, *m;* -ahyā, GS 48.10 51.16 53.7; -āi, DS 29.11 46.14
    51.11. *From* maga, *n,* a hole ?

magāunō, of a Magian tribesman, 33.7,—GS magavan, *m.*

magavabyō, to *or* from Magian tribesmen, 51.15.

mahmāi, to me, 50.7, DS.

mahmī, in my, 32.1, LS.

mahyā, of me, 32.9 48.12 50.6 GS.

ma*h*yā*e*, of my, 44.10 46.18 50.9; *or* of mystic, *see* māyā.

maibyā(cā), to *or* from my, 28.7,8 46.17 49.8.

maibyō, to *or* from me, 28.2 31.4 43.14 46.3 48.8 51.10.

Maidyōi-mā*e*nhā, relative of Zarathushtra, a missionary; 51.19 VS.

mainis, punishment, 31.15 44.19, NS -ay, *f.*

mainyañtā, they think, 34.8,—man.

mainy*ê*us, of the spirit, *frequent,* GS mainyav, *m.*

mairishtō, who best remembers, 29.4,—NS -a, *adj.*

manā*e*, mind, 45.2,—NS manah, *n,* which forms

manahīm, spiritual, 53.6,—AS manahya, *adj.*

manaothrīs, monitresses, 44.5,—NP -ī, *f.*

mana*n*hā, with the mind, IsS; -hō, of the mind, GS manah.

mana*n*hascā, mind, GS NAP, 43.3 46.7,18 etc.

m*a*narōis, of the message, 48.10,—GS -ray, *f.*

mānayeitī, he causes me to think, wait; hinders.—49.2, man.

manō, abode, B. 30.4 34.8,—NP manah, *n.* abode ?

manōi, according to my mind, 32.1,—DS -na, *n.*

mañtā, thought, 31.7,19 33.6 51.16,—*from the verb* man; *or*
mañtā, guardian, counsellor, manager, IsS -tav, *m.* which forms
mañtū, 46.17, IsS; mañtūm, AS 33.4.
manyāi, I will consider, 43.9,—man.
manyātā, may be considered, 45.11,—man.
manyetē, he shall be thought, 44.12. ib.
manyêus, of the spirit, *frequent,*—GS mainyav, *m.*
marakaēcā, to death, 31.18,—DS -ka, *m,*
maraxtārō, the destroyers, 32.13,—NP -tar, *m.*
maredaitī, it destroys, 51.13,—mared.
mareñtī, they mark, remark, notice, 43.14,—mar, *also*
mareñtō, 31.1,—NP PrPart.
marexshaitē, he would wish to kill, 51.10,—3SK s-AorM marek.
maretaēibyō, to *or* from men, mortals, 29.7 45.5,—martiya, *m.*
maretaēshū, among mortals, men, 46.13,—LP ib.
maretānō, of human, mortal, 30.6 32.12,—GS maretan, *adj.*
mas, much, 32.3 34.9,—*adj.*
mashā, men, mortals, 29.11, VP; mashīm, 32.5, 46.11 AS.
mashyā, men, mortals, 32.4 NP; -āi, 48.5 DS; -āis, 29.4 34.5 48.1 IsP;
    -ascā, 45.11, -yêñg, 32.8 AP; -aēshū, 43.11 LP; -āenhō, 30.11 VP.
mat, always, with, 32.1 34.11 43.14 44.7,15 45.9 46.19 48.11 50.8.
mathra, (mystic) word, *m.* -rem, 29.7 31.6 45.3 AS; rascā, 31.18 AP;
    -rā, 44.17 50.6 51.8 IsS; -rāe, 43.14 AP; -rāis, 44.14 IsP.
mathran, word-speaker, prophet, *m.* -rā, 28.7 50.5 51.8 NS; -nascā,
    -nē, 50.5 DS; -nō, 32.13 GS.
mayā, 33.9. with me, B IsS*f* mā-yā; but, M, it may come from
māyā, *f,* joy, bliss, B; mystery, M ;mahyā, 32.9 IsS; mayāe, 43.2,
    AP; mahyāe, 44.10 GS.
maz, large, *adj.* -zōi, 29.11 46.14 DS; -zê, 30.2 GS (B); -ibīs, 32.11, Is
    P, adverbially.
mazā-rayā, possessing much wealth, 43.12, IsS*f.*
mazā-xshathrā, O much power-possessing, 49.10 VS.
mazdāenhō.dūm, you are to remember, 45.1, 2P s-AorM, mazdā.
Mazdāh, God, the Mindful One, *frequent,* see Table of Divine
    Names. -dā, VIs; -dāe, NGAbl ; -dam, AS ; -āescā, 33.11, GS?;

polytheistic plural -āescā, 30.9 31.4.

mazdāthā, memorable, 30.1,—AP -a, *n.*

mazdazdūm, to be remembered, 53.5,—s-Aor mand.

mazibīs, greatly, 32.11.

mazishta, greatest,— -tam, ASf 31.13; -tem, *m* 28.5 33.5 45.6 -tō, NS 49.1 53.8.

mazyō, greater, 31.17, NS -a, *adj.*

me, mê, me, NGS *or* conj. 29.5 44.8 50.1 53.6.

mêhmaidī, he shall be considered, 46.13,—man.

mêm, 53.4 my? AS?

mênāi.cā, I consider, 45.3,—ISKM, man.

mêñcā, I advise, 53.5, *below,*

mên . . dadē, I am mindful, 28.4,—1SPM, mand.

mêñ(cā)daidyāi, to memorize, 44.8 31.5.

mêñg, thou hast thought out, 48.2,—2SPrA, man.

mêñghāi, I would think, acknowledge, 43.4.

mêñghī, I thought, 31.8 43.5,7,9,11,13,15; mênghī, 29.10.

merashyāt, he will destroy, 45.1,—3SOA marek B Handb.67.4.

merazdyāi, to smite, 44.14, *inf* marez.

mereñgeidyāi, to destroy, 46.11, *inf* marek.

mereñgeduyē, you may destroy, 2PPrM, 53.6, ib.

merethyāus, of death, 53.8, GS -av, m.

merezdātā, pity me! 33.11,—marez.

merezdikā, pitying, 51.4,—NP -ka, *adj.*

mimagzō, thou shalt magnify, 45.10,—2S mang.

minas, thou wilt mingle, unite, 46.14,—2SPrA myas.

mithahyā, false, 33.1,—NPn, -ya, *adj.*

mithah-vacāe, false-worded, 31.12,—NS -cah, *adj.*

mithrōibyō, to *or* from engagements, contracts, 46.5,— ra, *m.*

mizdavan, compensating, 43.5,—APn of PrPart -vañt, mizda.

mizdem, compensation, 34.13 44.18,19 46.19 51.15 53.7 AS; -dē, 49.9 GS.

mizên, they care for, 44.20,—maēz.

mōi, conj. *or pron.* to me, 28.3 29.1 44.10 46.7,10,18,19 49.1 50.1 51.2,7,17,18,21.

mōist, he may send (in), admit, 46.12,—maēth, hêmithyāt.

mōithat, he may send (out), deprive, 46.4,—ib.

mōreñda*t,* he destroys, 32.9.10,—mar*ed.*
mōreñden, they destroy, 32.11,12,—ib.
moshu.cā, soon, 53.8.
mōyastrā baranā, bearing company, 30.9.
mraoc*as,* dodging, 53.7, NS PrPart -añ*t?*
mraoī, he tells, 32.14—mrav, *which forms*
  mraomī, I utter, 53.5.
  mraos, thou toldst, 34.13, 43.12.
  mrao*t,* he told, 32.2,10,12 45.5 46.9 51.19.
  mraōtā, you told, 43.11.
  mraotū, tell! 31.17.
  mrava*t,* told, 29.3 45.2.
  mravaitī, it is told, 51.8.
  mruitē, to tell, 49.6.
  mruyā*t,* he should tell, 46.5 51.8.
  mruyē, to tell, 49.3.
mūthrem, excrement, 48.10,—AS -ra, *n.*
myazdem, solid offering, 34.3,—A S -da, *m.*

N

na, nā, nāe, not, *conj, frequent,* 43.2,13,14,15 44.19 45.2 46.10 48.7 51.8,10,11, 19,21.

nā, man, 46.2,—NS nar, *m.*

nabāescā, atmosphere, clouds, 44.4,—AP nabah, *n.*

nadeñtō, imprecating, cursing, 33.4,—GS -dañt.

nāe, us, AP 29.11 33.7 34.7,8,12 43.3,10 46.18 50.5.

naēcīm, no indeed, 34.7.

naēcis, nobody, 43.6,13: naēcīt, 32.7.

naēdā, neither, none, 29.6 45.2 46.1 49.2.

naēshat, it may lead, 31.20,—3S Aor K nay.

nafshucā, among relatives, 46.12,—LP napāt.

nāidyāenhem, the weaker, 34.8,—AS -yah, *adj.*

nāmenīs, with *or* by their names, 51.22,—IsP, -man, *n.*

nanā, ? separated off ? B 48.4.

naptyaēshū, among descendants, 46.12,—LP naptya, *m.*

narem, a man, a hero, 30.2 AS; narō, 48.10 53.6 NP; narōi, 28.8, DS; —nar, *m;* nā, neres.

narepīs, diminishing, 53.9, AP -pis, *n, from verb,* narep.

nasat, he attained, 51.16, 53.6,—nas; anasat, ēnāxshtā, vīnē-nāsā.

nāshāmā, we may drive off, 44.3,—nāsh.

nasvāe, they have perished, 51.13,—nas.

nasyañtō, they who disappear, 32.4,—NP PrPart nas.

nazdishtam, nearest, 33.4 50.3,—AS -ta, *adj.*

nê, *conj. or pron.* to *or* of us 29.8 30.2 31.11,17 44.1 45.8,9,10 48.5 50.1 51.16,20.

nemahvaitīs, reverent, 33.7,—NPf, -vañt, *from* nam.

nemah, reverence, *n, forms*

   nemanhā, IsS 28.1 34.3 50.6,8 51.5,20.

   nemanhō, GS 43.9 44.1 45.8.

   nemascā, GS AP 49.10.

nemê, I may revere, 44.1,—nam.

nemōi, to flee. 46.1,—*inf.* nam.

neras, men, 45.7,—AP nar, *m.*

neres, of a man. 29.9 34.2, GS nar.

nī, down, 32.14 48.7.

nī-dāmā, I will lay down, 45.8,—dā.

nī-dātem, set down, 49.3,—AS PfPA nī-dā.

ni-pāanhē, I am to protect, 28.11 49.10,—1SK s-AorM nī-pāy.

nī-varānī, B's reading of varānī, 53.4.

nīs, off, 44.13, *with* nāshāmā.

ni-shasyā, settled down, 50.2,—AP PfP shāy. B *derives from* nis-hasya, fut. *of* hant, to remove.

nōit, not, 28.9 29.1 30.3,6 47.4,5 48.7 49.2,4,9 51.6,12,14 46.1

nū, nū.rêm.cīt, 31.7 45.1,8 51.1.

nū-nāe, now to us, 29.11.

O

ōyā, tn result of this, 47.2,—IsS a, this.

P

padāis, with verses *or* verse-feet, 50.8,—IsP pada, *n.*

padebīs, with verses *or* verse-feet, 51.16,—IsP, pad, *m.*

pafrē, he hindered, 49.1,—Pf par.

pairī, around, from, under, 29.5 34.8 46.1 51.22.

pairī-āis, the former, those that I did earlier, *adverbial verb,* B.

pairī-cithīt, earlier, 29.4.

pairī-gaēthē, in the outer realm, 34.2,—LS -tha, *n.*

pairī-(cā)-jasāi, I will come around, 28.2 50.8 51.22,—gam.

pairī-jasat, he came around, 43.7,9,11,13,15.

pairī-matōis.cā, of thinking beyond, pride, 32.3,—GS -tay, *f.*

pairyaogzā, thou commandedst around, proclaimedst, 43.12,— 2SPr aog.

paithī, upon, beside the path, 50.4,—IsS *after* ā, pathī, *f.*

paithyaēcā, to a master, 53.4,— DS patay, *m.*

paitī, again, to, at, for, with, but, 30.2 33.11 34.6 48.7 49.11 50.9 51.22.

paitī-eretē, who has opposed, 44.12,—NSf -ta, PfP ar.

paitī-mraot, said again, answered, 32.2,—mrav.

paitī-mrāvat, said again, answered, 29.3,—mrav.

paitise, the master, 44.9,—NS patay, *m.*

paitishāt, he receives, 44.2,—aēsh, to seek.

paitī-zānatā, you recognize, 29.11,—2PPrA zān.

paityaoget, rebounding, answering, 46.8,—*adverb from* aog.

paity-ā-stêm, impressed, obedient, 53.3,— AS -stay, *f,*—stā.

paityeiñtī, they go again, meet, 49.11,—3PPM ay.

paouruyāe, the first, 46.6,—AP parav.

paouruyāis, with the first, 46.15,—IsP parav.

paouruyehyā, of the first, 33.1 48.6,—GS paourva.

paourvīm, at first, 29.10 30.4 31.11 43.5,8,11 44.2 51.2,— *adverbial* AS of paouruya, *adj; see* pourvīm.

parā, out, through, before, away, 30.2 43.12 48.2 51.15 53.6,7.

paracā, before, 53.7.

parāhūm, in the future, 46.19,—AS parāhva *from* parā, anhav

paraos, of much, powerful, 47.4,—GS*m.* parav, *or* paourva, *meaning* much *or* first.

parê, out, before, 33.7 34.5.

parshtā, to ask, 43.10,—*inf.* fras, *for* PfP.

parshtêm, to ask, 43.10,—*absolute* fras.

pas*ê*us, of cattle, 31.15 50.1,—GS pasav *m.*

pasūs, cattle, 45.9,—AP ib.

pā*t,* he will keep, 32.13 46.4,—pā(y).

patā, father, 44.3 45.11 47.2,—NS patar, pitar.
  patarêm, 31.8 45.4,—AS ib.

path*a*m, the path, 31.9,—AS pathā, *f.*

pathō, of the path, 51.13,—GS path, *n.*

pathō, the paths, 33.5 34.12 43.3 53.2,—AP ib.

pathmêñg, the paths, 46.4,—AP pathman, *n.*

patōis, of the master, 45.11,—GS patay, *m.*

paurvatātem, the first-fruit, 33.14,—AS tā*t, f.*

pāyā*t,* he guards, restrains, 46.8,—3SKA pā(y) pā*t*pōi nipā*e*nhē

pāyūm, guardian, 46.7,—AS pāyav, *m.*

perenā, thou fulfillest, 28.10,—2SIA par,

perenā*e*nhō, full, 44.13,—NAP -na, *adj.*

peresā, I asked, 31.14,15,16 43.10 44.1-20,—fras, *which forms*
  peresaētē, 31.13, *as passive,* 3DPM.
  peresāi, I ask, address, 44.12.
  peresāitē, he counsels, keeps watch, 31.12; in 13 Barthlo. reads
    peresaētē.
  peresas, asking, 51.5,—NS PrP.
  peresa*t,* he asked, 29.2 43.7.
  peresmanêng, deliberating, 30.6,—AP -na, *adj.*

peretāe, 51.13, peretō, 51.12, at the bridge,—LS -tav, *m.*
  peretus, 46.11, NS; peretūm, 46.10, AS.

perethā, compensations, 48.2,—NP -tha, *n.*

perethūs, wide, 50.7,—AP -thav, *adj.*

peshō-tanvō, body-forfeited, 53.9,—NP -va, *adj.* tanū.

pis*h*yasū, let them see, appreciate, 50.2,—pāh.

pis*h*yeiñtī, they behold, 44.20,—pāh.

pithā, 53.6, ?

pithrē, to a father, 44.7,—pitar, fedrōi.

pithwā, with food, 44.5, IsS -tav, *f,*— arêm-pithwā, noon, *as right time for* food?

pōi, to protect, 44.15,16,—*inf.* pā(y).

pouru, much, *first consonantal stem-form of* parav, *which forms*
    pourubyō, 34.8 DAbIP.
    pourūs, 43.15 NS*m.*
    pourūs, 47.6 NP.
    pourushū, 50.2 LP.
    pouruyē, 30.2 44.19 45.2 LS *temporal.*
    pouruyō, 28.11 GS?
    pouruyō, NS 30.7 31.7 44.3,11 46.9 51.3,15.
    pourvīm, AS *adverbial,* 28.1 31.8 45.3; *see* paourvīm.

pourū-aēnāe, of many violences, 32.6,—NS -nah, *adj.*

Pouru-cista, third and youngest daughter of Zarathushtra, the bride of Frashaoshtra, 53.5 (*much wisdom,* 'Sophia').

pouru-temāis, as much as possible, 34.1.

puthrem, a son, 44.7, AS puthra, *m.*

R

rāda*t*, he prepares, adapts, 51.6,—rād.
rāda*n*hā, with ready willingness, 46.13,—rādah, *n.*
rāda*n*hō, of a Preparer, 46.17 45.7,—GS rādah, *adj.*
rādem, a Preparer, 29.9,—AS rāda, *m.*
rādeñtī, they prepare, 33.2,— rād.
rāe*n*ha*n*hōi, thou wouldst grant, 28.8,—2SKAorM, rā.
rāe*n*hayen, they would cause to apostacize, 32.12,—rah, *caus.*
raēxenāe, the inheritances, 34.7,—AP -nah, *n;* raēk.
raēxena*n*hō, of the inheritance, 32.11. GS ib.
rafedrahyā, of support, assistance, 28.1,—GS -dra, *n.*
rafedrāī, support, 28.3 33.13 46.12,—DS ib *or* Inf rap.
rafedrêm, support, 46.2; -*dr*em, 51.20,—AS.
rafenō, of assistance, 28.6 43.8,14,—GS -nah, *n.* with aojōñghva*t*,
    NA*n*, 'strength of assistance.'
raithīm, a way, (of understanding), directions, 50.6,—AS -thya, *m.*
rajīs, 53.9 ?—isolated ones, M; B *reads* arejīs, valuable, *from*
    AP arejay, *adj? Verb* are*g*, arejat.
rāmā-dāe, peace-giving, 47.3,—AS -dāh, *adj. n.*
rama*m*cā, peace, 29.10 48.11 53.8,—AS rāman, *n.—Verb* ram
rāmemcā, cruelty, 49.4, AS rāma, *m. Belongs with* rema.
ra*n*ayāe, of both contending parties, 31.19—GD rāna, *m.*
rānōibyā, to both contending parties, 31.3 47.6 51.9,—DD, ib.
rānōibyō, 43.12,—DP ib.
rānyō-skeretīm, fortune-bringing, 44.6 47.3 50.2,—AS -tay.
raocāe. the lights, 50.10; raocāescā, 44.5,—AP raocah, *n.*
raocebīs, with the lights, 30.1 31.7,—IsP ib.
raostā, it lamented, 29.9,—raod.
rapañtē, for support, 34.4,—DS PrP rap.
rapañtō, 28.2, of support,—GS ib.
rapên, they may support, 51.18,—rap.
rāreshō, apostate, 49.2,—NS -sha, *adj. with ablative.*
rāre*sh*yan, that they may apostacize, 32.11,—Pr29 rah.

rāreshyeiñtī, they have apostacized, 47.4,—rah.
rashō, the harm, 30.11,—AS rashah, *n.*
rāshayēnghē, to injure, 49.3 51.9,—*inf.* rash.
rashnā, with an abservance, command, 46.5,—IsS rāzan, *n.*
rashnam, an observance, command, 34.12,—AS ib.
rāstī, he belongs to, 53.9,—3SPA rath.
rātam, oblation, service, 33.14 43.9,—AS rātay, *adj.*
rātayō, serviceablenesses, 33.7,—NP ib,
rāthemō, belonging to, 44.17, NS; 53.6 NP;— -a, *adj.*
ratōis, of serviceableness, 29.11,—GS -tay, *adj.*
ratūm, judge, judgment, 31.2 44.16 51.5,—AS ratav, *m.*
ratus, judge, 29.2,6,—NS ib.
ratūs, judgments, 33.1 43.6,—AP ib.
rāyō, riches, 43.1,—AP (B, GS) rāy, *m.*
rāzarê, command, decree, 34.12,—NS rāzar, *n.*
razishtā, the most right, 33.1,—AP erezav. *sup.*
remem, cruelty, 48.7, AS; remō, 29.1, NS;—rema, *m. Belongs*
with rāma.
rōithwen, to saturate, fill, 31.7,—*inf.?*

S

sādrā(cī*t*), pain, grief, torment, 34.7 43.11 45.7,—AP -ra, *n.*
sāhī*t*, he may teach, 50,6,—sāh.
sa*h*yā*t*, he may pronounce, 44.19,—s*a*h.
sa*h*vārê, plans, 29.4,—AP -var, *n.*
sā*h*vênī, I teach, 53.5,—sa*h*; *or* AP sā*h*van, *n.*
saocaya*t*, he may burn, 32.14,—saok.
saoshyañ*t*, helper, savior, PfP sav; *in* sing. *of* Zarathushtra, *in plur. of* his helpers. *See*
   saoshyañ*t*am, GP 34.12 46.3.
   saoshyañtō, GS 45.11.
   saoshyañtō, NAP 48.12 53.2.
   saoshyas, NS 48.9.
sarê, to commune, 49.3,—*inf.* sar, *which forms*
   sar*e*danāe, 43.14, scorner, B; princely chief, M; society-giving church-organizing.—AP -na, *adj.*
   sar*e*dyayāe, companions, 33.9, GDu. -ya, *m.*
   sar*e*jā, helper, 29.3,—NS sar*e*gan, *m.*
   sarêm, 49.8,9; sarem, 53.3, 'united society, association, commun-ion,—AS sar, *f.* (B, GP 49.9).
   sāremnō, being in communion with, 32.2,—PfP NS -na, *adj.*
   sāreñtē, to him who is communing with, 51.3,—PrP DS.
   sarō, associations, 31.21,—AP sar, *f.* (B, GS).
   sarōi, to commune, 44.17,—*inf.*
   sārshtā, he communes, 49.5.
sas, the effecting, doing, 43.11 46.19,—sand, NSPrP *or* 2Ss-AorA
sashathā, you have familiarized yourselves, 30.11,—sak.
sasheñcā, they may learn, 53.1,—sak.
sāsnāe(scā), teachings, commands, 29.8 31.18 49.9,—AP -nā, *f.*
sāsnan*am*, of teachings, 48.3,—GP ib.
sāsnayā, with the teaching, 29.7,—IsS.
sastā, you procure, 29.1,—2P s-AorA sand.
sāstārō, the princes, 46.1,—NP -tar, *m.*

sastē, in the consummation, 30.8 46.12,— sasta, *n.*
sāstī, he is teaching, 48.3,—*sah.*
sastis, teacher, 32.9 45.1,—*adj. in comp.* NS -tay.
sastrāi, to fulfil, consummate, 46.3,—sand.
sāstū, may he teach, 45.6,—*sah*, sāstī.
savā, the profits, 44.12 45.7,—AP savā, *f.*
savacā, the profits, 30.11,—NS*f*, ib.
savāis, with profits, 48.1 51.15, —IsP ib.
savaṇhō, of profit, 43.3,—GS savah, *n.*
savaṇhō, the profits, 51.2,—AP ib.
savaṇham, of profits, 28.9,—GP ib.
savayō, to procure profit for, 51.9,—*inf.* sav.
savōi, in the place of profit, 43.12,—LS sava, *f.* (B, AD*f.*)
savō, a profit, 34.3 51.20,—NS savah, *n.*
sāzdūm, to be opposed, 31.18,—sā.
sazdyāi, to fulfil, 30.2 51.16,—sand.
scañtū. they strive, 53.2,—hak.
sêñdā, they effect, 51.14,—sand.
sêñghā, with the teaching, 44.16,—IsS sêñgha, *m.*
sêñghā, teachings, 45.2,—NP ib.
sêñghāeṇhō, teachings, 48.3,—AP ib.
sêñghahyā, of the teaching, 43.14 44.14 48.12,—GS ib.
sêñghāis, with the teachings, 46.3 51.14,—IsP ib,
sêñghaitē, he declares. 32.7,—M sah.
sêñghāmahī, let us formulate, 31.1,—ib.
sêñghanāis, with the teachings, 32.9,—IsP sêñghana, *m.*
sêñghānī, I declare, 46.17,—sah.
sêñghascā, the teachings, 31.11,—NP sêñgha, *m.*
sêñghō, the teaching, 32.6 51.14,—NS ib.
sêñghūs, through the teachings, 34.7,—IsP sêñghav, *m.*
sêñnhē, in the teaching, 51.7,—LS sêñgha, *m.*
seraoshā, with obedience, hearing, *or* Sraosha, 46.17,—IsS -a, *m.*
seraoshānē, I will hear, 50.4,—srav.
Seraoshem, Sraosha, 28.5 33.5,14 45.5,—AS -sha, *m.*
Seraoshō, Sraosha, 43.12 44.16,—NS ib.

sevīshtāi, for the strongest, 28.5,—DS -a, *sup.* sura.
sevīshtō, strongest, 33.11,—NS ib.
shaētī, he dwells, 33.5 (43.3); shaēitī, 46.16,—3SPA shay.
shōithrahyā, of the clan, 31.16 46.4,—GS shōithra, *n.*
shōithrem, the clan, 31.18, AS ib.
s*h*yaomam, of the deeds, 32.3,—GP s*h*yaoman, *n.*
s*h*yaothanā, deed, NS *f,* 45.4.
———— nā, with deed, IsS 31.22 34.1,14 48.4 51.21.
———— nā, deeds, NP 45.2.
———— nā, deeds, AP 28.1 31.11 33.1 34.2,9,10,15 43.5 44.10 47.1,2 53.1.
———— naēshū, LP 31.8.
———— nahyā, GS 33.14 45.8.
———— nāi, DS, 34.5.
———— nāis, IsP 30.5 31.20,21 34.8 43.6,16 44.6 45.5 46.4,7,8,11,15 47.5 48.5,12 50.9 51.1,3,5,13,14,19 53.2.
———— nam, GP 28.4 48.8.
———— nascā, NP 31.6.
———— nāt, AblS 32.12.
———— nem, AS 32.5.
———— nēñg, AP 49.11 (*adj.*)
———— nōi, LS 30.3 46.9.
s*h*yas, those dwelling, 44.9 (47.5),—NS PrP shay.
s*h*yātō, he rejoices, 51.8,—s*h*yā.
s*h*yavāi, to treat, move, 33.8,—*inf.* shav.
s*h*yēitibyō, to those rejoicing in, 53.8,—s*h*yā.
sinam, destruction, 44.14,—AS sinā, *f.*
sīshā, do thou reveal, teach, 28.11 34.12,—sāh.
sīshōit, he would reveal, teach, 43.3,—O ib.
sīzdyamnā, they are driven back, 32.4,—NP *adj* PfPM sīzdyā.
skeñdō, a break, 30.10,—NS -da, *m.*
snaithishā, with the weapon, 31.18,—IsS -ish, *n.*
spādā, both armies, 44.15,—ND -da, *m.*
spanyāe, the holier, 45.2,—NS -yah, *comp.* speñta.
spashuthā, you discover, spy, 53.6,—2PPA spas.
spaṣyā, I discover, look on, 44.11,—ib.

spathrahyā, of success, 30.10,—GS -thra, *n.*
spên.cā, fortune, success, 45.9,—AP -spā, *n.*
spenishtā, through the most bountiful, 33.12 43.2 51.7 53.3,—IsS -ta,
    sup. speñta.
    spenishtahyā, GS 47.2.
    spenishtō, AS*n*, 30.5 43.16.
speñtā, bountiful, VS 33.13,—-ta, *adj.*
————tā, IsS 43.6 44.7 45.6,11 47.1,5,6.
————tā, NS*f.* 51.4,11.
————tahyā, GS 28.1 34.2.
————t*a*m, AS*f*, 32.2 34.9,10 49.2.
————tā*t*, AblS 47.4.
————tem, AS*m.* 43.4,5,7,9,11,13,15 46.9.
————tō, NS 43.3 44.2 47.3 48.3,7 51.16,21.
speñtō.temō, more bountiful, 45.5,—NS -ma.
spênva*t*, he promotes, 51.21.—spā.
spereda(nĭ), with zeal, down, 53,4,—spere*d*, *f,* or I will emu-
· late, *verb.*
Spitāma, tribe *or* family of Zarathushtra, 'whit-ing'? 29.8 46.13,15,
    51.11,12,19 53.1,2,3.
sraotā, hear! 30.2 33.11 45.1,—srav, *which forms*
    sraotū, 45.6,9 49.7,9, Imp.
    srāvī, 32.7,8 45.10 53.1, is heard, recognized,—PrP pass.
    srāvayaēmā, we may cause to be heard, 49.6 *caus.*
    a-srūdūm, heard badly, 32.3, *augm.* pass.
    sruidyāi, to hear, 34.12 45.5 (46.13) *inf.*
    sruyē, to be heard, 33.7 *inf.*
    a-srvāt*em*, both of them heard, 30.3,—3DAugm.
sravāe, words, 28.10,—NP -vah, *n.*
    sravāe, AP 32:9,10; -vāescā, 34.15.
    sravahī, LS 30.10.
    srava*n*hā, IsS 32.12.
srāvahyeitī, to become heard, notorious, 32.6, srav, inf.
srāvaye*n*ghē, to cause to be heard, proclaim, 29.8,—ib.
srevīm, hearing, 28.7,—AS -vay, *f.*

sruidyāi, to hear, 34.12 45.5 46.13,—srav.

stā, you are, 32.3 34.6.—Pr ah.

stāenhaṯ, they stood, 50.4,—3P s-AorA stā, axshtaṯ 3P 51.4.

staomyā, praisings, 33.8,—AP*n* -ya, *adj.*

staotācā, praising, 30.1,—NP -ta, *adj.*

staotāis, with praises, 45.8 49.12,—IsP -ta, *m,* stav.

staotā, praiser, 50.11,—NS -tar, *m, late word.*

starêmcā, star, 44.3,—AS star, *m.*

staumī, I praise, 43.8,—stav, which forms

  *sta*va*s,* praising, NS PrP, 34.6 45.6 50.4,(9).

stêñg, places, 50.2,—AP stay, *f,* a-stīs, 43.3.

stōi, to be, 31.8 33.9 34.4 45.10 46.16 49.2 50.2,6; LS stay.

stūt*am,* praising, praying, 28.9 34.2,—AS *adj.*

stūtō, praising, praying, 34.12,15 41.1,—AP *ib.*

sūcā, with sight, 30.2,—IsS -ca, *adj.*

sūidyāi, to be useful to, 44.2 49.3,—*inf.* sav.

suxrā, with red (fire), 31.19 51.9,—IsS -ra, *adj.*

suyē, to profit, 49.9,—*inf.* sav.

syascīṯ, 32.16, ? sā, it is teaching, ?

syazdaṯ, he goes backwards, he shuns, 34.9,—syazda.

syōzdūm, let it be opposed, 48.7,—s-Aor sā.

T

tā, this, IsS;P; 30.1,3,4,10 31.1,5,14 32.5,9 33.6,8 34.15 43.4 44.8 45.7 46.8,9 47.3,5,6 49.3 51.2,5,10,12,13,15,22.

tā-cā, 34.10 45.7 47.5; **tā-cīt**, 31.5 44.3 46.19.

tāe, these, NAVDu 31.14.

taē-cīt, these certain, 32.11,—NP.

taēbyācā, to both these, 51.2.

taēibyō, to *or* from these, 34.1 44.18.

taibyō, ib. 30.8 44.6 53.3.

tāis, thus, 34.11 44.7.

tāis(cā), with these, IsP 30.11 32.6 34.8 43.14 46.10,15,16 49.5 50.9.

tam, this, AS,GP 28.7 44.10 46.7 48.5 49.6 51.16,18.

tanūm, body, 33.10,—AS **tanū**, *f*, **tanus**, *n*, *whence*
    tanushicā, about the body, 43.8,—LS.
    tanuyē, for his own body, personally, 30.2,—DS.
    tanvascīt, of his body, 33.14,—GS.
    tanvêm, body, 46.8,—AS.

tarê-maitīm, 'thinking beyond', arrogance,—33.4,—AS -**tay**, *f*.
    Contrariness, as special opponent of gentle Ar-maiti, Y.60.5.

tarê-manyañtā, those scorning, 45.11,—NP PrP **man**.

tarê-mastā, those scorned, 45.11,—AP PfP **man**.

tashā (gêus), the Shaper of the Cattle, 29.2 31.9 46.9,—NS -**shan**, *m*

tashat, shaped, 29.1,7,—**tash**.
    tashō (gam). thou didst shape the Cattle, 31.11 44.6 51.7,—ib.
    tāsht, shaped, 44.7,—PfP,
    tashtō, he was shaped, 49.9.

tat, that, 31.3,5 32.16 34.6,14 43.1,10,11 44.1-19 46.2,5,9,18 49.7,8,10 51.1,18,19,20 53.5,9.

tatashā, I shaped, 29.6,—Perf. **tash**.

taurvayāmā, we may overcome, 28.6,—**tar**.

tavā(cā), I am able, 28.4 43.14 50.11 51.18 53.9,—**tav**.

taxmem.cā, heroism, 43.4,—AS -**ma**, *adj*.

tayā, furtive, 31.13,—NP*n*, -**ya**, *adj*,

têm, therefore, this, 29.7 31.20 33.9 34.7,13 43.13 45.8,9,10 46.13 51.21 53.4,7.

temāescā, darknesses, 44.5,—AP **temah**, *n*.

temaṇhō, darkness, 31.20,—NP ib.

têmcā-tū, do thou —— this, 53.3.

têñg, those, AP 32.1 44.11,13 46.4,14.

teviscā, violence, 29.1,—NS tevish, *n.*

tevīshī, vitality, 34.11 51.7,—ND -shī, *f.*

——, through vitality, 45.10,—IsS ib.

tevīshīm, vitality, 33.12 43.1 48.6,—AS ib.

thraoshtā, you mature, 34.3; it matures, 46.7,—thraosh.

thrāta, protector, 50.1,—NS -tar, *m.*

thrāyōdyāi, to protect, 34.5,—*inf.* thrā.

thrāzdūm, protect! 34.7,—s-Aor ib.

thwā, thee, thy, 28.5,7,11 43.4-15 44.3-19 46.1,3,9 49.8 51.4,9 53.3.

thwahmāt, from thy, 28.11 43.9 46.7 47.5.

thahmī, in thy, LS 32.6,8 33.10 34.10 43.4,13 48.4,7 49.5,8,10.

thwahū, in thy, LP 43.7.

thwahyā, of thy, GS 31.3 32.13 34.8,9 43.4,6 44.14 48.12.

thwahyāe, of thy, GS 48.8.

thwam, thee, AS 29.10.

thwarōzdūm, did you fashion, create, 29.1,—s-Aor thwareṣ.

thwatcā, thee, thy,—ASn 33.4 44.3 50.1.

thwāvas, like thee, 31.16 43.3 44.1,9 48.3,8,—NS PrP thwāvañt.

thwaxshaṇhā, through zealous, 33.3 46.12, IsS -shah, *n.*

   thwaxshō, zeal, 29.2,—AP ib.

thwê, thy, 31.9,—NS.

thwisrā, shining, 31.13,—AP -ra, *adj.*

thwōi (astī), (is) to bless, 34.11,—*inf.* B. *Doubtful.*

thwōi, thy, NP 31.9 32.1 34.11 44.11 48.8.

thwōreshtā, creator, 29.6,—NS -tar, *m.*

tkaēshāi, to the false teacher, 49.3,—DS -sha, *m.*

   tkaēshō, the false teacher, 49.2,—NS ib.

tōi, to *or* of thee, thy, 29.2 30.7 32.15 33.2 46.2,9 48.1,8,12 49.4,11 51.8 53.9.

   Also 30.9 33.6,9 43.10.15.

tū, but, 46.10,16; thou, 28.6,7 32.7 49.7 51.3.

Tūrahyā, of the Tura tribe, 46.12,—GS -ra, *m.*

Tushnā-maitis, silent thought, *or* devotion, 43.15,—NS -tay, *f.*

tvêm, *emphatic conjunction*, thee ? 28.11 46.19 47.3 48.2.

U

ubē, for both, 34.11,—DS uba.
ufyācā, I am lauding, 43.8,—vaf.
ufyānī, I will sing hymns, 28.3,—ib.
ugréňg, strong, 50.7,—AP ugra *adj.*
ūitī, thus, 45.2.
upā, in, into, up, 45.5 53.8.
urūdōyatā, they have caused to lament, 44.20,—raod.
urunascā, the souls, 49.10,—AP urvan, *m.*
urūpayeiñtī, they practice deceit, 48.10,—*same as* diwzaidyāi.
urūraost, he refused, 51.12,—3SPrPfA raod.
urushaēibyō, for the hungry, 29.7,—DP -sha, *adj, hvarethra.*
urvādanhā, the joys, 43.2,—AP -dah, *n.*
urvāidyāe, (I, the) more joyful, 34.6,—NS -dyah, *adj.*
urvaēsē, at the crisis, turn, change, 43.5,6 51.6,—LS -sa, *m.*
urvā, soul, 34.2 44.8 45.7 46.11 50.1 51.13,—NS urvan, *m, whence*
   urvānē, DS 31.2.
   urvānem, AS 28.4.
   urvanō, NAP 33.9 45.2 49.11.
uruarāe(scā), plants, 44.4 48.6 51.7,—AP -rā, *f.*
urvāshat, he is encouraged, 44.8,—*see* urvāxshat.
urvātā, commands, 30.11 31.1,—AP -ta, *n.*
   urvatahyā, GS 34.8.
   urvātāis, IsP 31.1 44.15.
   urvatem, AS 31.3.
urvāthā, friendly, 51.14,—NP -tha, *adj.*
   urvathō, a friend, 31.21 44.2 45.11 46.14 50.6 51.11,—NS ib.
urvatōis, of a vow, 46.5,—GS -tay, *f.*
urvāxshat, it is rejoicing, 34.13,—ASn PrPart.
urvāxs-uxtī, with cries of joy, 32.12,—IsS -tay, *f,*
urvāzā, bliss, 30.1,—NS,AP -zā, *f.*
urvāzema, bliss, 32.1, IsS,AP -zeman, *n.*
urvāzishtam, most blissful, 49.8,—AS -ta, *adj. supell.*

us, up, out! 33.12 46.11.

usêmahī, we wish, 34.4,—va*s*.

usên, in his wish, 44.10 45.9,—LS [usan, *n.*

ushā*e*, dawn, 44.5,—NS ushah, *f.*

ush*e*urū, 34.7; M, in wide mental light? sophistries, IsS.

ushtā, desired, beloved, decided, success! 30.11 33.10 43.1 46.16 51.8,16,
   —2PPrA *and* PfP va*s*.

ushtānā, by living, 43.16,—IsS -nā, *f. whence*
   ushtānāi, for life, DS 34.14.
   ushtan*e*m, life, AS 31.11 33.14.

ushtis, will, 48.4,—NS -tay, *f.*

ushtr*e*mcā, a camel, 44.18,—AS -rā, *m.*

ushuruyē, ? 32.16 wide light? DS.

us*h*yāi, to proclaim, 43.15.

Usixs(cā), an opponent of Zarathushtra, 44.20,—NS.

ustānāis (za*s*tāis), with stretched-out, 29.5,—IsP PfP us, tan.

ustāna-za*s*tō, with outstretched hands, 28.1 50.8,—NS -a, *adj.*

usvahī, we desire, 46.16,—va*s*.
   usyā*t*, he desires, 50.2,—ib.

utayuitī, enduringness, AS*n* 33.8; IsS 43.1; ADu 34.11 45.10
   51.7— -tay, *f, whence*
   utayuitīm, AS 48.6.
   utayuitīs, AP 30.7.
   utayūtā, 45.7, LS.

ux*d*ā, through utterance, 32.9 44.19,—IsS ux*d*a, *adj, whence*
   ux*d*ā, NP 45.2.
   ux*d*ā, AP 43.5 44.8 51.20 53.1.
   ux*dah*yācā, GS 33.14 45.8.
   ux*d*āis, IsP, 28.6 43.11 46.14 47.2 51.3,21 53.2.

uxshā, a bull, 50.10,—NS uxshan, *m.*
   uxshānō, the bulls, 46.3,—NP ib.

uxshyā, thou causest to grow, 33.10,—vaxsh, *whence*
   uxshyeitī, to grow, 44.3,—*inf.*
   uxshyō, thou causest to grow, 31.7.

uz-āreshvā, arise up! 33.12,—*imp.* ar.

uzemêm, reverence, 44.7,—AS -ma, *adj.*

uzemōhī, we consider, regard, 46.9,—1PPA aoz.
uz-ere(i)dyāi, to rise up, 43.12,14,—*inf.* ar.
uz-jên, he may go up, 46.12,—3SPrA gam.
uz-ūithyōi, to protect,, 46.5,—*inf.* av.

V

vā, or, *frequent.* 51.11, you?

vacāe, words, speeches, 31.1 33.8 49.7,—AP vak, *m.,f.*

vacahicā, word, 30.3,—LS vacah, *n. whence*

    vacanhā, IsS 31.22 32.5 33.2 34.1 47.1 48.4.

       vacanham, GP, 31.19, —uxdāi *as inf,* 'to speak truth of the words of his tongue.'

    vacanhō, AP 49.11.

    vacê, AS, 45.5.

vacem, AS 29.9 31.12 50.6,—vak, *m.,f.*

vācī, it is said, 43.13,—vak, *verb.*

vacō, NP 31.20,—vacah, *n.*

vacō, AP 53.7,—ib.

vadarê, the weapon, 32.10,—AS -dar, *n.*

vādāyōit, may repel, 29.2,—vādāya.

vademnō, counselling, 53.5,—NS *adj. to* vādati, he speaks.

vāe, you, NAP 28.2,9 31.2 32.1,3,5 43.13 49.6 50.4,8,9.

vaēdā, he knows, 28.10 31.2 34.7 45.4 46.2 48.9.—vaēd.

vaēdem, as provider, 29.10 32.11,—AS -da, *m.*

vaēdemnō, knower, expert, 28.5 31.22 43.14 48.3 51.19.—NS PfP vaēd.

vaēdenā, knowing, 34.7,—NP *adj.*

vaēdishtō, most knowing, 32.7 46.19,—NS.

vaēdōdūm, is to be known, 53.5,—vaēd, *whence*

    vaēdyāi, *inf,* to know, 44.8.

vaēm, we, 30.9, NP.

vaēnahī, thou seeest, 31.13,—vaēna.

vaēnanhē, to see, 32.10,—*inf.* ib.

vaēpyō, a pederast, ? 51.12,—NS -ya, *adj.*

vaēshō, place of decay 53.9,—AS -shah, *n.*

vafūs, sayings, decrees, 29.6; vafus, 48.9,—AP vafav, *m.*

vahishta, best, *frequent.* 28.7,8,9 30.2,4 31.1,4,6,7 32.6,11,12,16 33.3,6,7,9 34.15 43.2,11,15 44.2,10 45,4,5,6 46.6,10,18 47.1,2,5 48.3,5 49.9,10 50.1,4 51.1,4,22 53.1.

vahmē, praying praise, adoring, 34.2 45.6,—LS -ma, *adj,*

vahmahyā, of praying, praises, adoring, 50.7,—GS -ma, *whence*
   vahmāi, DS 46.10,17 50.10 51.2 53.2.
   vahmem, AS 48.1.
   vahméñg, AP 45.8.
vahyō, better, 30.3 31.2,5 43.3 48.4 51.6,19 53.9.
vaiñtyā, supplicatory, 28.10,—NP -ya, *adj.*
vairīm, at choice, 34.14 51.1,—AS as adv.
vairyāe, 'choice,' valuable, 43.13,—GS -ya, adj.
vanaēmā, we may overcome, 31.4,—van.
vananam, victory, 44.15,—AS -na, *f,*
vanhāu, good, 30.10 31.19 33.2 47.6 49.8, IsS NAP vanhav, *whence*
   vanhaovē, DS 43.5.
   vanhêus, GS, *see* 28.1,7,8,10 30.1,19 31.10 33.3,5,13,14 34.7,9,10,11,12,13,14 43.1,2,3,4
      44.4,13 45.4,5,8,9 46.2,14,16 47.2 48.3,6–9,11 49.3 50.8,9 51.3,6,11,16 53.5.
   vanhuyā, IsS *f,* 33.12 51.10.
   vanhuyāi, DS 53.4.
   vanhūs, AP 34.2.   *See* vohū, vanuhī.
vañtā, with praise, 51.22,—IsS -ta, *m.*
vanuhī, good, *f, all cases:* 32.2 43.5 48.2,5 49.1 51.10,17,18,21 53.1,4.
vaocā, say, speak, 31.3,5 34.15 44.1-19 48.2,—vak, *also*
vaocacā, 45.3 ib.
vaocanhē, to proclaim, 28.11,—*inf.* vak.
   vaocat, he speaks, 29.6 34.10 45.3; vaocāt, 31.6.
vaorāzathā, you have rejoiced, 50.5,—2PPfA urvāz.
vaoxemā, through onr preaching, 34.5,—IsS -ma, *from* vak.
var, *a,* to choose, *wnence*
   varatā, 3PPrM 30.5 32.12.
   varemaidī, 1PPrM 32.2.
   vāurōimaidī, 28.5 ?
   verenātā, 3P, 30.6.
   verenē, 46.3.
   vereñtē, 3SPM 43.16 51.18.
   verenvaitē, 3DPM 31.17.
var, *b,* to convert, *whence*
   vāurāitē, 47.6.
   vāurayā, 1SOM 31.3.
   vāurōimāidī, 28.5.

var, *c,* general choosing, *whence*
    varānī, 1SP 53.4.
    fra-varetā, 31.10.
vārāi, for the will, 33.2 51.6,—DS vāra, *n.*
varecāe, help, 32.14,—AS*n* -cah, *n.*
varedaitī, she prospers, 28.3,—var*ed, whence*
    varedayaētā, they may increase, acquire, 50.3.
    vareden, they increase, 49.4.
    varedemam, to increase, 46.16.
vārem, the will, 46.18,—AS vāra, *n.*
varenāi, for conviction, manner of life, 49.3,—DS -na, *m.*
    varenêñg, 31.11 48.4,—AP.
vareshaitē, they have been performed, 29.4 33.1—3PA or var*ez:*
    vareshaitī, he works, 33.2 46.19.
    vareshā, I may have done, 50.10.
    vareshānē, I may work, effect, 51.1.
    varesheñtī, they practice, 45.3.
    var*ez*ayañtō, of the working, 45.4, GS PrP.
vas, overcoming, 49.4,—NS vañ*t,* PrP van.
vasāe, the chooser, 31.11, —NS -ah, *m.*
va*sase,* arbitrary, powerful, 43.8,—*in comp. from* vasê.
va*sat,* he wills, 29.4,—vas.
va*sê,* at will, arbitrarily, 43.1 50.9 53.9,—*adv, see* vasō.
va*sê*-itōiscā, of freedom, 53.9,—GS itay, *f,* (going).
vasemī, I wished, 29.9 43.1 44.3,—vas.
    vashī, thou wishest, 34.12 43.9 44.16.
    vashtī, he wishes, 29.8 46.14.
va*sh*yetē, it was announced, 44.11,—va*sh.*
vasnā, through *or* with will, 34.15 46.19 50 11,—IsS -na, *m.*
vasō, at will, 31.19 32.15,—*adv. see* vasê.
vāstā, shepherd, 29.1,—NS -tar, *m.*
vastē, to clothe oneself in, 30.,5—vāh.
vāstrā, with the pasture, 29.2 32.10,—IsS -tra, *n.*
    vāstrāi, DS 47.3.
    vāstrā*t, verb? or* AblS 33.4 51.14.
vāstravaitī, with a pastoral realm, 48.11,—IsS *f* PrP. -vañ*t.*

vāstravaitīm, a pastoral realm, 50.2 AS ib.
vāstrē, in a pasture, 33.3,—LS -tra, *n,* *whence*
  vāstrem, a pasture, 44.20,—AS ib.
vāstrīm, the pastoral man, 31.10,—AS vāstrya. *whence*
  vāstryā, AP 29.1 33.6.
  vāstryāi, DS 29.6.
  vāstryā*t*, AblS 31.9.
  vāstryaēibyō, DP 53.4.
  vāstryehyā, GS 31.15.
  vāstryō, NS 51.5.
vātāi, to a wind, 44.4,—DS vāta, *m.*
vāunus, supplicating, 48.8,—Part. van.
vāurāitē, 47.6; vāurayā, 31.3; vāurōimaidī, 28.5;—*see* var.
vāverezōi, to perform, 29.4,—*inf.* varez.
va*x*edrahyā, of a sppeech, 29.8,—GS -dra, *n.*
vāxs, it may grow, 44.17,—vaxs, to grow.
  vaxsha*t*, it may grow, 31.6 48.1,6.
  vaxshentē, for growing, are becoming known, 32.4, DS PrP.
vaxshyā, I will utter, 30.1 46.15 51.8,—F vak.
vaxsht, caused to grow. 34.11.
vayōi, woe! 53.7.
vayū-beredubyō, crying woe, 53.6 DP b*er*et, *adj.*
vāzā, both driven, 51.12,—NDu -za, *adj.*
vazda*n*hā, enduring, 49.10,—IsS -dah, *adj.*
vazdrē̃g, promotive, 46.4,—AP -dra, *adj.*
vazdvarê, enduringness, 31.21,—AS -dar, *n.*
vāzishtō, most prospering, 31.22,—NS -ta, *adj.*
vazyamnābyō, to those who are being driven, (in marriage),
  53.5,—DP PfP vaz.
vê, *conjunction,* indeed, 45.3 49.12 51.15 53.4,5,7.
vē̃gha*t*, he may overcome, 48.2,—van.
  vē̃*n*haitī, he shall overcome, 48.1, ib.
veredā, with the increase, 31.4,—IsS vered, *f. or from* var?
verenātā, that they should choose, 30.6,—var.
  verenē, I may choose, 46.3.
  verentē, he may choose, 43.16 51.18.

verenvaitē, they both choose, 31.17,—3DPM.

verethrem-jā, 'come with victory,' victoriously, 44.16,—NS gan.

verezdāis, with increasing, 46.3,—IsP PfPA varez.

verezênem, group of laborers, 32.1,—AS -na, *n.*

verezênyō, a laborer, 33.3,—NS -ya, *adj.*

verezênahyācā, of the group of laborers, 33.4,—GS -na, *n.*
>   verezênē, LS 34.14.
>   verezênyāe, GS *f,* -ya, *adj* 45.9.
>   verezênā, NP 46.1.
>   verezênāi, DS 49.7.

verezyat, he works, 47.2,—varez.

verezyātam, agriculture, 48.5,—AS -ātā, *f.*

verezyō, activities, 30.5,—AP -zyah, *n.*

verezyeidyāi, to work, act, 33.6 43.11,—*inf.* varez.

vêstā, 46.17, ? M, with recognized; B, of your; vê-stā, will have stood for you.

vī, out, 43.12.

vī-cayathā, he may sift out, 46.15,—kay, *whence*
>   vī-cidyāi, to sift out, 31.5 49.6, *inf.*
>   vī-cinaot, he may sift, 46.17.

vīcirō, he who is sifting, 29.4 46.5,—NS -ra, *adj.*

vī-cithahyā, of the sifting, 30.2,—GS -tha, *n.*
>   vī-cithem, 46.18,—AS *ib.*
>   vī-cithōi, in the sifting, 32.8,—LS *ib.*

vīdā, thou? fore-knowest, 49.1,—vaēd.

vīdāitī, he distributes, 51.6,—dā.

vīdāitīm, a distribution, 47.6,—AS dātay, *f.*

vīdam, it shall be distributed, 32.6,—3SIM vī-dā.

vīdas, distributing, 33.3,—NS PrP ib.

vīdat, he may distribute, acquire, 51.5; vīdāt, 53.4.

vīdātā, in a distribution, 31.19, LS dātay, *f.*

vīdāyāt, he may distribute, 34.12 43.12.

vīdīshemnāis, with the distributers, 51.1,—IsP PfP.

vīdō, partaking in, 51.18,—NP vīd, *adj.*

vīdus, who knows, 28.4 45.8,—NS PfP -av, vaēd.

>   vīdushē, for the knower, expert, 30.1 31.17 51.8 DS.

vīdushō, of the knower, expert, 34.9, GS.
vīduyē, to comprehend, 29.3 31.5 44.3, *inf.*—vaēd.
vīdvāe, the knower, expert, 29.6 31.6,12,17,19 32.6 34.10-44.19 45.3 48.2,3.
vī-dvaēsh*a*m, of opponents of enemies, 34.11,—GP -shah, *adj.*
vīdvanōi, to know, 31.3,—*inf.* vaēd.
vīdyā*t*, he would (like to) know, 48.9,—ib.
vī-jêmyā*t*, she will extend, 44.11,—gam.
vī-mereñcaitē, they would destroy, 31.1,—3PPM mar*e*k.
vīnastī, they can find, 31.15,—vaēd, to find.
vī-nênāsā, I will cause to disappear, 32.15,—1Pf na*s*.
vīrāa*t*cā, 'hands,' serfs, men, 31.15,—GD -ra, *m.*
  vīrêñg, AP 45.9.
vī*s*en, they would reduce, 31.18,—vaēs, *whence,*
  vīseñtā, they·reduce, raise, 32.14, 3PPrM.
  vīseñtē, they will gain, 48.10, 3P s-AorKM.
vīspa, all; *all cases:* 28.1,8 31.2,3,13 33.5,10 34.2,3,5,6,10 43.2,14 44.3,7,11 45.1,6
  46.10,11,19 49.3,5,8 51.20 53.4.
vīspā-hish*a*s, all-detecting, 45.4,—NS PrP.
vistā, known, 48.2,—NS *f.* PfP vaēd.
  vistō, knowingly, rightly, 29.6,8 50.1,—NAS *ib.* PfPass.
Vīsht-āspa, chief of Magians, 28.7 46.14 51.16 53.2.
vīzibyō, to villages, 53.8,—DP vīs, *f.*
vī*sh*yātā, let him discriminate, 30.3,6,—vaē*s.*
vīvāpa*t*, he destroys, 32.10,—vāp, to raise.
Vīva*n*hushō, son of Vivahvant, 32.8. NS.
vī-vareshō, thou shalt seek to gain, 45.8,—var*e*sh.
vī-vêñghatū, you shall be happy, 53.5,—van.
vī-vīduyē, to know, understand, 43.9,—*inf.* vaēd.
vohū, good, 28.3-6,11 29.1,10,11 30.7,8 31.5,6,22 32.2 33.7,8,10-12 34.5,6,8,15 43.7,9,11,
  13,16 44.1,6,8,9,16 45.6,9,10 46.3,9,10,12,13,18 48.12 49.1,2,5,7,10,12 50.3,6,10,11 51.1,2,7,15,20,
  21 53.3,4.
vōistā, thou knowest, 28.10 32.6 46.10,—s-Aor vaēd.
  vōivīdāitī, he learns to know, 30.8,—3SKA.
vōi*z*da*t*, he raises, 32.10,—vaē*s.*
  vōi*z*dyāi, to raise, 43.13, *inf.*
vouru-cashāne, wide-glancer, 33.13,—VS -nay, *adj.*

vōyathrā, hopes, 34.10,—AP -thra, *n.*
vy.ā.dar*esem*, I shall behold, 45.8,—dar*es.*
vy*a*m, reward, distribution, 48.7,—AS vyam, *f.*
vyānayā, with guidance, wisdom, 29.6 44.7,—IsS -nā, *f.*

X

xrafstrā, savages, 28.5 34.9; M, vermin-polluted; B, small
   beasts of prey;—AP -ra, *n.*
   xrafstrāis, IsP, 34.5.
xraoda*t,* shall terrify, 46.11,—xraod.
   xraodaitī, it shall tremble, 51.13,—3SKA.
xraoseñta*m,* let them cry up, 53.8,—xrao*s.*
xraozdishtêñg, the firmest, hardest, 30.5,—AP -ta, *adj.*
xratav, xrathwa, *m, f,* understanding, *whence*
——tāe, LS 48.4.
——tavō, NP 45.2 46.3.
——têus, GS 32.4 34.14 43.6 46.18 49.6 50.6.
——thwā, IsS 31.7 48.3 53.3.
——tū, IsS 45.6 48.10.
——tūm, AS 28.1 32.9.
——tūs(cā), AP 31.11 32.14. 31.9
xrūnyā*t,* from bloody deed, 46.5,—AblS -ya, *n.*
xrūneramcā, bloodshed, 53.8,—AS -rā, *f.*
xrūrāis, bloody, 48.11,—IsP -ra, *adj.*
xsāi, I will·teach, 28.4,—1SKM xsā; *see* ā.xsō, 46.2.
xsha*n*mênē, to put up with, 29.9, *inf.*
xshapā.cā, with the night, 44.5,—IsS -pā, *f.*
xshathra, *n,* (*m,* 48.10,11) ruler, realm, kingdom, power, an Ahura.
xshathrīm, a ruler, 29.9,—AS -thrya, *m.*
xshayā.cā, O ruler, 28.7,—VS -ya, *m.*
xshayā, I shall rule, 50.9,—xshā(y), *whence*
——yamnêñg, ruling, 32.15, AP PfP.
——yamnō, he who is ruling, 31.19, NS ib.
——yañtāe, they who are ruling, 33.9, AP PrP.
——yañtō, of ruling, 29.2, GS ib.
——ya*s,* ruling, 32.16 43.1,10 46.5 51.5,17.
——yathā, thou rulest, 48.9.
——yehī, thou hast ruled; 44.15.

xshayō, to destroy, 32.5, *inf.*

xshéñtā, xshéñtām, let them rule, 48.5, xshā(y).

xshmā, with You, 43.11 50.5, IsS.

xsmaibyā(cā) to *or* from both You, 28.10 29.1 46.15 53.5. DADu

xshmākā, through Your, 34.15 IsS.

    xshmākahyā, of Your, 49.6 GS.

    xshmākāi, for Your, 50.10, DS.

    xshmāk*a*m, of Your, 44.17 34.14 GP.

    xshmāk*e*m, Your, 46.18 51.2 AS.

xshma*t*, by, from ? You, 29.1 44.17 AblS?

xshmāva*s*ū, among such as You, LP. 34.3. -vañ*t*.

    xshmāvat*a*m, of such as You, GP. 46.10.

    xshmāvatō, of One like You, 33.8 34.2 44.1 49.6 GS.

xshnaoshāi to satisfy, 46.1,—*inf.* xshnav, *whence*

    xshnaoshemnō, I am satisfying, 46.18,—NS PfP.

    xshnaosh*e*n, they satisfy, 30.5,—3PKA.

    xshnāus, (he is) satisfying, 46.1,13 51.12,—s-Aor.

    xshnevīshā, I may satisfy, 28.1.

    xshnūm, so as to satisfy, 48.12 53.2.

xshnūt*e*m, satisfaction, 31.3,—AS xshnū*t*, *f.*

xshus*t*ā, melted, liquid, 51.9,—IsS -ta, *adj.*

xshvīdemcā, milk, liquid food, 29.7,—AS xshvīd, *m.*

xshyō, to destroy, 31.20,— *see* xshayō.

Y

yā, who, *frequent.*— IsS NAP, ya.

yā-cā, *above,* 33.14 43.5 44.20 48.10 50.10.

yadā, when, as soon as, 30.8; as far as, 31.4,16 50.9.

yāe, yāescā, which, 31.14 33.10 34.3 43.4 44.5 46.8 53.1.

yaē-cā, 30.5 45.1 53.1; yaē-cīt, who, 48.3.

yaēibyascā, to *or* from both of whom, 28.8 DAbID.

yaēibyō, to *or* from whom, 28.3 44.11, DAbIP.

yāenhō, (before the great event) of the crisis, 30.2,—GS yāh, *n.*

yaēsham, of whom, GP 32.7 49.4 51.3.

yaēshū, in which, LP 33.5 34.8·

yāhī, in the crisis, 46.14 49.9,—LS yāh, *n.*

yahmāi, to whom, DS 29.3 43.1 44.16 46.6.

yahmī, in which, LS 43.6.

yāis, as, 32.7 44.20.

yāis, with which, IsP 28.2,11 32.3,6,7,12 44.12,20 46.15 51.20.

yāis ā, *adverbial verb,* in the manner which, 28.11.

yam, a hold, 49.8,—AS yam, *f.*

yam, *pron.* which, AS,GP 31.3 44.9 48.3 49.8 50.3 51.9,16,17 53.2.

yā-nāe, which us ? 50.5.

yānāis, with benefactions, 28.9,—IsP -na, *m.*

yaoget, he joins, 44.4,—3SPrA yaog, *whence*

   yaojā, I join, 50.7.

   yaojañtē, for the meeting, 30.10,—DS *or* LS *f.* PrP.

yaos, I will sanctify, 44.9,—yaozdā.

yaos, age, final conclusion, concessive, 46.18,—NS yav, *n.*

yaos—dānē, I will perfect, 44.9,—yaozdā.

yaozdāe, thou who perfectest, 48.5,—NS yaozdāh, *adj.*

yāsā, I will entreat, 28.1,8 49.8 51.21,—yās, *whence*

   yāsas, entreating, 49.12,—NS PrP.

   yāsat, he entreats, 32.1.

yascā, which, AP, 32.3,10 46.10 51.6.

yasnā, hymns, 34.1,—NP -na, *m. whence*
  yasnahyā, GS 34.12.
  yasnāis, IsP 45.10 50.9.
  yasnascā, AP 53.2.
  yasnem, AS 33.8.
yas-tā, whoever, 31.7 45.11.
yas-tat, he who, 44.19.
yas-tē, I who,? 33.5 43.16.
yas-têm, whoever, 46.4,6.
yāt, since, 32.4.
yathā, how, as that, 29.4 30.4,7 31.2,14-16 33.1 34.5,6 44.1,18 45.3 46.9 48.9 49.6 51.5.
yathāis, *for* yathā-āis, 33.1, in accordance with these,
yathanā, such as, 31.22 43.10.
yathrā, where, 30.9 31.11,12 46.11,16,17 53.7.
yāus, of an age, ever, 43.13,—GS yav, *n. whence,*
  yavā, for ever, 29.9 49.1,—IsS.
  yavaētāitē, in perpetuity, 28.11,—LS *f.* -tāt. *f.*
  yavat, as far as, as much, 28.4 34.9 43.8,9 50.11 53.7.
  yavē, for ever, 28.8, DS.
  yavōi, for ever, 46.11 49.8 53.1,4,—LS.
yayāe, of which, 33.9 45.2 46.7,—Du;P.
yazāi, I will worship, 33.4 50.4 51.22,—yaz, *whence*
  yazaitē, he worships, 32.3.
  yazemnāenhō, being worshipped, 51.20,—NP PfP.
  yazemnascā, adorations, 34.6,—AP *ib.*
yê, who, *frequent.*
ye-cā, and who, 30.1 51.2.
yehyā, of which, GS 31.4,5 32.16 33.1 34.2,13 43.6 45.6,7 48.7,9 51.13,22.
yêm, which, AS 28.8 29.9 34.13 43.13 45.2,8.
yêmā, twin, 30.3,—NDu -ma, *adj.*
yême, 53.6, *is* yê-me, who me.
yêñg, which, AP 28.10 32.5,15 43.3 46.4,11,16.
yêñgs-tū, whom thou,? 46.14.
yesnē, hymns, 51.22,—NAP yasna, *m, whence*
  yesnyācā, hymns, 30.1,—AP.
yezī, when, if, since, 31.2 32.6 34.6 44.6,15 48.1,9 53.1.

yezīm, when, 31.8.

yezivī, when, 53.3.

yim, which, 31.6, AS.

Yimas-cīt, a certain Yima, 32.8.

yōi, who, *frequent*, 28.9 30.8,9,10 31.1 32.1,12 44.16,20 45.3,5,7,11 46.1,3 48.12 49.4 51.3,22.

yōithemā, we would hasten, 28.9,—ya*t*, 1PPfA.

yūjên, they join, accustom, 46.11 49.9,—yaog.

yūs, your, 32.3 46.15.

yūshmaibyā, for both of You, 32.9,—IsDAblDu.

yūshmākahyā, of Your, 50.7,—GS; *also*

    yūshmākāi, for Your, 50.5 DS.

    yūshmākem, Your, 34.5 AS.

yūshma*t*, You, 34.7 AblS? AS*n*?

yūshmāvat*am*, of Such as You, 29.11, GP *see* xshmāvañ*t*.

yūs-tā, you that, 32.4.

yuxtā, let him be joined, 49.9,—IsS PfP yaog.

yūzêm, You, NP 28.9 29.10,11.

Z

zaēmācā, through waking, 44.5,—IsS -man, *n,*

za*h*yācā, abandoned, 53.8,—NP za*h*ya, *adj.*

za*m*cā, earth, 44.4 46.1,—AS zam, *f.*

zaoshā*t,* from the delight, 47.5,—AblS -sha, *m, whence*
  zaoshē, for the delight, 33.2,10,—DS.
  zaoshēñg, delights, 48.4,—AP.

zaotā, (as) priest, 33.6,—NS -tar, *m.*

zaozaomī, I invoke, 43.10,—zav *or* zbā.

zaranaēmā, we would vex, 28.9,—zar.

Zarath-ushtra, 'old camels,'? 28.6 29.8 33.14 43.8,16 46.13,14,19 49.12 50.6
  51.11,12,15 53.1,2,3.

zaraz-dā*e,* heart-given, 31.1,—NP da, *adj.*

zaraz-dāitis, heart-faith, 43.11,—NS day, *f.*

zar*e*m, purpose, effort, 44.17,—AS -ra, *f.*

za*s*ta, hand, *m. all cases;* 29.5 30.8 33.2 34.4 43.4 44.14 47.2 50.5,8.

za*s*tava*t,* 'handy,' energetic, 29.9,—AS*n* PrP.

za*s*tā-ishta, 'hand-wish'? laborious, token, 34.4 IsP; 50.5 IsS.

zbayā, I invoke, 33.5 46.14 51.10,—
  zbayeñtē, for invoking, 49.12, DS PrP.

zavêñg, calls 28.3 29.3,—AP -van, *m.*

zavō, strength, 33.12,—AP -vah, *n.*

zazeñtī, they shall attain, 30.10,—Pr5 haz.

zdī, be! 31.17,—*imp.* ah.

zemō, of the earth, 51.12,—GS zam, *f.*

zeredācā. with the heart, 31.12,—IsS zered, *n.*

zevīm, invokable, 31.4,—NS*n* zaoya.

zevīshtīm, swiftest, speediest, 46.9,—AS zevīshtya, *whence*
  zevīshtyāenhō, NP 28.9.
  zevīshtyêñg, AP 50.7.

zī, for, *frequent.*

zīt, 45.8, *for* zī-īt. however it,—ay, *pron.*
zōishenū, trembling, shivering, 51.12,—NDu zōishenav, *adj.*
zushtā, beloved, darling, 32.4,—NP PfP zaosh.
zūtā, in the call, 50.1,—LS zūtay, *f.*

Meaning *and* Termination *of* Declensions.

Singular.

Nominative. subjective case,—s, *or loses consonant.*

Accusative. objective case, —m, *am, em,* im.

Instrumental, *by means of, through, with,*—ā, ayā.

Dative, *to, for,*—āi, ē, ōi.

Ablative, *from, by,*—āt, or like Genitive.

Genitive, *of,*—as, s, s.

Locative, *in, at, among,*—i, u, r, m, s.

Vocative, *O!*—indistinct, like instrumental, nominative, etc.

Dual. For two objects; a pair; both.

Nominative, Accusative. ī, ai, e.

Instrumental, Dative, Ablative, ibyā.

Genitive, āe.

Locative, ō.

Plural.

Nominative, as, ō, ā, āe.

Accusative, ēng, ns.

Instrumental, bīs.

Dative, Ablat⁺ ⁺byō.

Genitive, am, ām.

Locative, su, hu, shu, shvā.

Vocative, *indistinct.*

These general terminations change according to contraction with the preceding stem, or following particle cā *or* cīt; according to the accent, or the degeneration of the language.

Nouns *and* Adjectives,—A-Declension.
Singular.

Nominative. M. ō, F. a, ē, ēhya, ā; N, ō. ADJ. ō, uyō; yē, ecā; ō

Accusative. M,N, em, êm, em, im, īm, aom, um; F, am, ām.

Instrumental, M,N, ā, ācā; F, a, aya, ayā, ē; ADJ uha.

Dative, āi, N, āshā*t;* ADJ. *f.* ayā, *n.* .asyāi.

Ablative, ā*t,* a*t.*

Genitive, M,N, ahē, ahyā, ehē, ehyā, ācā; F, āe, escā, ē.

Locative, M, ā, ē, ōi, ayā, a, ya; F, jya, uya, ē, āe; N, ēcā, ayā

Vocative, a, ā; F, ē; ADJ. are?
Dual.

Nominative. M, a, ā, ācā; āenhō, āe, uyē, irē; F, ē, āe, escā
    ya, e; N, ā, a, ē.

Accusative. M, a, ya, ē, cā; F. ē, ara, ācā; N, a, ā, ē;
    ADJ, a*n*hā, acā, uyē.

Instrumental, Dative, Ablative, byā; F, ābyā; ADJ. ibya, ibyā

Genitive, M,N, as, escā; āe, a*t*cā; F, ām, āhū, ahu, āhva.

Locative, āyō; ADJ. ōyō.

Vocative, M,N, anā; F, ascā; ADJ, amnā, acā.
Plural.

Nominative, M, ya, yā, *en*hō, ē; F, āe, escā; N, ā, ē, dhā, āe, sc

Accusative, M, ê*n*g, a, ā, escā, āscā, a*n*, acā. ās, e, ē; F, ā
*e*scā; N, *like M,F.* ADJ. m,*f,* ō, āe, *a*n, azis; *n,* ūtā, wya, ā, ē

Instrumental. M, āis, iscā, ibīs; F, ābīs; N, āis, ibis.

Dative, Ablative, M, ibyō, F, ābyō, ascā; N, ibyō, ascā.

Genitive, *a*m, ām.

Locative, M, ēshū; F, āhū, āhvā; N, *like M,F:* ADJ, eshvā.

Vocative, a, ā. ADJ. *m.* e*n*hō, *f.* āe.

Nouns *and* Adjectives,—I-Declension.

Singular.

Nominative. i, is, is*e*; F, i, ī, is; N, shnī; ADJ, yō.

Accusative. M,F, im, īm; N, i, ī, ā.

Instrumental, M, i; F, i, icā, ī, dya, yē; āca. N, yā.

Dative, M,N, e, ē, āi, ōi; F, e*e*, aēcā, ayē.

Ablative, M, ōi*t;* F, ēdhcā, aēdhā; ya*t.*

Genitive, M, ōis, āis, ayō; F, ashōis, ā*e*, ascā.

Locative, M, ara; F, āta, ūtā, ātā, ācā, ūtī, ō; N, *ê.*

Vocative, M, azhi, ē; F, aitē, ashi; N, *ê.*

Dual.

Nominative. F, ūitī.

Accusative. M, aitī; F, ūitī; N, ashi, fshaonīca.

Instrumental, Dative, Ablative, ashibya, ā.

Plural.

Nominative, M, ayō, a, īs, es; F, ayō, āyō, ascā, ā, āitis; N, ī.

Accusative, M, (a)yō, īs, iri, aya; F, īs, ayō, ōyō, iscā, īs, ā, ā*e,* yō, ashē.

Dative, Ablative, ibyō, ascā.

Genitive, *am.*

Locative, ishu, ishva.

Vocative, M, ayo. F, ayō.

Nouns *and* Adjectives,—U or V-Declension.
Singular.

Nominative. M, us, use, u, ū, āyu; F, us, u, āos; N, u.

Accusative. M, ūm, āum; F, aom; vêm; N, u, ū, ucā.

Instrumental, M, ū, vā, vō; F, anhu; N, ā, āyū.

Dative, M, uhē, uyē, avē. wē, aēcā; F, anvē, uyē, havē; N, avē, aēcā, ōi, aovē.

Ablative, M, aot; F, aot, vat.

Genitive, M, êus, aos, yaos, thwō, āus; F, êus, nvō, ascīt, ascā, anvā; N, êus, aos-cā, ā, us.

Locative, M, vō, vā, hō, i, uyā, ās, avō; F, anvī, anhvō, āvō, āe.

Vocative, M, yō, vō, u, mainyū; F, ō, āe, a.

Dual.

Accusative. M, u, ū, ūcā; F, yu; N, vohū.

Instrumental, M, ubyā, uvē.

Dative, Ablative, M, ubya, ubyā.

Genitive, M, ahvāe; anhāe.

Locative, M, anhuyaos, anhvō.

Vocative, mañtū.

Plural.

Nominative, M, avō, ascā, āyō, a, āvō; us; F, avō, āvō; N, u, ū.

Accusative, M, ūs, us, avō, avā, wā, u, uscā; F, avō, vascā, ava; N, ū.

Instrumental, ubis; ūbis.

Dative, Ablative, ubyō, ascīt, iwyū.

Genitive, am.

Locative, ushva, āhū; F; ushvā, ushu.

Vocative, avō.

Nouns *and* Adjectives. — Consonant-Declension.

Singular.

Nominative. *loses consonant;* ā, ē, ō. -ah, *or* ā(y), *becomes* āe: the Present Participle stem añ*t*, makes *as*.

Accusative. em-cā. N, a, ā, acā, ê, āe, ō.

Instrumental, nā, a, a*n*hā.

Dative, ē, ōi, aēcā.

Ablative, a*t*-cā, acā; N, man, ba*r*esman.

Genitive, ō, a*n*hō; N, ascā.

Locative, M, i, a; F, ē; N, i, ni.

Vocative, a, aom, acā, ma.

Dual.

Accusative. a, ā.

Instrumental, āe.

Dative, Ablative, ibyā.

Genitive, āe.

Plural.

Nominative, ō, a*n*hō. M, ascā, acā, a*n*ō. F, na, nō; N, —*consonant,* as dama*n*, ā; āe, i, īsh.

Accusative, ō, a*n*hō. M, ascā, ā, van, īnō. F, nō, nascā, ō, ām. N, a*n*, ma*m*, enī, enis, āe, ê.

Instrumental, ebīs, īs, a*n*.

Dative, Ablative, ibyō, oyō, abyō, êbyō.

Genitive, a*m*.

Locative, ōhva, ōhū, aha, ōhva, as(h)ū.

Vocative, ō.

VERBS.

Few, if any, Avestan verbs are found complete; so that tabulations are unsatisfactory. The reader will find the many collateral Present-stems in the Dictionary, while the chief terminations follow. It should be noted that the quantity of final vowels is uncertain.

There are three *numbers:* singular, dual, plural.

There are several *voices:* active, middle, passive.

There are many *moods:* indicative, optative, desiderative, causative, iterative, conjunctive, injunctive. If a form is taken in the sense of the latter, it may refer to present, past, or future.

There are so many different conjugations as to throw uncertainty over the whole. Reichelt's *Awestisches Elementarbuch* gives most occurring forms grouped together in one table.

TABLE OF TERMINATIONS

		PRIMARY		SECONDARY		IMPERATIVE		PERFECT	
		Active	Middle	Active	Middle	Active	Middle	Active	Middle
S	1	mī	ē	m	i, a			ā(nī),a	ē,K āi,
	2	hī, sī,	(n,s)hē	s, sh,	(n,s)ha	dī,	nuha, shvā,	tha,	—
	3	tī,	tē,	t,	ta(ī),	tū,	tam,	a, ā(u)	ē,
D	1	va(s)hī,	—	vā,				—	
	2								
	3	t(h)ō,	āthē,	tem,	ātem,			atar,	aitē,
P	1	ma(s)hī	maidē	mā,	maidī,	—	—	mā,	
	2	thā,	thwē,	tā,	dwem,	tā,nā,	dwem,	ā,	—
	3	añtī,at,	ñtē, atāi,	n,	ñtā,	ñtū,	ñtam,	are(sh),	

Infinitives end in ō, ē, ōi, āi, etc.

Present Participles have as stem añt-; Nom.Sing. *-as;* ASn, -at.

Past Participles, Active, -ta, *adj;* Middle, -mna, *adj.*

L E Ap'33

APPRECIATIONS

AS BOOK ARTIST

You tempt the learned poor and the cultured rich by the rich and solid literary savories in your catalogues. What a piece of typography!
—Jerome Goldstein.

AS A POET

etry, did you say? Well, What did the poetess Edith M. Thomas think of this 'ry?

This modest title does not adequately entitle these quite unusual collections of poems. I am struck by the variety of notes sounded, and by the excellence of poetic art achieved in both intimately religious strains and class race affect a reader appealed to by the excellence of clear thought in verse as crystalline. A humorous satirical note is lent by his frank declaration against Mediaeval Art. I find a deal of wisdom in My Unseen Passengers, with its crisp beginning. The most individual and striking of these poems is Woodland Vision; but each poem could be singled out for some characteristic excellence."

Rejoice, Reader, for you too can share Edith Thomas's enthusiasm by sending Three Dollars to the Platonist Press, Teocalli, No. Yonkers, N. Y., for the magnificent Collected Poems of Kenneth Sylvan Guthrie, entitled

VOTIVE GARLANDS

Hung on the World-Temple's Walls.
It is a book you will want to keep handy on all occasions to entertain all your friends. Those interested in politics, sociology, art, you can start performing with the Garland of Thistles; the Garland of Roses will charm your lady-friends; the Garland of Nocturnes are for your moon-light walks; the Garland of Oracles will attract to you mystics and dreamers; your clergyman will want to enjoy the Garland of sons; the afflicted will come to you for the consolation of the Garland of Bitter-sweet; philosophical historians will discuss the Chaplet Forget-Me-Nots; and when all alone, you will revel in the Garland of Fancies. No one will be disappointed.

Doctor Kenneth S. Guthrie's book of poems "Votive Garlands" is a remarkable book of verse. Doctor Guthrie is a prolific writer of prose and verse with the happy gift of what may be termed a felicitous gift of poetic colloquial expression. Doctor Guthrie never hesitates to use a poetic license whenever it helps to clarify his ideas. Those who can not understand and appreciate high-brow and exaggerated poetic phrases will find Doctor Guthrie's etry delightfully different. The poems in collection contain a wholesome philosophy d a practical moral. —Anton Romatka.
I have read it with pleasure. . . . Your poems re spontaneous and original.
—David W. Cade.

Refreshingly bold in its utterance of philosophical and social views not yet accepted by ruling majority; radical in a constructive ther than destructive sense.
Dr. Marion M. Miller.

Splendid, succinct. —Marcus M. Cass.
A source of great inspiration to me,—thanking you for many hours of happiness and leasure. —Alfred Eichler.
Delightful passages, pages,—thank you so uch for this pleasure. —Benjamin Musser.

Thank you most heartily;—greatly enjoy them,—they cover so much ground and comprise so many subjects you would seem to be versatile and informed as Sir Francis Bacon himself. Rarely does a poet prove so comprehensive and widely cultured! With much appreciation, —Laura Simmons.
What a genius you are! A rare poet indeed!
—Lida C. Hosea.
Surely prolific, often interesting, sometimes inspiring. —Flora Louise Hunn.
I should like to have a copy.
—Scottie McKenzie Frasier.
I trust that a personal meeting with you may sometime be effected: I fully appreciate,—
—Charles Alva Lane.
Here is universality of thought, joyous spontaneity of expression, hopeful idealism and refreshing originality of idea.
—Helen Frances Doherty.

Most interesting book,—Greatly enjoyed, . . . They have that rare and much sought after quality of being different. The frequent glint of humor and the individual philosophy are very intriguing. Again and again the beauty of some lines would flash up from the page.
—Della Eulalia Thomas.
Very good and very devout expressions of personal religion, which I like and enjoy very much. I must confess to a naughty joy in your description . . .
—Marion Courtenay Smith.
Very original and interesting.
—C. G. Blanden.
My own regards! —Lillian Whiting.
I want that copy.—We might become very good friends. —Royal Dixon.
Very beautiful book of poems, I should like to have the pleasure of meeting you sometime to tell you personally how much I admire your work. Your generous gift,—I shall treasure it, you may be assured. I should like you to visit me at the College of the City of New York, where I am conducting a class in Poetry Writing. Perhaps you will read some of your favorite poems. —Morris Abel Beers.
Charming volume, I appreciate the gift, and found so much in the book that was modern, sympathetic thoughtful and alluring—I congratulate you on your gifts in poetry and aesthetics. —Frederick Petersen.
Great learning, a philosopher of lofty thought and aspiration . . . Splendid ideas, fine lines . . . —Mary Sinton Leitch.
With appreciation,—Marilla W. Freeman, Cleveland Public Library.
Pleased, — Louisa Remondino Stabel, State Vice President, So. California, League of American Pen Women.
Gratefully, . . . They are verily as though 'your image in the glass should linger when yourself are gone!' Thank you for this Vision of Beauty! —Edwin Lathrop Baker.
Your book has been with me constantly. How have you managed to accomplish so much! It is very wonderful! Thank you greatly for the pleasure you have given me, for the pleasure the book will always give!
—Winifred Russell.
I am much arrested by its originality. I am reminded of Walt Whitman by your outspoken views, . . . infused with right thinking and with freedom from old cant. I like your Platonic atmosphere. It sounds good in the day

of loud-mouthed piety. Your Moon-poem strikes me as going deep into the essence of things. I enjoy your twinkling satire. It was much to have won the praise of Edith M. Thomas. —Harrison S. Morris.

There are so many books of verse issuing from the press, that say and mean absolutely nothing that is a great relief to come across a book like this that is so far ahead of the general run of books. Let me congratulate you on your achievement, and trust that you will write many more poems so clear-cut and fine as these. —J. M. Moreland.

I have spent a very pleasant and profitable afternoon reading your Votive Garlands. Many beautiful thoughts, well expressed,—I admire your independence and individuality. —Dr. Alexander de Menil, Pres't, The Society of St. Louis Authors.

Happy to receive it, most welcome. —Alice Brown.

Grateful.—John F. Wilson.

Like to read them.—Agnes La Fere.

I feel . . . mighty . . . prominent . . . after a bath in your Garlands. —Ivan Swift.

I have read some of them with interest. —Nathan Haskell Dole.

A great deal of interest and pleasure.—It is quite unusual, and your field is wide and varied. The thought is clear, and you are not afraid to mention Christ. There are many poems that I like, some for excellency of thought, and some that just in a certain way appeal to me,—exceptionally fine and striking. Nicely gotten up.

Thanks for your interesting volume. —Larry Chittenden.

I enjoyed reading it; cordial appreciation,—original, lovely. —Viola C. White.

Very real pleasure — particularly struck. — They disclose a depth of power of appeal that range all the way from vagrant fancies to the intimate desires of the soul. —Winifred Russell.

Glad to see your volume.—Ben Field.

Delightful, invigorating, inspiring. Your versatility is amazing, and your thought conveyed always in a most happy manner. —Anna Spencer Twitchell.

Devotional poetry is scarce. Pious folk are not always poets, and poets are not always pious. All these poems are in good verse, and some of which are of real merit, none of them being without spiritual worth of some kind. Not every reader will endorse every sentiment expressed but no reader will fail to find something to his taste and much to his comfort and religious stimulation. The author is a man of intense inner life, and not without the literary gift wherewith to give it attractive utterance.—The Church Chronicle, Cincinnati.

I have enjoyed them very much. Delightful imaginative touches, flashes of genius, mysterious perceptions, which gave me great joy. Your interior life must be very wonderful. Only the real mystic can play with divine things as you do. I shall always treasure it. —Elsa Barker.

It is filled with beautiful thoughts; . . . expresses a great concept . . . in harmony with Oriental ideals . . . —Estelle Duclo.

. . . So completely to my liking I am sure I shall enjoy the rest. —Theda Kenyon.

Poetic instinct urges them forth. He maintains the true poet's calling in his choice of subjects. He writes on subjects which are really worthy of the attention of a thinker, and

not on trivialities. The Garlands are full of interest and real poetic feeling; they can be dipped into here and there to find refreshment, and many a weary half-hour may thus be passed.—W. G. Raffé, in Hindustan Review.

AS A LITERATEUR

SPIRITUAL MESSAGE

Now you will see how grateful I am to you in spite of not having written you earlier. I found your chapter on the Message of Great Dramas quite useful in preparing my Introduction to Aeschylus's 'Prometheus,' and I took the liberty of appropriating one or two paragraphs, with due credit of course.—Nathan Haskell Dole.

WHAT IMPORTANT JOURNALS SAY

The Springfield Republican:

An unusual and interesting book, which appears to be the result of a great amount of labor and of many years of thought. The author endeavors to distill from the great literary masterpieces of all languages and peoples their peculiar and individual quality of inspiration. In developing this plan the author presents brief and well-condensed synopses of a considerable number of recognized master-pieces. They are well and appropriately made. From the outline of what the book aims to present, it might be suspected of being a volume of interminable length, but in reality it contains but 300 comparatively short pages. It is an interesting, and in many ways an inspiring study.

The Living Church, Chicago, Ills.:

A work of amazing erudition and labor, on the evolution of humanity's aspirations . . . It would take too much space even to summarize the specific discussions of the separate national sources of the 'racial prophetic elements,' and the 'lyrical prophetic' are from a hundred authors . . . He points out in what manifold ways human salvation is taught by international writings . . .

New York Times Review of Books:

The author apparently has aimed to make it another one of those links, constantly growing more numerous, which knit the school more closely to outside life . . . Teachers who wish to get away from the microscopic method of dealing with literature, will find in it much to help them.

Normal Instructor and Primary Plans:

The book is thoroughly wholesome and decidedly uplifting, valuable to every student for his study, and every scholar for reference. It is a splendid gift-book for literary people and lovers of books.

Scholars and deep thinkers would enjoy the book. —Henry Wood, the author.

Very interesting and informing reading. —Dr. George Davis, President Normal College.

I prize them very much. They are enchanting. How profitably you have spent the years for others! —Harriette E. Hodgson.

Very inspiring. Your book appeals to me as almost the only example I know of the scholar's attempt to show the underlying ideals toward which the greatest seers in all lands have been striving, each in his own way enriching the values on the common goal. I can think of no figure more needed to-day than the true Prophet.

—Dr. J. H. Randall, of Columbia University

PLAYLETS

Fine!—Medora L. Ray, Head of Modern Language Department, W. I. High School.

You gave us a beautiful and inspiring evening and we are indeed most grateful
—Theodor Heline,
Leader of Rosicrucian Fellowship.

I have read your play with interest. It has good atmosphere and good theme.
—Florence A. Boole.

Very clever.—Miss Wells.

I have heard many comments in praise of its presentation, not only in respect to its authorship, but to its dramatization.—Edward Cornell Zabriskie, Principal W. I. High School.

Very effective, I read it with pleasure.
—Mary H. Johnson.

Thanks for a glorious evening. Never did I enjoy a play more (the Tempest), and what a sermon it did get over! You are a wonder!
—Agnes Wood.

Sayonara is a charming little play,—and recommend it for presentation by amateurs, where opportunity arises.
—Edith S. R. Isaacs,
of Theatre Arts Magazine.

I am going to produce it at Goucher College just as soon as I can. It is admirably suited for production by colleges and clubs, and it gives me pleasure to recommend it.
—Florence Louisa Speare, Goucher College.

AS A PROGRESSIVE

A ROMANCE OF TWO CENTURIES

I offer my earnest congratulations. It shows thought and skill; and what to my mind is even better,—a knowledge of peoples and conditions. Then also I admire the fact that you are not afraid to look ahead. May you prove a prophet indeed, and may your glorious visions for the future of our race be realized. If what you predict is Utopian, it must be remembered that your vision is a large one, and that you write with the pen of an idealist. Scholars, teachers, thinkers will all welcome your book, and therein find much food for earnest thought.
—Ernest Laycock.

It contains suggestive ideas as regards the future course of events in the world.
—United India and Indian States.

He has formed a very readable and interesting survey of what his country might be like in a hundred years.—Real imaginative power which the learned author displays with the utmost ease and facility . . . worthy of Jules Verne himself. Considerable degree of ingenuity and indeed of real artistic inventive faculty in both scheme and details. He has not allowed his undoubted scholarship to overwhelm him, and he keeps his artistic productions commendably free of all reference, or appeal to any classical or other authority. He has many pointed criticisms to make in passing. His comments upon advertising are full of a humor not unsupported by facts. Throughout the whole of this interesting volume, we meet with the remarks of a sympathetic and educated man on the life of today as he has seen it in his wide travels, contrasted with what he thinks it should and could be, in the administration of wiser men.
—W. G. Raffé, in Hindustan Review.

An entertaining yarn. The author has traveled all over the world, and his story contains much of practical conclusions, based on careful observation, and little of the piffling Utopia of romantic idealists.
—N. Y. Tribune.

Interesting. On lines of his own, for he imitates nobody, he has set forth the future

with great ingenuity, and a strikingly faithful care for particulars.
—Mr. Osborne, critic in N. Y. World.

Most timely now, during the Peace Conference. He manifests French clearness, British practicality, Italian suavity, Spanish brilliance, and Yankee raciness. No one will lay it aside unfinished.
—E. J. Burrowes, of N. Y. Times, 12 years.

Prophecy, reduced in a material way to something tangible and concrete.—N. Y. Call.

Profoundly interesting . . . A thrilling romance that has a natural and intriguing climax. The author's scholarship would command attention in any literary relation.
—Brooklyn Eagle.

Many of his ideas are original and daring; they deserve the attention of any one whose interest runs along social lines. One is amazed at his wealth of vocabulary, his fertility of phrase, his sustained high diction. He is always brilliant and fecund. Those who delight in peering into the vistas of the future will find in it many a matter that will arouse antagonism or approval, and will render its reading a distinct and unusual pleasure.
—Mr. Marvin, Editor, in Troy Record.

Suggestive ideas.—Baltimore Sun.

AS A LECTURER

SOME PRESS COMMENTS

He carried his audience with him by that simplicity, directness and personal magnetism which are the mark of a superior and creative mind.
—The Enquirer, Cincinnati, Ohio.

Charmingly portrayed by the scholarly speaker . . No lecture at the Centennial Club has been more successful. He made his audience feel as if he was carrying it bodily with him. Should he ever visit Nashville again he will find a most cordial welcome.
—The Nashville (Tenn.) Banner.

Dr. Guthrie, a world-traveller and scientist, familiar with seven languages, delivered a remarkable lecture to an audience of teachers and physicians. French, German and English foibles and points of view were presented wittily and charmingly.
—The Philadelphia (Penna.) Inquirer.

Interesting, entertaining, instructive, delivered to an appreciative audience.
—The New Harmony (Ind.) Times.

His polished diction and magnetic presence awakened lively interest and marked enthusiasm.—The Evening Bulletin (Phila., Penna.).

He is a man of solid scholarship; his viewpoint is fresh and original, and his style is charming. —The Matawan (N. J.) Journal.

The legends of the country were told by this accomplished raconteur in the most dramatic manner. Many who went as casual listeners came away determined to go deeper into this interesting study.
—The Nashville (Tenn.) Democrat.

I heard him deliver it for the New York Board of Education, and in giving it for our church, he offers us a high intellectual enjoyment and privilege.
—Rev. K. Jaeger, in (Brooklyn) Ebenezer Bote.

The audience represented the cream of Nashville culture, who were enthusiastic in their applause and praise of the entertainment.
—The Nashville (Tenn.) Tennessean.

He is a man of solid scholarship; his viewpoint is fresh and original, and his style is charming. —The Matawan (N. J.) Journal.

APPRECIATIONS OF DR. KENNETH GUTHRIE—4
AS A SCHOLAR
PLOTINUS

I congratulate you; you have gotten ahead of me!—Stephen McKenna.

I marvel at the scholarship that your writings constantly evidence.—Edward Cornell Zabriskie, Principal W. I. High School.

We will make a record of our appreciation of your noble work.—A. G. Cummins, Editor Chronicle, Poughkeepsie.

Dr. Guthrie has placed the whole English theological world in his debt. His work is one which no theological or philosophical library can afford to be without.
—Rev. Dr. Leicester C. Lewis, in May 1919, Anglican Theological Review.

May the immortal Gods expedite the publication of your Plotinus! I hope it will soon issue from the press.
—Thos. M. Johnson, the great Platonist.

The work of Dr. Guthrie in bringing Plotinus, the most important representative of Neo-platonism, and its best exponent,—to the attention of a wider circle of English readers is beyond praise. Dr. Guthrie's translation is the first complete English rendering ever made. American and British scholarship,—for they are both combined in Dr. Guthrie, are to be congratulated on this necessary and excellent piece of work. Dr. Guthrie has not only given a good translation, but he has also arranged the material in chronological order, has furnished a careful study in sources, development, and influence of Plotinic thought, and has appended an excellent concordance to every important point in the complete works.—Rev. Dr. Samuel, A. B. Mercer, in Living Church, May 3, 1919.—

In an anthology which I am about to publish I have taken the liberty of using portions of your valuable versions.—Grace H. Turnbull.

Dr. Guthrie has done a very great service to the thinkers and students of the English speaking peoples. Here we have Plotinus complete in English for the first time, and translated in a most sympathetic and clear manner. Also the writings are grouped in chronological order, by which one may trace the development of idea. Without wishing to appear fulsome, the reviewer considers that no reader of this magazine who is seeking mentally to grasp the fundamental law of Cosmos, or attain a reasonable conception of philosophic truth, should fail to possess himself of these volumes, and possessing, study them assiduously. Dr. Guthrie has done his work completely and most excellently.
—Michael Whitty, in Azoth.

American and British Scholarship—for they are both combined in Dr. Guthrie are to be congratulated on this necessary and excellent piece of work.
—Living Church.

Complete and with much clearness, faithful to the text.—M. D. Roland, Gosselin, O. P., Revue des Sciences Philosophiques et Theologiques.

I am delighted with it; one of the best additions to my library. I am sure you have done a great work for mankind in making this splendid translation, and I desire to express my sincere thanks and appreciation.
—Dr. W. A. Butler.

A fine piece of scholarly work.
—Congregationalist and Advance.

His magnificent work has attained an international homage. As a classicist he ranks with the foremost.—Dr. Plummer in the Mercury

PHILOSOPHY OF PLOTINUS

A most useful summary of the leading ideas of the Enneads grouped under convenient and systematic headings. There are many who will appreciate this service, for no other such book exists in English.—Mr. Mead, in the Quest.

A very concise and scholarly statement of the doctrines of Plotinus, in connection with the preceding Greek philosophy.
—Dr. Paul Carus, in Open Court.

Too great praise could hardly be bestowed upon this scholarly contribution to Platonic literature. Students will do well to procure this book and read it closely.
—Universal Brotherhood.

A multum in parvo of philosophy. It simplifies and correlates the leading philosophies from that of Plato to that of Constantine, and Christianity. It may well be called a text-book on the Philosophy of God, man and things,—or Spirit, Soul and Matter.
—The Christian Metaphysician.

I think that your condensed statement of the contents of the Enneads of Plotinus will be of service to all students of philosophy.—W. T. Harris, U. S. Commissioner of Education.

The summary is the clearest and most intelligent which has yet appeared. His happy phrasing of Platonic terms and his deep sympathy with Platonic thought proclaim the presence of a capable translator. So lucid and capable a compendium . . . As accurate as anything in a digest can be expected to be. Those who desire to enter the Plotinian precincts of the Temple of Greek philosophy by the most expeditious path cannot do better than take this for their guide. It is the best that has yet appeared. To our Platonic friends and colleagues we say not only 'you should,' but 'you must' read it.—G. R. S. Mead, in the Theosophical Review.

I must compliment you on the passages translated,—a most wonderful selection as an introduction to the whole Hellenistic, Platonic philosophy, as regards selection, order and rendering. I had them read to the Freshman philosophy classes at Columbia, and made the deepest impression.
—J. H. Randolph, of Columbia University.

Again I long to taste of the rarely beautiful philosophic fare therein,—will you send me another?
—Jerome Goldstein.

NUMENIUS

A good deal of interest and instruction.
—Prof. Chas. C. Torrey, Yale.

PAGAN BIBLE

It is a keystone to the fallen arch, and a new light for the living.—John Rotzer.

A remarkable little volume. We take pleasure in commending most strongly this excellent and valuable work to all and singular.
—Dr. Plummer, in the Mercury.

PHILO

Your valuable outline,—I hope to make good use of it.—Prof. H. A. Wolfson, Harvard.

The plan to put them in all Hebrew Institution libraries is commendable.—Dropsie College, Philadelphia.

A carefully classified note-book or index of Philo, who must have been an inspirational writer.
—Light, London.

Dr. Bloch of the Jewish Division of the N. Y. Public Library liked it so much he made a list of individuals and institutions to receive it.

Useful to give a first idea of the philosophic and religious ideas of Philo.—M. D. Roland Gosselin, in Revue des Sciences Philosophiques et Théologiques

PROCLUS

Fascinating.—Jerome Goldstein.

This is an unique book. It is the best work on Proclus we have had before us, and much of it consists of original translation now given for the first time in English. Every classicist and every truth seeker who values the wisdom of the ancients, should possess a copy, for it contains a rich philosophy, the fruitage of a mature mentalism developed at a time when it was at its height. No better start could be made than by way of an intensive study of this Proclus volume. —Dr. Plummer, in his Mercury.

ZOROASTER

The writer has issued this translation, not for the scholar, but for the average intelligent man and woman, he gives the transliterated text of the Gathas along with his translation, and all sufficient apparatus to enable every intelligent man to check the translator's reliability. —United India and Indian States.

A most commendable piece of work, done with extreme care. I like the make-up and get-up of the work,—the little decorations are a happy thought;—and altogether it will please me to produce a very full and complimentary notice or two. —W. G. Raffé.

I have read your critical analysis and your interpretation with great interest. I have gotten from them a new point of view. —Prof. Crawford Howell Toy, Harvard.

AS A RELIGIONIST
COMMUNION
AN ORIGINAL CRITICISM
by the highest Literary authority and its Sequel

The Rev. Kenneth Guthrie's little devotional handbook "Of Communion with God" is not unworthy to be laid alongside of "Gold Dust" and the "Imitation" AS FOOD FOR THE SOUL IN ITS MOST SACRED HOURS. Are these meditations all your own, Mr. Guthrie, or are they translations or adaptions?

—Literary World, Boston, June 13, 1896.

Not very long ago, in speaking what were intended to be words of high commendation for a little devotional work by the Rev. Kenneth S. Guthrie, of Philadelphia, entitled "Of Communion with God," we used language which has been erroneously and unfortunately interpreted as implying a doubt of its originality. Perhaps our language was open to that interpretation, though in comparing the book with "Gold Dust" and "The Imitation," and asking the author in a tone of friendly familiarity whether his meditations were his own or the adaptations or translations of another's, we meant not disparagement but compliment, and to signify our sense of the unusual merit of his pages. We wish now to make the expression of that sense plain and unequivocal, and to say in so many words what we aimed to say then by implication, that THE BOOK, though small and easily to be overlooked, IS ONE OF THE STRIKING AND REMARKABLE BOOKS OF ITS CLASS, THE LIKE OF WHICH SELDOM APPEARS, and that Mr. Guthrie is its true author.

—Literary World, Boston, Sept. 5, 1896.

"A devotional treatise, or rather a series of meditations and soliloquies. It expresses tender spiritual sensitiveness, and a deep sense of the importance of humility, fidelity, and Christian love. It will be found helpful by many, and it is prettily printed."
—The Congregationalist.

"A valuable little book to promote devout meditation on the way and counsels of God, with prayer and adorations. It is by a Church clergyman of Philadelphia, and is concerned in Book I, with Love; Book II, the Presence of God; III, Adoration; IV, Peace."
—The Living Church.

"Moulded after Thomas à Kempis. Very good, with wise and excellent thoughts."
—Southern Churchman.

"These 'Communions' will be breath and life to many souls. And you have woven into them some precious inspirations—and the eyes and the hearts will catch at them and be made thoughtful and more holy."
—Rev. Augustine Caldwell, Ipswich, Mass.

"Your little work is admirable, and reminds us of Thomas à Kempis. I like it very much and believe that it will be helpful to all devout people."—Rt. Rev. Thomas F. Gailor, D.D.

"I have read it with as much interest as edification, and cannot but congratulate you for having thought, felt, and written it. All the characteristics of a truly Christian life are there presented in an attractive and impressive manner. Though short, it is complete. The double Commandment which sums up the Law and the prophets is there shown in all its application. The spirit of Christ breathes throughout all its lines. It should become the 'Vade Mecum' of every earnest Christian. It will become so."
—Rev. Dr. Miel. Editor L'Avenir, Philadelphia.

"The very first page fastened my attention upon it, and touched my spirit with the deepest sympathy for the one who filled for me that hour with heart-felt devotion. With many of your meditations I could follow you both unto their heights and depths. I was glad to see a little book of its kind, that was equally removed from mystic pietism on the one hand, and sacramental musings on the other: the spirit of the believer brought 'directly into touch' with the spirit and the presence of his blessed LORD, anywhere and at any time. It may seem to some that your language as well as subject is too exalted and intense to be practical, but in a measure surely every one can enter into the sanctuary of thought which you suggest, even if not conscious of the fulness of feeling that you express. Keble says that there are 'souls by nature pitched too high, by suffering plunged too low.' I think both kinds may meet half-way 'between' while reading ever so rapidly the pages you have printed."
—The Rev. Dr. J. K. Murphy. Germantown.

It is pure gold and diamonds, pearls and rubies. Have read it many times, and want a copy for my daily use. I would like to send a copy to every thoughtful and earnest soul I know. It should be, and in time undoubtedly will be translated into all languages to be studied along with the Bibles of all nations.
—Mrs. Townsend Allen.

They are very good and helpful.
—Henry Wood, the author.

DEVOTIONAL MEDITATIONS

Your excellent pamphlet is a great help, and I start in to-day with a full determination to reach Eternal Consciousness, and I wish to thank you for extending so helpful a hand.
—Stanley B. Huber.

MYSTERIES

He has put us greatly in his debt by the publication of the wonderful work, which has for many years been put only in the hands of accepted students. He has further added to its value for students by generously including a set of questions which he arranged for his own students, so that a kind of correspondence method of study is suggested. There is a question for each day, and the passing of each phase of degrees is to take one month in order deeply to impress it by slow and thorough study. The work bears the impress of scholarship and erudition, but far more than these, of a guiding wisdom.

—W. G. Raffé, in Hindustan Review.

A world of delight!—I read two chapters of it every evening.—Mr. Ames, Librarian Bosler Memorial Library, Carlisle, Penna.

PERRONIK THE SIMPLE-HEARTED

This legend is, by the experts, considered to be one of the chief bases of the other Holy Grail legends, for the reason that it claims a definite location, the castle of Kerglas, near Jannes. After years of effort, Dr. Guthrie succeeded in locating it, made some sketches, and has reproduced one of them as frontispiece.

The story is of absorbing interest to all. The more mature minds are charmed and refreshed by its contact with nature, while the interest of the young is held by the skill of the telling of the story. It has never failed to arouse and hold the interest of groups of people.

'It is a most charming tale related in a fascinating way. The style is so breezy and original that it is calculated to charm both old and young. Every child should be entitled to peruse this beautiful legend.'

—Florence van der Veer-Quick, London.

Stimulation for the intuition is in every paragraph,—rich in inspiring imagery.

—M. H. D., in The Messenger.

'I am very glad to hear that you are to publish the story of Perronik; for due to its action and veiled moral it will be enjoyed by both young and old. We need more of such charming old legends for readers to-day.'

—Jane Haven, High School Principal.

THE REUNITING PILGRIMAGE
A Prose Poem of Human Initiation

Skilfully making use of time-honored traditions and expressions, it studies the problem of the justice of the administration of the universe, as revealed in our human existence. It then indicates a possible solution, which inevitably culminates in social communion.

Its object is to supply a working basis for life strong enough to yield courage and inspiration to the unfortunate and discouraged, while the alluring beauty of its diction and setting gives it a universal appeal. It has been used as private text-book by groups of students of the higher life.

It is printed ornamentally, and bound daintily. Its net price is 80 cents, carriage paid. Large reductions for orders by the dozen, addressed directly to the publishers.

'I am so anxious to have you re-publish this sublime work that I am enclosing a cheque to cover the necessary expenses. I wish everybody to have an opportunity to receive its inspiration to high endeavor, its consolation in affliction, and support in times of trial.'

'I have rated your book so high that I have for years read it in full as the crowning or concluding lesson in the study-classes in spiritual culture which I have been holding all over the country. I could sell very many copies for you if you were only willing to publish it. Do you not realize that this is a public duty?'

—Mrs. Rudolph, Philadelphia.

RELIGIOUS EXPERIENCES

With deepest interest I have enjoyed reading this interesting book. It proves many things for all. The outstanding features are—you have overcome great obstacles, you have kept a close observance on your happenings, and these years of experience will always make you popular because you can so thoroughly understand the sufferings of your fellow-beings. The mightiest proof is, God reigns supreme!

—Magdalena Schweyer.

Fresh proof of the existence of the Living God, an object lesson in practical religión, an added refutation of atheism, and additional proof of natural religion.

—United India and Indian States.

Such a wealth of unusual and arresting material, that I am promising myself a more careful perusal.

—Estelle Ducio.

Your interior life must be very wonderful. Only the real mystic can play with divine things as you do.

—Elsa Barker (about Poems).

Stimulating and helpful article on the Eucharist.

—Beatrice E. Carr.

CHARACTER WORK

I enjoyed your articles in the Mercury. Keep at it!

—Agnes Wood.

REGENERATION

I realize that you are teaching Hidden Wisdom, and opening up to Seekers of Truth important new paths of investigation.

—Mrs. Maud Westrup, London.

Truly it is the first time I have ever seen the old argument presented in a logical, scientific form such as would appeal. The research, the actual amount of accumulated fact, in your book is greater than I ever saw in so small a compass.

Having recognized for some time that continence in its widest sense is the true path to eternal life, I am glad that at last we have a work which fearlessly proclaims this, and at the same time gives scientific and philosophical reasons why men should live the life.

—Richard T. Prater.

"Regeneration, The Gate of Heaven," is a carefully written work on the subject of Chastity which the Author deals with from various standpoints. Every chapter in it is full of valuable interest. It is the only work that I know, published on the subject, giving so much precious information in a single volume. Every person interested in the regeneration of humanity should read this book.

VIRCHAND R. GANDHI,
September 19, 1897.   of Bombay, India.

We thank the author for giving us in REGENERATION, if not the last word the New Science may have for us concerning the deeper uses of the creative powers, containing a mass of valuable physiological and biological parts showing exhaustive research, your precise methods making the book a necessity to those seeking light upon the most vital of problems. REGENERATION will bring to many a vision of possible freedom, and without freedom there can be no liberty to share.

Sincerely, ALICE MAY,

AS UNIVERSITY PROFESSOR

SOME UNIVERSITY ENDORSEMENTS

from University of the South, at Sewanee. This is to certify that Dr. Kenneth Sylvan Guthrie of New York City, delivered a course of lectures during the Summer Session of the University Extension Department of the University of the South this year; and that his lectures were universally enjoyed and commended. Doctor Guthrie is a man of the widest culture, and speaks of what he has seen and known. His illustrated lecture on Brittany was especially delightful.—Thomas F. Gailor, Chancellor of theh University, and Bishop of Tennessee.

In his lecture 'The Vanished Splendors of the Ancient World, whatever was most picturesque in myth, legend and history was thrown on the screen,—skillful restorations, maps, panoramas; and by illuminating comment the audience was carried through Babylon, Syria, Asia Minor, to Greece, Carthage, and Rome, mistress of the ancient world. The lecture was calculated to arouse a desire for historical study, the greatest merit of a University Extension lecture dealing with history. The lecture on 'National Interpretations of Human Destiny' endeavored to read from carefully analyzed select masterpieces representing modern Hungary, Germany, France, Spain, England and the United States, the trend of that inevitable drift of thought, which goes on irrespective of individuals and schools, and shapes lives of men and nations. Particularly suggestive was the endeavor to show a culmination of such modern thinking in Moody's Masque of Judgment.' The lecture was full of memorable phrases and brilliant epigrams, rousing a lively interest, and proving suggestive and stimulative.

One of the best lectures delivered at the Extension Session of the University of the South in 1911 was the sympathetic interpretation of the spirit of 'Brittany.' The illustrations were exceedingly beautiful, excellently chosen, and their sequence was so superbly ordered as to convey a glamor of the ancient magic.
—William Bonnell Hall,
Vice-Chancellor of the University.

I admire and respect and hope for disciples for you. I hope you will always show the same courage and that the ways will get more and more straightened for your feet.
I often think of you and your lone fight. I respect your heroism.
—Prof. Wm. James, Harvard.
Harvard University, Cambridge, Mass.

I knew Dr. Kenneth Guthrie rather intimately when he studied at Harvard some dozen or less years ago. I have not seen him since then, but he has always been a man of great power of work and will, and of ardent moral and intellectual character, able doubtless to wield great influence on certain kinds of students. He is unquestionably fitted to teach modern languages, economics, and psychology in an institution like yours. His experience has been wide, and his information various.
Believe me, dear Sir, sincerely yours,
(Signed) William James.
Tulane University of Louisiana, New Orleans.

I take pleasure in commending most heartily Dr. Kenneth S. Guthrie. He holds degrees from his University, from the University of the South, Sewanee, Tenn., and from Harvard. Dr. Guthrie studied under me here in graduate work in Latin, pursuing other subjects at the same time. His breadth of learning is very remarkable. He has a good knowledge of Latin,

Greek, and the modern languages of Europe. He has also made a study of Economics and Psychology. As to his ability in the natural sciences and mathematics, I have no personal knowledge. He taught one year as an Assistant in Tulane, and has, I believe, done some private teaching since. For a few years he was in the Episcopal Ministry, but he now desires some regular work in a school or college. He is a man of high ideals and is thoroughly conscientious in any duty he may undertake. Very respectfully,
(Signed) James H. Dillard, Dean Prof. of Latin.

AS A TEACHER

A man with a whitish beard beneath a little moustache, with very agreeable features, representing the head of a learned man. If there is a person worthy of the teaching profession, it is he. In spite of his advanced age, to judge by his white hair, he is devoted to his vocation, and he instructs us with the zeal of a youth. The moment we enter his class, we always find him cheery, so that we feel at home.

During the recitation, to impress us with the words and idiomatic expressions he often recalls us quotations, and historic events. His profound erudition in the French language, and his literary taste have so raised my estimation of him, that I treasure my lessons with almost religious devotion. His pupils' questions he answers with convincing thoroughness.

From time to time he amuses us with jokes composed of impromptu instructive quips.

All his pupils are the objects of his affection, and the weakest of us he cares for as if they were his own children. He shakes hands with all of us, especially those who have been absent. We are very happy with him.
By his pupil Harry Aremenakian, March, 1828

You will never know the happiness I have derived from such generosity of heart and mind as you have given me the unusual privilege to experience.—May I venture to hope that you might still in the future continue to inspire me.
—Agnes Long.

From that time on I became interested in the study of the French language.
—Imre Braun.

I have been reading your book recently.
—Gustave Straubenmüller,
Associate Superintendent, N. Y. City.

A man I can conscientiously recommend. Extremely painstaking and thorough in teaching. He is worthy of the greatest trust.
—Frank V. Chambers.

Permit me to express my appreciation. The spirit shown by you in your teaching was of the finest kind, and was inspiring to your class. Your enthusiasm and earnestness were contagious, and was reflected by the amount and character of the work accomplished during the season. A number of the students express themselves as well repaid for the time spent with you.
—W. R. Hayward,
Principal Curtis Evening High School.

I couldn't resist the temptation to write and tell you how much assistance to my work with you this summer has proven itself. I am only now beginning to realize how much I learned, and the interest acquired in the study of the French language. Till now I hated it. Now I love it and am at the head of my class, thanks to your wonderful teaching.—Helene Barker.

WASHINGTON IRVING HIGH SCHOOL

Since February 1910 I have been associated with Mr. Kenneth S. Guthrie in the Department of French in the Washington Irving High School, New York City. I have always found

Mr. Guthrie courteous, kind and enthusiastic in his work; and I take pleasure in recommending him to an institution desiring earnest, faithful work in the Department of French.
—Nannie G. Blackwell, Head of Department.

Dr. Kenneth S. Guthrie taught in the Grand Street Annex for about five years. I found him very conscientious, painstaking and earnest. He was always considerate and kindly in his manner, and had the respect of his pupils. He was thoroughly conversant with the subject he taught.　　　　　—Idelette Carpenter,
In Charge of Grand Street Annex.

SOUTH BROOKLYN EVENING HIGH SCHOOL

This is to certify that Dr. Guthrie taught German and French for one term during the season 1909-1910 in the South Brooklyn Evening High School for Men. His personal interest in the students who reported to him for instruction, and his enthusiasm in his work made his services most valuable to us. His control of the classes under his charge was excellent.
—Joseph T. Wingebach, Principal.

AS A GENERAL LECTURER

Our people are still talking of the living, loving and informing portraits you gave us of Pythagoras and Plato,—no mere musty biographical details mixed with cribbed bookscraps. We seemed to meet the men and hear them illuminate our present-day problems. Come soon again with more!
—Theodore Heline,
Director of Union Centre, New York City.

Your lectures have been a source of great inspiration to all. They would reflect credit on the curriculum of any college or university. Your rare pictures and maps have helped to make the Platonic message real to us. We are looking forward to the coming lectures with high anticipation.　—Malcolm B. Schloss,
Director North Node Philosophical Gatherings.

SOME UNIVERSITY ENDORSEMENTS
Harvard University

I knew him rather intimately. He has always been a man of great power of work and will, and of ardent moral and intellectual character, able to wield great influence. His experience has been wide, and his information various.
—The late Professor William James.

Tulane University, New Orleans
His breadth of learning is very remarkable. He is a man of high ideals, and is thoroughly conscientious in any duty he may undertake.
—Former Dean James H. Dillard.

University of the South, Sewanee
His lectures were universally enjoyed and commended. He is a man of the widest culture, and speaks of what he has seen and known.
—Bishop Thomas F. Gailor, Chancellor.

The lecture was full of memorable phrases, and brilliant epigrams, arousing a lively interest, and proving suggestive and stimulative.
The lecture was calculated to arouse a desire for historical study, the greatest merit of a University Extension Lecture. — Dr. William Bonnell Hall, Vice-Chancellor.

Captivating, well-balanced, among the best ever given at Sewanee.—Wm. Norman Guthrie, Rector St. Mark's, N. Y., Director of the University Extension Department, Sewanee University.

A PERSONAL APPRECIATION

Among the many prominent men who have been in Grantwood during the past winter, there has been no one of so versatile genius and achievements as he. A trained physician, teacher and preacher, he is also a composer of music, a poet of no mean ability, and a linguist of great distinction.

—The Palisade Post (Grantwood, N. J.)

BRITTANY

His lectures Vanished Splendors and Natural Interpretations of Human Destiny) were universally enjoyed and commended. He is a man of the widest culture and speaks of what he has seen and known. The Brittany lecture was especially delightful.—Bishop Th. F. Gailor, Chancellor University of the South.

I consider it both a privilege and duty to extend to you my hearty appreciation of the superb lecture on Brittany. The enthusiastic and repeated applause of the audience only feebly corresponded to my personal feelings.
—Rev. Dr. Charles Jaeger.

It gives me great pleasure to furnish a testimonial as to your ability as a public speaker.
—Dr. Stuart Close.

DUTCH U. S. TRAITS

Your very interesting masterful speech on Dutch Origins in the U. S. is still ringing in our ears. We bring due homage to your versatile intellect. I extend to you our gratitude and appreciation.　　　—Th. Fabry de Jonge,
Secretary of Club Eendracht maakt Macht.

I commend your program, to which I have nothing to add.
—Prof. L. C. Van Noppen, Columbia.

The best lecture we have had in seven years. As valuable for us Dutch as for you Americans.

Sure to fructify the interaction of both races.
—Club 'Union Makes Power.'

FADS AND FANCIES

Thank you for your interesting and entertaining lecture on Fads and Fancies. We all enjoyed it immensely and will long remember it.—President Chas. S. Armstrong, Dragon Club, St. Stephen's College.

AS A CLERGYMAN

The spiritual overtones were indeed manifest as you celebrated to one at least of your communicants.—Beatrice E. Carr.

I was very much impressed by the service in your church yesterday. I think it was very beautiful in its simplicity. I hope you will be rewarded some day for your noble work.
—Aurelia Somers.

We were deeply moved by the beauty of the service as you conducted it and by your own attitude of affection and graciousness toward the young people who were strangers to you. If they are ever to be won to the love of Christ, it will be through their respect for such men as you, and not through contact with the rigid and formal dogmas of the average clergyman.
—Irene Hagopian.

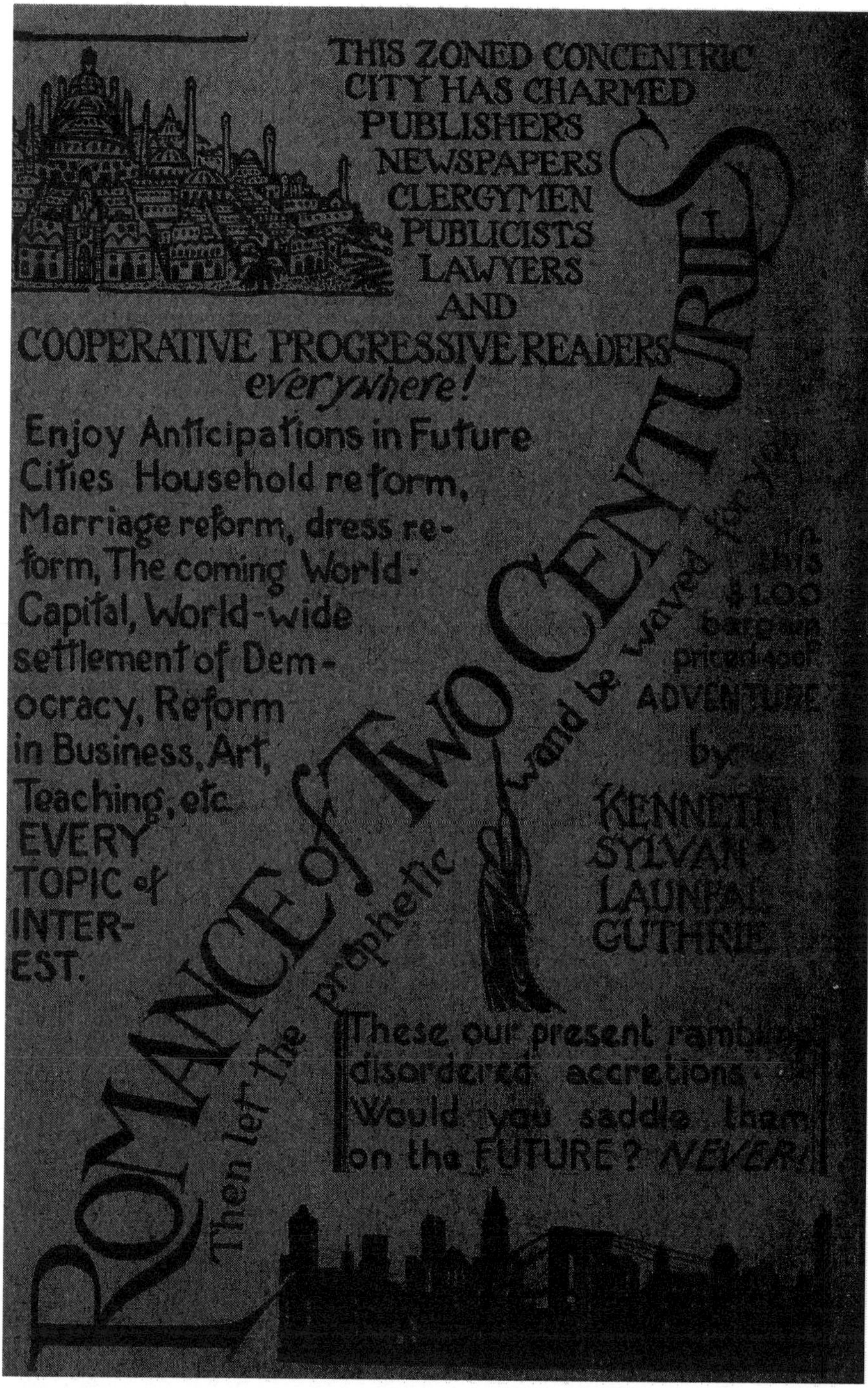
THIS ZONED CONCENTRIC
CITY HAS CHARMED
PUBLISHERS
NEWSPAPERS
CLERGYMEN
PUBLICISTS
LAWYERS
AND
COOPERATIVE PROGRESSIVE READERS
everywhere!
Enjoy Anticipations in Future Cities Household reform, Marriage reform, dress reform, The coming World-Capital, World-wide settlement of Democracy, Reform in Business, Art, Teaching, etc. EVERY TOPIC of INTEREST.
ROMANCE of TWO CENTURIES
Then let the prophetic wand be waved for you
this
$1.00
bargain
priced
ADVENTURE
by
KENNETH
SYLVAN
LAUNFAL
GUTHRIE
These our present ramb
disordered accretions
Would you saddle them
on the FUTURE? NEVER!

Lightning Source UK Ltd.
Milton Keynes UK
UKHW022149250919
350467UK00004B/124/P